Race and the Writing of History

RACE AND AMERICAN CULTURE
Arnold Rampersand and Shelley Fisher Fishkin
General Editors

Race and the Writing of History

RIDDLING THE SPHINX

— — — — — — — — — — —

Maghan Keita

OXFORD
UNIVERSITY PRESS

2000

OXFORD
UNIVERSITY PRESS

Oxford   New York
Athens   Auckland   Bangkok   Bogotá   Buenos Aires   Calcutta
Cape Town   Chennai   Dar es Salaam   Delhi   Florence   Hong Kong   Istanbul
Karachi   Kuala Lumpur   Madrid   Melbourne   Mexico City   Mumbai
Nairobi   Paris   São Paulo   Shanghai   Singapore   Taipei   Tokyo   Toronto   Warsaw

and associated companies in
Berlin   Ibadan

Copyright © 2000 by Maghan Keita

Published by Oxford University Press, Inc.
198 Madison Avenue, New York, New York 10016

Oxford is a registered trademark of Oxford University Press

Library of Congress Cataloging-in-Publication Data
Keita, Maghan.
Race and the writing of history :
riddling the sphinx / Maghan Keita.
p.   cm.
ISBN 0-19-511274-1
1. Afro-Americans—Historiography.   2. Blacks—Historiography.
3. Historiography—United States.   4. Culture conflict—
United States.   I. Title.
E185.K38   2000
973′.0496073′0072—dc21   99-19277

9 8 7 6 5 4 3 2 1

Printed in the United States of America
on acid-free paper

Preface

the Sphinx. . . . had flown to Thebes
from the uttermost part of
Ethiopia. . . . she now asked every
Theban wayfarer a riddle. . . .[1]

Frank Edward Moorer. When I was a young master's degree student, Frank Edward Moorer seized me and shook me with the intent, possibilities, and responsibilities of being an intellectual—and a black one at that. It was Frank Moorer who introduced me to William Edward Burghardt Du Bois. To be sure, Moorer had help. His colleague, and my former junior high school teacher, Curtis Wilson, had provided some prep. He was seconded—maybe in some ways preceded—by the mentor of all of our family's children, Larry Barclay. Larry made sure that all the tools and all the opportunities possible were known to my working-class parents.

I had been passed along to Larry by the very able faculty at Glenville Senior High School—a black school in the midst of one of Cleveland's black communities. There were many people who taught me, many people responsible, in part, for my successes—too many to name in entirety: Mrs. Clemens, Mr. Cap, Mr. Newsome, the inimitable Mr.

---

1. Robert Graves, *The Greek Myths,* Vol. II, (Mt. Kisco, New York: Moyer Bell Limited, 1988), 10.

Bohi, and, of course, the guidance counselors' guidance counselor, Mrs. Harpole.

Glenville's students were blessed. There were people who believed in us as we read Homer. We knew Herodotus. Bulfinch's *Mythology* was well worn, as was Edith Hamilton's work. Some of us even studied Latin—some, including myself, not nearly enough. And, of course, we all knew where Egypt was.

We also knew Oedipus. We imagined him shuffling along, his feet swollen, standing before the walls of Thebes, answering the riddle of the Sphinx. We knew Egypt. We knew Thebes. We knew the Sphinx. Somewhere in a black, shining classroom questions were being posed that could only find voice decades later.

Finding voice. In many ways, that is the fundamental intent of this volume: to find voice, recognize it, and celebrate it. For me, such a task could not have been accomplished without the help of a great number of friends and colleagues. I hope I am forgiven for those I have forgotten or neglected to mention; the act is not purposeful.

However, I must acknowledge Shelley Fisher Fishkin and Arnold Rampersad, the editors of this series for Oxford University Press. It was Professor Fishkin who thought that I had an idea worth expressing. She asked me to write about it and then invited me to the University of Texas at Austin to talk about it. Professor Rampersad supplied more encouragement and was gracious enough to invite me to Princeton to try to explain myself.

Seth Koven and Larry Little, my colleagues in the Department of History at Villanova University, have been in the trenches with me from the very beginning. Seth must have commented over and again on every idea and concept, on phrasing and clarity, on the notion of giving this intellect some life. Larry did all that he could to make the ideas and the concepts readable. The two did all that they could; in the end, the shortcomings of this project are mine, not theirs.

I also need to acknowledge my good friends, Kenneth Curtis of the University of California, Long Beach, and the late Gerald Davis of Rutgers University. Ken's comments guided the manuscript in many ways. It is to Jerry Davis that this work is dedicated. Jerry gently prodded, cajoled, encouraged, and mentored the process, and, most of all, the author. He provided a singular wish: to be able to tell this story, and any other, with the beauty and lucidity he employed.

In many ways, this work was inspired by the pioneering efforts of William Leo Hansberry and Frank M. Snowden, Jr.. I am indebted to both Gayle Hansberry, Professor Hansberry's daughter, and Professor Snowden for their time, wisdom, and aid in what I've attempted here.

It is, I am sure, quite clear that the faults in the analysis are my own and in no way reflect the guidance they attempted to provide me.

Finally, I must express my thanks to Mr. Robert Milks and his editorial team at Oxford University Press. Their comments were straightforward and helpful and their attitudes always steady and calm. All this made the process somewhat less anxiety-laden.

To my wife, Nzadi, and my sons, Najja and Cabral, this is for you as well.

Contents

Race and the Writing of History

Introduction

Ways of Knowing—Race, the Construction of Histories, and Culture Wars

Until the princes shall come forth from Egypt and Ethiopia stretch out her hand unto God.

> Richard Allen and Absalom Jones,
> *A Narrative of the Proceedings of the Black People*
> *during the Awful Calamity in Philadelphia in the Year 1793*

. . . between memory and actuality

> Edward Said, *Orientalism*

Placed between Africa and Asia, and communicating easily with Europe, Egypt occupies the center of the ancient continent. . . .

No considerable power was ever amassed by any nation, whether in the West or in Asia that did not also turn that nation toward Egypt, which was regarded in some measure as its natural lot.

> Jean-Baptiste-Joseph Fourier, *"Preface historique"*

"The Talk of the Nation"

The epigraphs frame this discussion of America's culture wars. They are the talk of the nation. The March 4, 1998, National Public Radio broadcast of *Talk of the Nation* acknowledged America's culture wars. The issue was "are they over?" The March 6, 1998, edition of the *Chron-*

icle of Higher Education followed suit with a section that featured eight prominent academicians who responded to the question "Have the Culture Wars Ended?" On National Public Radio, Professor Alan Wolfe argued that they never began—at least not outside of the halls of America's intellectual centers. Lawrence W. Levine, on the other hand, writes that they never end.[1]

In his work *The Opening of the American Mind*, Levine answers *Talk of the Nation* host Ray Suarez's question "what's at stake?" Levine implies that the issues of the culture wars—pro and con—are profoundly epistemological. They are "tied to . . . a way of seeing the world, a way of understanding." One question linked to this observation is whether or not struggles over epistemology–struggles over ways of knowing—have any substantive, tangible effect on the lives of everyday Americans, or whether they are simply the sport, as Alan Wolfe says, of an elite.[2]

James Davison Hunter's conclusions support both Levine and Wolfe. The elite are the main actors here, but their actions have consequences for everyone. The questions of the culture wars center on what is to be known and *how* it will be known, particularly in the institutional sense. The historiographic issues focus on the how and why of knowing it. For Hunter, these questions have historical and political economic implications. The implications speak to ways of knowing and the privileging of a certain way of knowing—the granting of hegemony to a particular epistemology. In the real and tangible sense, Hunter writes that *"cultural conflict is ultimately about the struggle for domination.* . . . The power to define reality is not an abstract power." Indeed, that power of definition, that ability to *impose* identity, can determine if people eat or starve, live or die.[3]

For the past three centuries or so we have been treated to racialized ways of thinking. Race has become a way of knowing. Within this construction there has emerged, quite obviously and expectedly, epistemologies of blackness.

In the linear, dialectical, and polar discourses of our age, epistemolo-

1. "Culture Wars," *Talk of the Nation*, National Public Radio, transcript (March 4, 1998), 1–2. Lawrence W. Levine, "Struggles Are a Small Price to Pay for Diverse Universities," *Chronicle of Higher Education* (March 6, 1998), B5. Lawrence W. Levine, *The Opening of the American Mind: Canons, Culture, and History* (Boston: Beacon Press, 1996). Gertrude Himmelfarb, "The Vision of the University Is Still at Stake," *Chronicle of Higher Education* (March 6, 1998), B6.

2. Levine, *Opening*, 30. Wolfe, *Talk of the Nation*, 1–2.

3. James Davison Hunter, *Culture Wars: The Struggle to Define America* (New York: Basic Books, 1991), xii, 52; italics added.

gies of blackness are at least twofold. On one hand, they are representative of what can be seen as dominant and hegemonic, a discourse in which blackness is the embodiment of all that is negative.On the other hand, the epistemology is guided by argumentation in which blackness is a virtue and the origin of all we know and cherish. There is also the "blackness" that lies in between.

In the context of the conceptualization of these epistemologies, there should be little wonder that race has affected the writing of history over these several centuries. There should be little wonder that race has been crucial to our ways of knowing, crucial to the very construction of knowledge.

In the summer of 1976, as a young graduate student, I took the first of what would become many, many trips to Africa. Yet it was only while I was sitting in my living room in a mixed, but predominantly black neighborhood in Philadelphia in the summer of 1996, that it dawned on me how propitious that first trip was.

Even then, I had no doubt that I was in some way connected to that land and its history. Romantically, I gauged that even an Egypt Arabized for more than a millennium was still mine. Arabic-speaking peoples were still my "brothers" and "sisters." I felt, in my heart, that they would not deny me or my claim to Egypt.

My Egyptian resolve was reinforced in numerous and quixotic ways. In the arduous and daunting task of retrieving my lost luggage an old and grizzled guard, clearly recognizing me as an American and out of my element, attempted to put me at ease by way of sign language. Rubbing his bare arm and then mine, he indicated that we were one and the same people. We could see this. On the streets of Cairo, when people approached to ask directions that I could not give, it never occurred to me that they could be asking these questions of anyone other than a "child of Egypt" come home.

Then came the one event of my stay that indicated that there was more to Egypt and its own history than my superficial and romantic expectations. I was sitting on the rooftop terrace of the hotel. The young boy who was the porter had brought me a *"Bepsi"* (Pepsi). It was then that I attempted to improve the fluency of my Arabic by engaging him in conversation while he swept the roof. My first and only question to him (one he understood perfectly—some indication of the fluency of my elementary Arabic) changed the entire perspective from which I would come to understand contemporary and historical Egypt, Africa, and the world.

"Anta Arabi?" ("Are you Arab?"), I asked—anticipating the answer to a question I assumed to be almost rhetorical. He shocked me with a

force and power that seemed to cause his chest to swell immensely in spite of his chubby, preadolescent frame. *"Leh! Leh! LEH! Aina Nubi! AINA NUBI...!"* ("No! No! NO! I am Nubian! I AM NUBIAN . . . !"), he replied, his voice trailing off almost in the practice of a polished orator, his audience hanging on his very word.

I understood him precisely as well. Then I looked at him and realized that I, a black American—unabashedly and identifiably "black"— was fairer than my young Egyptian—my Nubian friend. I was never so clearly understanding of the concept of race and its multifarious consequences as I was that day. With a series of short expletives, my young friend had prepared me for an examination twenty years in the future.

This work is about race and the ways in which it affects our writing of history and the construction of whatever we choose to call knowledge. In our recent intellectual history, we have come to realize that there are different ways of knowing and constructing knowledge; some of us even accept the notion that race is a fundamental construct in epistemological formation. There exist epistemologies of race in which race becomes the pivotal way of knowing. This body of racialized knowledge is essential to both individual and group identity, private and public lives, and institutional, structural, and systemic development.

Conventional epistemologies reflect the status quo; alternative epistemologies contest it. This is a useful way to approach a discussion of epistemologies of blackness. Epistemologies of blackness are constructions of knowledge, ways of knowing, that descend from a general epistemology of race. While their variation might be infinite, within the framework of this discussion the purpose of this argument is served if we approach epistemologies of blackness as two competing yet, paradoxically, complementary forms: the conventional and its alternative.

The conventional epistemology of blackness is a construction of the modern age. Its source is that great Age of Enlightenment which brought with it notions of science, progress, and race. In the attempt to scientifically classify existence, some of the most superficial characteristics of human physical and social interaction were given vaunted positions in intellectual and social life as key indicators of how society should be regulated. Race as a key component of that social order came into being as we now know it.

In this modern racial epistemology oppositional categories ruled: science versus superstition, civilization versus barbarity, progress versus backwardness. All of these abstractions could be abstracted to white versus black, and in this, blackness as a way of knowing emerged. The conventional epistemology of blackness argues that "blacks" are fundamentally, inherently, biologically both infantile and bestial. They are to be cared for and subjected to tutelage, or simply controlled. The source of control has been racism, the ideological component of a system of knowledge constructed on race; it is the system's defense mechanism. It is also used to expand the powers of this system of knowledge.

At the same time, one must realize that the alternative epistemology of blackness functions in basically the same way in promoting and expanding a construction of knowledge that opposes the conventional characterizations. In sum, the alternative epistemology argues for "manhood" (to use its nineteenth-century terminology) and the responsibilities and potential of black peoples to function in and contribute to the progress of civilization. The paradox is that because both epistemologies take as their starting points the modern construction of race, race becomes the ideological barometer by which the defense and expansion of both epistemologies is mounted. The histories that seek to explain and rationalize these epistemologies are ideological and propagandistic. They arise from a need inherent to any system of knowledge, and the power it confers, to protect itself.

My observations are supported, in part, by those of Ellen Somekawa and Elizabeth A. Smith. They urge historians to acknowledge the intrinsic propagandistic character of their work—to acknowledge that within the construction of knowledge, they are architects of ideology. In regard to the evolution of the historians' craft they argue that "what was once explicitly ideological now masquerade[s] as objective." They remind us that "our own social and political positions have everything to do with what stories we choose to tell"[4] and that those stories may lend themselves to domination, or to resistance and liberation.

Within the realm of idea and classification, "blackness" and "whiteness" are *imagined* forms; they are abstractions, and the context in which they presently occur, that of Western thought and imagination, is fundamentally a construction of the modern age. And though we believe, as aficionados of the forms, that they are given inherently to the exclusion of the "other," they are in large part formed and formulated by "outside constituencies." The exclusivist nature of the forms is attenuated in two ways. First, in the necessity of characterizing itself oppositionally, the West must have the "other"; the "white" must have

---

4. Ellen Somekawa and Elizabeth Smith, "Theorizing the Writing of History Or, 'I Can't Think Why It Should Be So Dull, For a Great Deal of It Must Be Invention,'" *Journal of Social History*, 22 (Fall 1988), 154.

the "black." Second, historically, the cultural and physical evolution of the West is one in which the "other" is inextricably lodged.[5] Since the Enlightenment, the quest for a new epistemology of "modernism" has involved the dislodging of intrinsic elements deemed incompatible with the construction of modern Western identity. These elements can be described as anything that might be characterized as "black," or carry its connotation.

If race is constructed, then the same must be said of culture. The construction of culture is an ideological imperative. Amilcar Cabral stated this explicitly when he wrote of culture as a weapon.[6] The notion fits perfectly with W.E.B. Du Bois's observations on art and history. History, as William Appleman Williams noted, is "a way of learning" ("knowing," if you will). And in the American context of which Williams wrote, much of that history has become apologia for the American "predicament", a key tool in the construction of an American weltanschauung.[7] Here history and culture collapse upon one another. The history of culture (or race) becomes ideological and propagandistic, and the propaganda, in itself, becomes a way of knowing. Ideology is a tool of epistemology. If, as Cabral asserts, culture may be forged into a weapon, is it not conceivable that its manufacture might be for culture wars?

Denial has been extremely important to the construction of Western history and modern thought.[8] Within that denial, and as a consequence of it, an epistemology of blackness was erected. However, the construction of Western history and the epistemology it supported was challenged from its very beginning. In what would become the United States, people of African descent began the challenge before they set foot on these shores. Their very presence, epitomized in the intellectual productions of such men and women as Olaudah Equiano and Phyllis Wheatley, gave rise to a "race conscious" body that Du Bois would describe as the "talented tenth." This group's commitment to the acquisition of education indicated their recognition of the power of the construction of knowledge. Their task was broadly epistemological: the construction of knowledge and, therefore, a new way of seeing, defining, articulating, and solving *their* problem and determining the black's place in the world. This centering was both historical

5. Toni Morrison, *Playing in the Dark: Whiteness and the Literary Imagination* (Cambridge: Harvard University Press, 1992).

6. Amilcar Cabral, *Return to the Source: Selected Speeches of Amilcar Cabral* (New York: Monthly Review Press, 1973), 59.

7. William A. Williams, *History as a Way of Learning* (New York: New Viewpoints, 1973).

8. William L. Hansberry, "The Material Culture of Ancient Nigeria," *Journal of Negro History*, 6, 3 (July 1921), 261–262, 290–295.

and contemporary. This articulation of race and its capacity to resolve the crucial issue of the age—race and racial discrimination—was not a project of the masses. It was, however, for their "uplift."

What Du Bois and company articulated, what they were heir to, was the construction of an *alternative* epistemology, a response to the fundamental premises of the historical construction of the conventional epistemologies of blackness whose *blackness as a way of knowing* centered on the negation of Africa and peoples of African descent.[9] The alternative project has centered on the construction of a historical consciousness, and as such, a consciousness of identity. In the modern age, such a historical and identity consciousness are the equivalents of racial consciousness.

It is misleading to consider this process as *one* project. Even if that were the case, we would have to recognize the *many* voices. The "history of [a] race" becomes a vehicle in the construction of the epistemology of blackness. Yet even early African American works show that there were, indeed, different ways of reading "blackness" and the histories associated with it. All of these readings, however, focus on the reclamation of "language," its inversion, and its re-creation in all its forms. These are acts that pose danger. These actions force new readings, and from there flow alternative epistemologies. We are witness to the realization that not only had the "old" epistemology—the epistemology of the dominant order—already been "read" and "deconstructed" by those it was meant to dominate, but the result was and is the construction of new ways of knowing, defining, and creating identity that were at hand long before the coming of our intellectual lives. These historical readings, deconstructions, and constructions began what Shelley Fisher Fishkin has articulated as the "interrogation of whiteness."[10]

So the expectation, in the face of oppressive epistemologies and historiographies, and the ideologies and propagandas that are part of their train, is that the oppressed will put forth their own epistemologies and historiographies, and, of course, attendant ideologies and propagandas, based on their own experiences. The notion of a "Negro Renaissance" carries all these implications, as does the theme of "Black is Beautiful," and the thesis of Afrocentrism. They are constructed one upon the other and reflect the historical and cultural lives of African Americans. These epistemologies, historiographies, ideolo-

9. George W. Frederickson, *The Black Image in the White Mind* (Hanover: Wesleyan University Press, 1971).

10. Shelley Fisher Fishkin, "Interrogating 'Whiteness,' Complicating 'Blackness': Remapping American Culture," *American Quarterly*, 47, 3 (September 1995).

gies, and propagandas, in many ways, are inversions of convention, which help to provide a more holistic conceptualization of society and reality.[11] They also speak to the inherent agency of black peoples. Such epistemologies move blacks from being solely victims or survivors of history to the acknowledgment that they produce history as well.

Within the context of culture and the epistemology of blackness are rooted "ideological concerns over identity." Most certainly, blackness is key to American identity; remove the blackness and the identity is no longer American. We might speculate if the same can be said of the modern world in general.

Said reiterates what others have already pointed out: imperialism as a form of domination requires an "impressive ideological formation . . . as well as forms of knowledge affiliated with domination."[12] The fundamental problem for those of us who analyze this material is our refusal to see the ideology inherent in the aesthetic forms of the periods in question. This is the manifestation of ideology at the "very significant levels . . . of national culture." The epistemological structure reflects a "privileged, genealogically useful past." Ideology is a sustaining force of domination. It is a necessity of resistance as well.

Valentine Mudimbe's observations on the "invention of Africa" correspond and in many ways are synonymous with the "invention of blackness" and its epistemological constructions. As Said, Frantz Fanon, Cabral, and Du Bois have observed, as the cultural and intellectual historians have illustrated, there is the "native's" ability for resistance and the reshaping of knowledge, especially in what have been termed the "marginalized" spaces—spaces that are marginalized because they cannot be dominated, a refusal to be dominated that gives these spaces a "dangerous importance." This dangerous importance can be characterized in the least in the ability of the marginalized to produce knowledge and in so doing challenge our ways of knowing while constructing alternatives to them.

The marginalized challenge the "white norm," as Mudimbe puts it. The marginalized are representational of the white norm's oppositional counterpoint: new epistemologies of blackness. Their "representational activities" and construction of "epistemological order" are ideological. They are challenges for the "new epistemological foundation . . . then functioning in the West" at the close of the seventeenth century, one in which the invention of race and racism as pseu-

11. Charles W. Mills, "Alternative Epistemologies," *Social Theory and Practice*, 14, 3 (Fall 1988), 259.

12. Edward Said, *Orientalism* (New York: Vintage Books, 1979), xxv, 9.

doscientific constructions emerged. As Mudimbe puts it, "system[s] of knowledge [are] . . . interdependent with systems of power and social control," and, of course, resistance to those systems.[13]

Knowledge is constructed. Much of what is constructed is "imagined" in that it is subject to its epistemological context. Once loosed from that context, it can be "read" anew in any number of ways. Again, within the context of the imagined community, Africa and peoples of African descent have been imagined as well. In almost immediate, and certainly sustained, reaction to this imagining and imaging has been the construction of alternative epistemologies of blackness. These epistemologies have been geared to offer different understandings of knowledge and its construction.

By necessity, epistemologies, ways of knowing, and the conditions under which knowledge is produced require ideologies to protect, project, and justify the power that is at their core and the uses of that power. By the same token, abuses of that power are met with alternative views of the world and the assemblage of knowledge around those views. "Black" peoples have consistently produced knowledge and constructed ways of knowing that have been consonant with their experiences and their need to control their own destinies. The historical record is replete with their examples, if only we are interested in "reading" them.

From this vantage, culture wars are about epistemological construction and reconstruction. They are about exclusion and inclusion. The historiographic denial that Hansberry wrote of and the invention of race itself provided paradigms for the construction of culture that would exclude certain peoples. These views have become "universal"—"canonized"—to the extent that the excluded parties are regarded as being without culture: uncivilized and barbaric; untutored and illiterate; and, therefore, without intellectual capacity.

Alan Bloom may not have introduced the term "culture wars," but his *Closing of the American Mind* certainly sounded the call to arms. Bloom, to the right, sounded vaguely reminiscent of Amilcar Cabral commenting on the "weapon of culture" when he declared that "culture means a war against chaos *and* a war against other cultures."[14]

Why are we at war? Bloom argues that it is to maintain the "universal or imperialistic claims" of Western culture.[15] Having read Bloom,

13. Valentine Y. Mudimbe, *The Invention of Africa: Gnosis, Philosophy and the Order of Knowledge* (Bloomington: Indiana University Press, 1988), 28.

14. Alan Bloom, *The Closing of the American Mind*, quoted in Levine, *Opening*, 18.

15. Ibid, 18.

who could wonder why Said wrote *Culture and Imperialism*? Having read Bloom, is there the possibility that there might be some exploration into what might drive serious Afrocentrism, postmodernism, postcolonialism, and so on? Bloom has certainly provided with the entrée for such inquiry.

Levine acknowledges the "hostility . . . attributed to any scholar who supplements the canon with the work of those who have been traditionally excluded from it." Keith Windschuttle sees such activities as a "murdering of our past."[16]

Windschuttle allows us to engage the historiographies of these wars. His title, *"The Killing of History . . . Murdering Our Past"* poses immediate questions: whose history; whose past? The answers to the questions are proscribed by the fact that "History [is] . . . among the most profound and enduring contributions that ancient Greece made . . . to the human species as a whole."[17] It may be, as Levine implies, that there are no other histories for Windschuttle and company. Then again, we might ask what it is that Windschuttle protests when he acknowledges that

> A great deal of the history of European expansion in the past two hundred years has been written from a strictly European perspective. . . . So today the question is not one of whether the repressed "other" should return or be revived. *It is more an issue of whether this return can be legitimately accomplished through the tools of traditional historiography, or whether the historical methodology nurtured by the colonial powers is so hopelessly compromised that it is useless for the task.*[18]

Again, we might ask Windschuttle is there a choice? The portion of Windschuttle's statement that I have italicized might be queried for its irony. Is Windschuttle writing tongue-in-cheek here as he makes the case for the new historiographies he denounces because they have rejected the principles of the Enlightenment—because they champion many histories and suggest that there is no absolute "truth"?[19]

And while Windschuttle concedes that there may be "a legitimate point buried beneath it all," he is clear that the source of all of his consternation—the major field on which this war is waged—is the United States as a center of "cultural studies." And, in spite of the French infusion, Windschuttle can, with the aid of Dinesh D'Souza's

16. Levine, *Opening*, 25. Keith Windschuttle, *The Killing of History: How Literary Critiques and Social Theorists Are Murdering Our Past* (New York: Free Press, 1996).
17. Windschuttle, *Killing*, 1.
18. Ibid., 12; italics added.
19. Ibid., 35.

"incriminating analysis" of black studies, give face to the most visible of America's cultural warriors: the "Afrocentric" perspective.[20]

Indeed, Afrocentrism is singled out on both sides of the political spectrum as the prime example of what is wrong in these culture wars, as possibly the cause of the culture wars themselves. With "know-nothing," "nonsensical" characters "directly from Central Casting" whose implied lack of sophistication is evident in their demagoguery, the racial nature of these wars is enjoined by those who would deny any racial intent whatsoever.[21] Yet in many ways they mirror the history and the historiography of these wars—wars that at their very best are fought for inclusion; wars fought over the right to "help shape public culture," over the right to engage in intellectual discourse; wars fought not simply to open the "private clubs" of the intellectual elite,[22] but to redefine and further democratize access to resources for those traditionally denied, for those denied by tradition.[23] The challenge to race as a way of knowing and the histories such racialized knowing has constructed is fundamental to today's culture wars.

20. Ibid., 19, 34.

21. Todd Gitlin, *The Twilight of Common Dreams: Why America Is Wracked by Culture Wars* (New York: Henry Holt, 1995), 170, 175. Levine, *Opening*, 25.

22. Nell Irvin Painter, "Battles Are Far From Over in Culture's Private Clubs," *Chronicle of Higher Education* (March 6, 1998), B7.

23. Evelyn Hu-DeHart, "Spotlight Is Shifting to Students of Color," *Chronicle of Higher Education* (March 6, 1998), B7. Annette Kolodny, "If Harsh Realities Prevail, We All Will Continue to Lose," *Chronicle of Higher Education* (March 6, 1998), B5. Todd Gitlin, "A Truce Prevails: For the Left, Many Victories Are Pyrrhic," *Chronicle of Higher Education* (March 6, 1998), B5.

ONE

Race and Historiography

Race explains nothing at all.
                    A. J. Kelso, *Physical Anthropology: An Introduction*

Undergraduates, seduced, as always, by the changing breath
of journalistic fashion, demand that they should be taught
the history of *black* Africa. Perhaps, in the future, there will
be some African history to teach. But at present there is none,
or very little: there is only the history of Europeans in Africa.
The rest is largely darkness. . . . And darkness is not a subject for history. (Italics added)
                    Hugh Trevor Roper, *The Rise of Christian Europe*

There you have it. It may be unfair to dredge up Sir Hugh again, but
his is the phrase that categorizes several generations of colonial and
postcolonial historians, some of whom are writing still. It also epito-
mizes popular thought on the history or histories of Africa as well. As
Sir Hugh has put it, there is no history of "black" Africa, and therefore
no need to entertain even more specious ideas such as "Egypt in
Africa," or "Africa in Egypt" for that matter.

This work begins with two contradictory notions that summarize
the historiography of the modern age. Both these notions center on
the concept of race. The first acknowledges, as does Kwame Appiah in
his book *In My Father's House* that race is an ill-gotten, unsubstantiated,
pseudoscientific configuration designed to justify and rationalize the

distribution of the world's resources in the modern age: [R]ace is an unavoidable element . . . and . . . racialist notions are grounded in bad biological—and worse ethical—ideas, inherited from the increasingly racialised thought of nineteenth-century Europe and America.[1]

The second notion of this work focuses on the "unavoidable" nature of race in the modern world. It is a challenge posed in this way: in spite of the deficiencies of "race" as a scientifically descriptive indicator of life as it is known in the wake of Columbus and others, it remains the most prevalent and powerful social, political, and economic manifestation of life in these times. In this context, in spite of Appiah's observations, it is a very real, "unreal" determinant in political, economic, and social apportionment. And in that, theoretically unsound or not, it has helped to guide the course of history, historical inquiry, and the writing of history. It is, as William Edward Burghardt Du Bois wrote in 1903, "*the* problem of the twentieth century."[2]

Even the field of world history is plagued with these questions and contradictions. In the structuring of a world history concentration, some of us are forced to ask what should be included. For peoples of African descent this is a pointed question. For those of the diaspora it is poignant. The case is particularized by African Americans.

Are African Americans to be included in the new configuration of the world? How should their history be treated? Then we are forced to ask how should African Americans who *write* history be regarded? How should those who write and yet have been the valid subjects of historical discussion be considered? Within such a context what does

---

1. Kwame Anthony Appiah, *In My Father's House* (Oxford: Oxford University Press, 1992), x. George Frederickson writes of racism as a "rationalized pseudoscientific theory positing the innate inferiority of nonwhites." *The Black Image in the White Mind: The Debate on Afro-American Character and Destiny, 1817–1914* (New York: Harper and Row, 1971), xi.

2. William Edward Burghardt Du Bois, *Souls of Black Folk* (Greenwich: Fawcett Publications, 1961), reprint of 1903 original, 23; italics added. Yet, in conjunction with this trenchant observation, Du Bois noted in a February 9, 1925, draft of a speech at Cooper Union:

> The best modern method of insuring this domination of dark labor is by spreading a propaganda which will hinder democratic development from crossing the color line. *A vast propaganda of this sort is going on. It is not scientific because science is more and more denying the concept of race and the assumption of ingrained racial differences. But a cheap and pseudo-science is being . . . [broadcast] . . . which makes the mass of people in civilized countries think that yellow people and brown people and black people are not human in the same sense that white people are human and cannot be allowed to develop or to rule themselves.*

> *The Correspondence of W. E. B. Du Bois*, Herbert Aptheker, ed. (Amherst: University of Massachusetts Press, 1973), 303; italics added. It might be allowed that Dubois's remarks could also be read as an indication that the "pseudo-science" of race denied the history of these peoples as well.

such a discussion say about our notions of historiography? How does the question of race reinforce the writing of history?

As Edith Sanders has pointed out, the question of the "black" in global historical development is so crucial "that it has become a problem of epistemology." It has become central to our definition of knowledge in the modern age. In the modern period it has been read in such a manner as to indicate that the presence of the black is ahistorical and characteristic of the absence of knowledge, whereas the absence of the black constitutes a bona fide historical event and is therefore worthy of being classified as knowledge. That is, the event, civilization, person, or peoples become *worth* knowing if there is *no* black presence. Black represents the extreme in this epistemological construction of histories, cultures, and civilizations, which moves from this point toward "whiteness" and which realizes the value of these histories, cultures, and civilizations in terms of their distance from "black"/"blackness."[3]

How did history and the writing of history come to this point? Are race and racism inherent to the historical process? The infusion of race into historiography, while not as recent as Appiah would have us believe, is a relatively short-lived phenomenon. It is associated with the expansion of Europe in the modern age, and its high point revolves around the colonization of the western hemisphere, new world slavery, and ironically, as Michael Biddiss indicates, the reaction against the processes of democratization.[4] The rationalizations that are formulated from the eighteenth through the twentieth century are based on conceptualizations and theories that seek to justify these major events—the events that epitomize *the* historical narrative of the modern age: exploration, capitalism, and the development of Western

3. Edith R. Sanders, "The Hamitic Hypothesis; Its Origins and Functions in Time Perspective," *Journal of African History*, 10, 4 (1969), 521. William Javier Nelson has argued that "American social practice through the nation's history has . . . focused . . . on biological factors such as the presence or absence of African ancestry." "Racial Definition: Background for Divergence," *Phylon*, 47, 4 (December 1986), 320. Jack D. Forbes, "The Manipulation of Race, Caste, and Identity: Classifying Afro-Americans, Native Americans, and Red-Black People," *Journal of Ethnic Studies*, 17, 4 (Winter 1990), 10–12.

4. Michael D. Biddiss, "Gobineau and the Origins of European Racism," *Race*, 7, 3 (January 1966), 256–257:

The invention of the concept of separate, biological "races" was also designed to exclude. . . . [O]ne can argue that the invention of biological races . . . has been a social and political process closely related to the spread of European imperialism and the perceived necessity for justifying slavery and conquest. (Italics in the original)

Forbes, "Manipulation," 7–8. Frederickson, *Image*, xi–xiii. In this regard, linking both Biddiss and Forbes, Laura Brown underscores the "necessary intimacy of structures of oppression and liberation in eighteenth-century culture." "Reading Race and Gender: Jonathan Swift," *Eighteenth-Century Studies*, 23, 4 (Summer 1990), 426.

democracy. The rationalizations and the concepts that accompanied them provided a rich mythology—a mytho-history—not only for the modern world but for all the periods that preceded it as well. In these very events we can realize our reluctance—our recalcitrance—in relinquishing these myths or allowing for their alteration. They are simply too important to our sense of who we are. And that, as Charles Tilly would put it, is central to the thesis of Western history.[5]

It is, in fact, in the early historical works of the modern age that the racial dynamic comes to the fore. Modern genetic and racial arguments were presented early on within the context of "history." Edward Long's *History of Jamaica*, published in 1774, is one example of this. The writings of Enlightenment figures such as Rousseau, Locke, Hume, and Jefferson would find resonance in a work such as Long's. As important, if not more so, as Stuart Gilman has argued, the "scientific" basis for their arguments would emerge in such notions as degeneracy theory, phrenology, craniology, eugenics, and social Darwinism. Gilman adds to this list the field of clinical medicine as an underlying feature of modern biological racism. The new sciences "validated race as a concept" and provided the foundations for the construction of the basic tenets of racial inferiority.[6]

Within this scientific and specifically biological nexus, the African was not simply inferior in his or her present condition; that inferiority was based on historical circumstance. The theory of evolution could be used to justify the African's present situation through speculation on that history: if the African were enslaved presently, then that enslavement spoke to inherent inferiority, which at best remained stagnant over time, or increasingly degenerated in contact with stronger, more vibrant intellectually and biologically fit "races." On the path of "historical evolution," the African was at the very beginning. There were no triumphs, no achievements, no great monuments to mark a journey that had not commenced, a journey that the intellectuals of the period doubted could be undertaken.

The histories that pointedly, and then over time nonchalantly, excluded the African relied on the "conquests" of science to confirm

5. Charles Tilly, "How (and What) Are Historians Doing?" *American Behavioral Scientist*, 33, 6 (July/August 1990). Forbes, "Manipulation," 10. C. G. Jung and C. Kerenyi, *Essays on the Science of Mythology* (Princeton: Princeton University Press, 1969), 18. Jung and Kerenyi speak to the importance of myth in the formation of national and supranational identity. "Myth" becomes essential to Jung's notion of the "collective consciousness." Freud even argued that dreams, at some levels, were the enactment of social mythology. Also see Martin Bernal,"*Black Athena* and the APA," *Arethusa* (special issue, Fall 1989), 25.

6. Stuart C. Gilman, "Degeneracy and Race in the Nineteenth Century," *Journal of Ethnic Studies*, 10, 4 (Winter 1983), 27, 30, 44.

their theories. The ways in which the new sciences were used underscore Tilly's assertion that the craft of history is "in general . . . a federation of overlapping disciplines." These sciences are, as Alice Littlefield et al. remind us, biased by "unconscious sociocultural influences which affect [researchers] especially when they have been steeped in the positivist faith that science is a neutral objective activity, largely immune to external influences."[7] This was never truer than in the eighteenth and nineteenth centuries, when "objectivity" became the standard and the proofs of scientific inquiry gained greater and greater currency. It was here, by way of degeneracy theory, eugenics, and the particulated studies of phrenetics and craniology, that Western biological and social sciences substantiated the inferiority of the African, the "Negro," the "black." And it was here that Africans and Africa were separated from civilization and historical progress.

The documents of naturalists, travelers, explorers, and colonialists became the staple fare of eighteenth- and nineteenth-century academic discourse. And while they were "accepted as objective testimony in travel literature and ultimately encoded in science in the most widely read volumes of travel and natural history through the middle of the [nineteenth] century," they remained "fiction . . . at least as disturbing, and much more offensive" than *Gulliver's Travels*.[8]

Degeneracy theory deserves particular mention here. It, more than any other concept, epitomized the historiography of the modern age. Gilman has pointed out that it was Long's *History of Jamaica* that first made the linkage between the theory of degeneracy and ideas of racial inferiority.[9] Long's treatment, in the company of works such as Georges Louis Leclerc Buffon's *Natural History* (1749–1760) and Janet Schaw's *Journal of a Lady of Quality*, prepared the stage for discussions of peoples of African descent in terms of their genealogical and evolutionary closeness to apes as opposed to humans beings. These discussions supposedly took place within the context of the writers having viewed the African in her or his "native habitat." This "scientific" assertion gave more veracity to the arguments, no matter how outlandish they might appear by today's standards. The weight and the wide acceptance of the authors gave the arguments even greater currency. So when they, like so many other writers of the period, referred to the tendency, proficiency, and frequency with which African women mated with apes; the ways in which black children resembled and

7. Tilly, "How (and What)," 686. Alice Littlefield, Leonard Lieberman, and Larry T. Reynolds, "Redefining Race: The Potential Demise of a Concept in Physical Anthropology." *Current Anthropology*, 23, 6 (December 1982), 653.

8. Brown, "Reading," 436.

9. Gilman, "Degeneracy," 30.

acted like monkeys; and the moral disposition of the adults being the same as "monkies and apes,"[10] they were illustrating what they viewed as the results of a certain and perpetually debilitating miscegenation among the *species* of African descent—human and beast. The result was a degeneracy that could not be overcome and that in itself threatened the very core of the civilized world.

While both Long and Schaw deserve particular attention here—in part because their observations coincided with the emergence of both the American state and the primacy of the institution of slavery in the modern world—it is Long's treatment of the policies of Jamaican planters toward Africans as primarily a defense of the institution of slavery that provides the most in-depth example of the reasoning of the period. As he noted, somewhat sardonically, "[T]he planters do not want to be told, that their Negroes are human creatures. If they believe them to be of human kind, they cannot regard them (which Mr. Sharpe insists they do) as no better than dogs or horses."[11]

Long's argument hinged on a "scientific" exposition of the racial (biological) and, therefore, social inferiority of the "Negroe," "black," "African," or "Aethiopian"—the terms were interchangeable. African biological and social inferiority manifested itself as degeneracy on several fronts. According to Long, the impact of this inferiority was witnessed through the most intimate and the most mundane contact between blacks and whites. Interbreeding caused biological degeneracy; shared customs, speech, and so in, resulted in cultural degeneracy.

Biological degeneracy was illustrated in Long's attempt to construct an argument based on the latest "scientific" thinking of the eighteenth century on race. Long begins with observations on the Spanish

---

10. Janet Schaw, *Journal of a Lady of Quality: Being the Narrative of a Journey from Scotland to the West Indies, North Carolina, and Portugal in the Years 1774 to 1776*, Evangeline Walker Andrews, ed., in collaboration with Charles McLean Andrews (New Haven: Yale University Press, 1934). Schaw's remarks on black children in Antigua circa 1774 epitomize exactly what I wish to convey here:

> Just as we got into the lane, a number of pigs run [sic] out at the door, and after them a parcel of monkeys. This not a little surprised me, but I found what I took for monkeys were negro children, naked as they were born. (78).

Schaw also makes her contribution to the degeneracy debate when she noted that the product of the union between "young black wenches" who "lay themselves out for white lovers" was a "spurious and *degenerate* breed, neither fit for the field, nor indeed any work as the true bred negro" (122). Brown, "Reading," 436–440. Along these same lines, it should be noted that Schaw and, specifically, Long would find themselves at odds with Buffon's theories concerning the "humanness" of the African. See the following Long discussion and *The History of Jamaica* (London: T. Lowndes, 1774; reprint London: Frank Cass, 1970), vol. 2, 349, 351–365.

11. Long, *History of Jamaica*, 270.

"science" of distinguishing racial intermixture. The science of intermixture consequently led to Long's assertion that the "oran-outang
and some races of black men are very nearly allied."[12] This is a conclusion that Long reaches after an extended discussion on the subject, a
discussion whose implications concerning such a genetic alliance for
whites would be echoed in the works of Gobineau and others, and
were stated most succinctly, according to Long, by the Dutch:
"[T]wenty or thirty generations . . . would hardly be sufficient to
discharge the stain."[13] Long could reason that this might be the case
because blacks were of a "different species belonging to the same
genus"—the "missing link," as it were, between man and ape: "[I]f he
is a creature, *sui generis*, he fills up the space between mankind and
the ape."[14]

Cultural degeneracy, Long asserted, was seen in the interaction
between blacks and whites, particularly white women, which resulted
in the adoption, by whites, of certain customs and mores. Long
illustrated these primarily through observations of language and
languidness.[15]

In Long's eyes, the potential cultural degeneracy of eighteenth-
century planter aristocracy had been witnessed historically. In spite of
the treatments that preceded him, Long was able to declare that the
record of Greek and Roman contact with Africans in the ancient period was one that underlined African inferiority: "[I]t is doubtful
whether we ought to ascribe any superior qualities to the more ancient
Africans; for we find them represented by Greek and Roman authors
under the most odious and despicable character."[16] The real irony is
that these ideas would receive support two centuries later in works
such as Grace Beardsley's *The Negro in Greek and Roman Civilization*
(1929) and Lloyd Thompson's *Romans and Blacks* (1989). Both assert
that blacks within the context of the classical world were seen as either
slaves or inferiors, characterized by negative depictions in the cultures
of the era.[17]

In this context, Long is finally able to illustrate the very point with

12. Ibid., 365.
13. Ibid., 261.
14. Ibid., 356, 363–365.
15. Ibid., 278–282.
16. Ibid., 354.
17. See Frank W. Snowden, *"Romans and Blacks*: A Review Essay," *American Journal of
Philology*, 3 (1990), 543–557. Also see in chapter 4 the treatment of Carter G. Woodson in regard to Grace Beardsley's work. Carter G. Woodson, *The African Background Outlined*
(Washington, D.C.[?]: The Association for the Study of Negro Life and History, 1936;
reprinted New York: Negro Universities Press, 1968), 4–6.

which Martin Bernal, his allies, and his critics contend: the rewriting of the history of the Classical Age to support the rationales that accommodate slavery and, therefore, racism, within the framework of capitalism. The ultimate notion of cultural degeneracy is evidenced in Long's treatment of Egypt by way of Goguet, who expands on the affinities between "Negroes" and Egyptians. There is a certain lack of clarity in this discussion: are we to suppose that the Egyptians are more Negro than the author is willing to explicitly state?

> The Negroes seem to conform nearest in character to the Aegyptians in whose government, says the learned Goguet, there reigned a multitude of abuses, and essential defects, authorized by the laws, and by their fundamental principles. As to their customs and manners, indecency and debauchery were carried to the most extravagant height, in all their public feasts, religious ceremonies; neither was their morality pure. It offended against the first rules of rectitude and probity; they lay under the highest censure for covetousness, perfidy, cunning, and roguery. They were a people without taste, without genius or discernment; who had only two ideas of grandeur, ill understood: knavish, crafty, soft, lazy, cowardly, and servile, superstitious in excess, and extravagantly besotted with an absurd and monstrous theology; without any skill in eloquence, poetry, music, architecture, sculpture or painting, navigation commerce or the art military. Their intellect rising to but the very confused notion, and imperfect idea of the general objects of human knowledge. But he allows that they invented some arts, and some sciences; that they had some little knowledge of astronomy, geography and the mathematics; that they had some few good civil laws and political constitutions; industrious enough adepts on judicial astrology; though their skill in sculpture and architecture, rose not above mediocrity. In these acquisitions, however imperfect, they appear far superior to the Negroes, who perhaps, in their turn, as far transcend the Aegyptians in the superlative perfection of their worst qualities.[18]

Long's treatment takes an interesting turn in that it allows Egypt to be debased because of its closeness to Africa—some might argue because of its "Africanness." By the same token, Long uses Egypt to illustrate its own degeneracy, and that of Africans in general. The gifts that an "odious and despicable" Africa might claim in ancient times came from a degenerate Egypt as well. Within this reasoning, the Aryan model, as Bernal has called it, was well underway by 1774.

Ironically, this was a degeneracy that Count Arthur de Gobineau ar-

18. Long, *History of Jamaica*, 355–356.

gued was essential to the progress of the civilized world. Yet he, too, saw it as the basis for the deterioration of that world and therefore argued vehemently against any interaction between the "races."[19] In Gobineau's thesis, the logic of the superior "Caucasoid" was tempered and enhanced by the artistic passions of "Negroid" peoples. This union provided for a fine, yet reasoned sensitivity to the arts, on one hand, and creative genius in logical pursuits, on the other. These were the qualities that accrued to whites; Africans simply benefited *overall*: there was "little compensation to be found in the fact that mixture frequently improves the lower race."[20]

In a nineteenth-century America where tensions were heightened by the issue of slavery, Gobineau's theories gained an audience in the rise of the new American School of Ethnology. The "school gained prominence under the tutelage of Samuel G. Morton (*Crania Americana*, 1839), George B. Glidden (*Types of Mankind*, 1840), and J. C. Nott," who "freely" adapted Gobineau's *Essay* for American consumption.[21] The upshot of two centuries of racial theorization rationalizing imperialism and slavery read, not altogether smoothly, something like this: the African and all peoples of African descent were incapable of independent civilization; where such a civilization was possible, it was the result of outside forces interacting with and "civilizing" inferior African elements. However, biologically and culturally, such interaction was doomed in that it created a hybrid race that was not only inferior intellectually and biologically, but was impotent as well. If these were the elements of miscegenation, then it became clear that the "great" civilizations of the world were those that had remained pure and sought to remain pure. Their longevity was a witness to their purity.

In that regard, it stood to reason that because Egypt was such an enduring civilization (Long and Goguet notwithstanding) it could not have been peopled by "hybrids," half-castes or mulattoes; and, because blacks were incapable of such a creation, Egypt must, therefore, be "white", that is, European. Writers such as W. G. Browne, in his *Travels in Africa, Egypt, and Syria*, written in 1806, "insisted that Egyptians were white." So "Egyptians emerged as Hamites, Caucasoid, uncursed and capabale [*sic*] of high civilization." Browne's insistence was joined by a chorus of voices adamant in their support of this position. The stridency of this view should be noted in Browne's title, where Egypt had

---

19. Biddiss, "Gobineau," 263.

20. Ibid., 263.

21. Gloria Horsley-Meacham, "Bull of the Nile: Symbol, History, and Racial Myth in 'Benito Cereno,'" *New England Quarterly*, 64, 2 (June 1991), 236–237. Biddiss, "Gobineau," 264.

already been separated from Africa.[22] It is a separation that continues to this day in some intellectual circles and in popular culture in general.

As Glidden remarked, "[T]he new ethnology . . . sought to take 'the whole question [of Nilotic ethnicity] out of the hands of the Greeks' and 'unscientific tourists'" and to place it in the hands of men of science who would provide objective veracity to the historical narrative of who and what the Egyptians were.[23]

Why was it necessary to take Egypt "'out of the hands of the Greeks'" and who were these "'unscientific tourists'"? Chief among the "Greeks" and "unscientific tourists" was Herodotus. It was Herodotus, or more precisely the *interpretations* of Herodotus, who allowed for a counterargument to the proponents of racial inferiority found in the new American School of Ethnology and those ideas and writings that preceded it. In fact, the arguments of Greek "tourists", poets, playwrights, geographers, and philosophers—not to mention the numerous Romans and Jews of antiquity—lent themselves to a conceptualization of Egypt and the entire eastern Mediterranean basin that was fundamentally different from the eighteenth-, nineteenth-, and twentieth-century rationalizations that form our standard histories.

Whenever a blow was struck for peoples of African descent in the struggle against the slavery and imperialism of the modern age, there was the evocation of the ancients. The use of Herodotus became so widespread in the defense of Africans that his very credibility could be questioned *again*. As A. R. Burn reminds us, on this account, the importance of Herodotus here is not whether what he recorded was true, but *"the fact that these stories were current is . . . historical fact."*[24]

While Herodotus is the source most prolifically used and most often

22. Horsley-Meacham, "Bull of the Nile," 237–238. Sanders, "Hamitic Hypothesis," 526, 527. Sanders's work on this point is extremely important in that it outlines the history of historical writing on the question of Egyptian identity in the transition and transmutation of the "Hamite." It forces us to refer to the history of the ideas under discussion in order to make sense of the discussion itself. Also see Dickson D. Bruce, Jr., "Ancient Africa and the Early Black American Historians, 1883–1915," *American Quarterly*, 36 (Winter 1984), 690.

23. Horsley-Meacham, "Bull of the Nile," 237–238. The two centuries of intellectual discussion and debate that preceded these conclusions included the work of some who have been regarded as the most brilliant minds of the Western enterprise. Biddiss lists them briefly as William Jones, Thomas Young, J. C. Pritchard, and Franz Bopp. They were followed by Edward Bulwer-Lytton, R. G. Latham, J. G. Rhodes, and W. von Schlegel. These scholars all lent themselves to the development and the rise of "Aryanism." Their work was augmented "scientifically" by Linnaeus, Buffon, and Blumenbach. Biddiss, "Gobineau," 257, 263.

24. As A. R. Burn indicates in his 1970 introduction to Aubrey de Selincourt's translation of *The Histories*, Herodotus had been called a liar repeatedly by some ancient sources, yet their "appellations" may have reflected the problems of *our* translations. In any case, it was within this context that Herodotus could be brought to task on the basis of what he heard and saw by modern critics who opposed the idea of an African Egypt. *The Histories*, 10,

rebuked, there are other ancient sources that lent themselves to the notion that Egypt was a "black" state, the most emphatic of which concerns the implications drawn from Diodorus Siculus's assertion that "the Egyptians are colonists sent out by the Ethiopians [i.e., the black peoples]."[25]

The notion of "blackness" as presented here relates directly to the terminology that the ancients used and that scholars such as Professor Frank M. Snowden corroborate as standard characterization of the time. It is the very word *Ethiopian* that in the classical lexicon defines the African more precisely than any other term, that is, the African in relation to modern racial categorization.[26]

The Frenchmen C. F. Volney, Dominique-Vivant Denon, and Henri Gregoire would bring the "scientific" proofs of an African Egypt to the world. Their conclusions, based on a firsthand exploration and review of Egyptian sites and artifacts, lead to conclusions that some would find rather astounding.

Volney wrote in 1802:

[A] people now forgotten, discovered, while others were yet barbarians, the elements of the arts and sciences. A race of men now rejected from society for their *sable skin and frizzled hair*, founded, on the study of the laws of nature, those civil and religious systems which still govern the universe.[27]

28–29. In reference to other classical sources, *Newsweek*, taking the pulse of the academic world, reported that "Bernal's critics treat the ancient texts more suspiciously." "Out of Egypt, Greece," *Newsweek* (September 23, 1991), 50.

25. *Diodorus of Sicily*: English translation by C. H. Oldfather (London: Leob Classical Library, 1935), vol. 2, 91, quoted in Basil Davidson, *African Civilization Revisited* (Trenton: Africa World Press 1991), 61–62. Frank W. Snowden, *Blacks in Antiquity* (Cambridge: Harvard University Press, 1970), 109.

26. Snowden, *Blacks in Antiquity*, 1–33. Snowden, *Before Color Prejudice* (Cambridge: Harvard University Press, 1983), 1–17.

27. C. F. Volney, *The Ruins: or, Meditations on the Revolutions of Empires: and the Law of Nature* (1802; reprint New York: Peter Eckler, 1926), quoted in Bruce, "Ancient Africa," 689. In an 1877 edition of Volney's *Ruins*, the editor quickly notes in a translation apparently sanctioned by Volney that the reference to "opulent cities, the pride of the ancient kingdom of Ethiopia" that implied the "negroness" of the Egyptians was recanted, as Du Bois indicated, in the face of more "scientific" information that enabled Volney "to correct many errors, in a later work published in Paris in 1814/15 entitled New Researches on Ancient History." The editor also used this revelation as an opportunity to cast doubts on credibility of both Homer and Herodotus, whose observations "necessarily induced the author of Travels in Syria to believe that this ancient people was of the negro race." *Volney's Ruins* (Boston: Josiah P. Mendum, 1877), 33. In this regard, it seems that the editor of *Volney's Ruins* may have concluded, much like Bovill in his treatment of another African population, that the Egyptians were "black" but not "Negro." E. W. Bovill, *The Golden Trade of the Moors* (London: Oxford University Press, 1968).

Both Denon and Volney concluded that the Egyptians were "Negroid"; and Gregoire enlisted Herodotus to prove this point.[28]

As Volney remarked, it would be with astonishment that "we reflect that to the race of negroes, at present our slaves, . . . our arts and sciences"[29] Within the context of the debate over American slavery, Denon and Napoleon were granted honorary membership in the American Academy of Science for "opening Egypt to scholarship."[30] All sides of a convoluted debate on slavery, abolition, resistance, and colonization would draw on classical sources and contemporary "scientific" evidence to make the same assertion: the African in America was descended from Africans who had raised one of the grandest civilizations of ancient times: Egypt.[31]

It was an "objective" argument that "fueled" what Gloria Horsley-Meacham has described as "the fiercest debate raging in nineteenth century America"; it was, as well, a debate that was manifested globally.[32] Then, as now, it was exceedingly difficult to view the Egyptian as "black" and to accept the "seeming paradox" that the "oldest civilization of the *West*" was African.[33]

28. Bruce, "Ancient Africa," 690, 691. Sanders, "Hamitic Hypothesis," 525.

29. Sanders, "Hamitic Hypothesis," 525.

30. Bruce, "Ancient Africa," 690.

31. Bruce, "Ancient Africa," 691. Horsley-Meacham, "Bull of the Nile," 235, 239. Frederickson, *Black Image*, 13. Among nineteenth century American writers who would use the same paradigm were David Walker, Herman Melville, Lydia Maria Child, and Frederick Douglass.

32. Horsley-Meacham, "Bull of the Nile," 236.

33. Sanders, "Hamitic Hypothesis," 525; italics added.

═══ TWO

Blackness in Ancient History
Criticism and Critique

> [T]he "blackness" of *Black Athena* stands as the most politically charged issue of the book.
>
> Molly Myerowitz Levine, "The Challenge of
> *Black Athena* to Classics Today"

The implications of blackness in historiography have been played out in the last three centuries in a manner that is both frustrating and confusing. There is the equation of "Africa" = "colored" = "Negro" = "black." With some variation, it becomes a definition that has gained general acceptance. Then within the subtleties and nuances of the debate there are some people who are "colored" and not "black"; and some who are "black" yet not "Negro." In all this, some people may be defined as "all of the above" and yet not be "African." Though, in fact, it is Africa that defines the geopolitical boundaries of their cultural, social, and political identities.

We need to acknowledge that "blackness" is a political definition as well.[1] So it should come as no surprise that the issue of "blackness" has been one of the most strident and galvanizing aspects of current historical debate. The criticism of Martin Bernal's *Black Athena*, in

---

1. As was the term "African" before it, and "colored" and "Negro" (both with lower and uppercase *n*). The two latest variations on the political theme are the "political blackness" of South Africa where "blackness" becomes a banner of political virtue worn by anyone who opposes apartheid. The other is seen in the choice of the term "African[-]American" as an expression of a certain political as well as cultural and social phenomenon.

large part, bears witness to this. That criticism is part and parcel of the legacy of the eighteenth- and nineteenth-century scholarship that has molded the intellectual and popular conceptions of the twentieth century. In a society driven by race, as it were—in a society regarded as anti-intellectual (even within some circles of the intelligentsia)—the superficial holds great sway.

Within that context, the public and the intellectual community have been taken with the title *Black Athena* and its various implications. Bernal, over and again, in what has become for me one of the weakest aspects of his defense of the work, has responded that the term "black" is the problem: "'Black' is, of course, a very ambiguous and loaded term . . . I am now convinced that the title of my work should have been *African Athena*."[2] Bernal's backpedaling on a seemingly insignificant issue has historical precedent that would have carried great weight in the eyes of one of his heroes, W. E. B. Du Bois. Du Bois noted that Volney, faced with withering criticism over his assertion that the ancient Egyptians were black ("negroid"), recanted his position.[3] Along these lines, given the tenor of her argument, Molly Myerowitz Levine offers this ironic insight: "One can easily sympathize . . . with the annoyance of non-white people at what may seem to be a peculiarly perverse pedantry over the application of the term 'black' to ancient Egyptians."[4] The terminology is, as she points out, key to the "most immediate and popular implications" of Bernal's work.[5] Yet we are forced to ask, even with the change that Bernal suggests from *Black Athena* to *African Athena*, just what implications would the reader draw from such a change? Would it clarify or further confuse? In modern communication, what are the reflexive vocabulary equivalences for "African"? Is "black" not one of them?

The crucial analytical essence of Bernal's response to the notion of "black" and "blackness" is that the response itself shows the confusion over physical definition and cultural determinant. That confusion has

2. Martin Bernal, *"Black Athena* and the APA," *Arethusa*, (special issue, Fall 1989), 31. Ellen K. Coughlin, "In Multiculturalism Debate, Scholarly Book on Ancient Greece Plays Controversial Part," *Chronicle of Higher Education* (July 31, 1991), A6.

3. "The Frenchman Volney called the civilization of the Nile valley Negro after his visit. But such a barrage of denial from later men met him that he withdrew his earlier conclusions, not because of further investigation, but because of scientific public opinion in the nineteenth century." W. E. B. Du Bois, *The World and Africa* (1946; rev. and enl. ed., New York: International Publishers, 1965), 118. Gloria Horsley-Meacham, "Bull of the Nile: Symbol History, and Racial Myth in 'Benito Cereno,'" *New England Quarterly,* 64, 2 (June 1991), 237.

4. Molly Myerowitz Levine, "The Use and Abuse of *Black Athena,*" *American Historical Review,* 97, 2 (April 1992), 454.

5. Ibid, 454.

prompted a broad array of criticism from various quarters centered on the "blackness" of Egypt. The cover story of *Newsweek* for September 23, 1991, was entitled "Afrocentrism: Was Cleopatra Black?" The nine pages of text were strategically accompanied by boxes that asked such pointed questions as "Were the ancient Egyptians black Africans?" and "Were the Greek gods actually Egyptian?" This issue of *Newsweek* was indicative of the questions that informed public opinion on supposedly scholarly, intellectual discourse. It made clear, as well, that public opinion and scholarly discourse also lend themselves to the most current debate over multiculturalism, diversity, and something called *Afrocentrism*. The underlying tone of a number of the articles, the scholarly commentary, and general public response was reminiscent of that of an article which appeared in the late nineteenth-century magazine *Popular Science Monthly* that posed the question in its title: "Are we to become Africanized?"[6] Again, another irony occurs here in that exploration of the "race" question is given to a journal that is not only "scientific," but "popular" as well. A. L. Chapin, in an 1883 review in *The Dial*, wrote in response to the "greatest question of the day, the future of the African in the United States," "that the article on this question in the 'Popular Science Monthly' prompts a few thoughts which may be fitly expressed in connection with our notice of the book before us." That book was George Washington Williams's *History of the Negro Race in America*.[7]

The tragedy of this debate on "blackness" is that it has yet to establish what it means to be "black" in real terms, as Jack Forbes might insist.[8] There is no hard, critical analysis of "blackness" as a multidimensional phenomenon in the modern age; and its best treatment for the classical period, by Snowden, is confined solely to the physical and is limited by notions of purity. So the debate remains, in some ways, the debate of two centuries ago, defined by the polemics and politics of the moment. Within it is a caricature of concepts such as multicultur-

6. *Newsweek* (September 23, 1991), 42–50. Coughlin, "Multiculturism Debate." David Nicholson, "'Afrocentrism' and the Tribalization of America," *Washington Post* (September 23, 1991). Robert Reinhold, "Class Struggle," *New York Times Magazine* (September 29, 1991), 26–52. H. Ganett, "Are We to Become Africanized?" *Popular Science Monthly*, 27, 145 (1883).

7. A. L. Chapin, "The Negro Race in America," *The Dial* (March 1883), 252. One of the most important items in the pieces in *Popular Science Monthly* and *The Dial* is the usage of the terms "African" and "Africanized." They speak to the fact that "African," "colored," "Negro," "black," and "Ethiopian" were regarded as synonymous. Chapin and his audience also accepted Williams's assertion that a considerable and important segment of the Egyptian population were black as well.

8. Jack D. Forbes, "The Manipulation of Race, Caste, and Identity: Classifying Afro-Americans, Native Americans, and Red-Black People," *Journal of Ethnic Studies*, 17, 4 (Winter 1990), 10–12.

alism, diversity, and Afrocentrism, rather than a valid assessment of what these ideas might really mean and how they might enhance our intellectual pursuit of who we are.

There has been in the discourse surrounding *Black Athena* a fear of "blackness." To paraphrase Molly Levine, one might regard black as "abusive."[9] It remains an unknown, undefined in relation to its reality and inadequately contextualized within given time and space. Therefore, within the setting of these discussions it remains representative of the "other." It is another characterization of the rise of the modern academy and its disciplinary structure, one that avidly plays itself out in popular culture. This fear of "blackness" and the potential of "blackness" to abuse are not far removed from the eighteenth- and nineteenth-century degeneracy anxieties of Long and Gobineau. These anxieties within the context of the academy might be characterized by the fear that "blacks" and "blackness" will interject elements into the intellectual discourse that will cause that discourse to degenerate. Historically, we can explain this notion through the conventionally assumed relations between "blacks" and "blackness," and history itself. How can those who, ostensibly, have no history enter into historical discourse? They cannot without the abridgement or the destruction of that discourse. Their interjection causes the degeneration of history. In the contemporary setting this rationale is echoed in terms such as the "canon" or the cry to raise and maintain "standards."

What I mean here is that "black" and "blackness" have been abstracted over the past two centuries or so to be oppositional. "Black" / "blackness" has never been defined in terms of itself or as a positive, but always in opposition to white—as its negative, as negation itself. This definition is complicated by the fact that within the realm of human physical reality, "black" and "white" do not exist. As terms, they are descriptive abstractions, just like "dark" and "light." Yet, because of notions of race, one is more likely to be "black" than "white," especially if one has to contend with the legal descriptions of a consciousness molded in certain corners of the Western world. However, even such an observation, as descriptive terminology, does not attribute "racial consciousness" to the Egyptians. It simply provides a contemporary definition for characterizing the Egyptian's physical appearance. Then, returning to the oppositional abstraction of "black" and "white," if Egyptians are not "black," they *must* be "white." These seem to be the only options, given the rigidity of definition, or as Bernal has put it, the tendency toward "misplaced precision."[10] And

9. Levine, "Use and Abuse," 454.
10. Bernal, *"Black Athena,"* 31.

they are the blunted tools with which most of the scholarly community and the general public work.

So within this scenario, there *can be* "blacks" in the United States, while there can*not* be "blacks" in Egypt. Egyptian "blacks" are not to be confused with West African "blacks."[11] Again we are faced with the "peculiarly perverse pedantry" to which Levine referred. In that perversion "black" is prohibitive and inhibitive. It is representative of overemphasis on race and it poses the danger of "reopening the nineteenth century discourse on race and its origins." "Blackness" allied to the controversy of *Black Athena,* "blackness" as the controversy of *Black Athena*, provides the perfect arena for the "misuse" or "abuse" of ideas: race and blackness.[12]

If we recall Glidden's pledge to free Egypt of Greeks and unscientific tourists, then just as we asked who those people were, we must ask who these people who would misuse and abuse the ideas of race and blackness are. For those making the claim, they are the "bad boys" of academe: the "radical Afrocentrists."[13] In good historiographic fashion, we are obligated to ask what makes them "bad" and what makes them "radical"? Bernal offers a key to this, and is supported by Levine.

Bernal recounts a chance meeting with Thomas Kuhn at which Kuhn remarked on Bernal's participation on the APA panel on *Black Athena* that "[I]t is all happening to soon. Disciplines should not respond so quickly to fundamental challenges." After further discussion, Kuhn blessed the gathering by saying: "[T]he important thing is that the meeting is being held." Bernal underscored Kuhn's analysis and provided insight into why some Afrocentrists might be considered "bad"/"radical" when he offered the following observation:

> Certainly, if a Black were to say what I am now putting in my books, their reception would be very different. They would be assumed to be one-sided and partisan, pushing a Black nationalist line, and therefore dismissed. . . .
>
> My ideas are still so outrageous that I am convinced that if I, as their proposer, did not have all the cards stacked in my favor, *I would not have enjoyed even a first hearing.*[14]

---

11. Bernal, *"Black Athena,"* 31. Clearly, the notion implicit here is that because "Egyptian blacks" (if there be such a thing) cannot be equated with "West African blacks," then, by extension, there can be no relation with "American blacks."

12. Levine, "Use and Abuse," 440–453.

13. Levine, "Use and Abuse," 453.

14. Bernal, *"Black Athena,"* 17–18, 20; italics added.

Levine addresses historiography as a culprit, though she is extremely ambiguous and sometimes hostile to those she labels as "radical Afrocentrists." She sympathizes with African Americans over the "omission and distortion of their history in American and European historiography" while she castigates "radical Afrocentrists" for their notions of the "irredeemable unreliability of 'European' historiography," a historiography that, she argues a few sentences later, had tremendous responsibility for engendering "an elitist and separatist attitude that marginalizes black scholarship and the arguments of Afrocentrists in the fallacious assumption that these are not and will never be part of the academic mainstream."[15]

In summary, some Afrocentrists have become "radical" because of the ways in which an "elite" and often "separatist" academy has characterized not only their works but many of the works that preceded them. As one of Bernal's most strident critics has put it, Bernal's greatest sin is that he has deliberately or inadvertently allowed himself to be used to advance "Afrocentrist theories that cannot be supported by historical, anthropological or archaeological criteria." Chief among these theories is the idea that there was "a significant role for blacks in Egyptian society."[16]

Robert Pounder goes on to exonerate the historiography that has brought us this far by adding:

> the reason we cannot accept his [Bernal's] theories is because they force the conclusion that racist historians counterfeited evidence. However imperfectly they may have construed evidence, however selectively they emphasized it, *the evidence itself remains.*[17]

The rancor of so very many of the reviews of *Black Athena* created the expectations that the special issue of *Arethusa* would dismantle Bernal's thesis. Interestingly enough, Pounder's assertion in 1992 that there was lack of support for Bernal's ideas across the spectrum is simply not borne out with the unanimity we are led to expect. Levine writes that in "the discussion . . . the most enthusiastically sympathetic, on occasion poignant support for Professor Bernal's work came from archaeologists."[18]

This support came, in part, from a paper presented by Professor

15. Levine, "Use and Abuse," 451, 453–454.

16. Robert Pounder, "*Black Athena 2*: History Without Rules," *American Historical Review*, 97, 2 (April 1992), 463.

17. Ibid., 484.

18. Molly Myerowitz Levine, "The Challenge of *Black Athena* to Classics Today," *Arethusa* (special edition, Fall 1989), 9.

Sarah Morris in which she concludes that the archaeological evidence suggests "more extensive Oriental influences on Greek prehistory than even Professor Bernal has assumed."[19] Morris argues that the

> archaeological discoveries, old and new, support Bernal's notion of how "Oriental" Greece was from the second millennium B.C. onwards. . . . The relationship between Greece and the Near East, including but by no means limited to the period called "Orientalizing" (the seventh century) is more palpable . . . for the archaeologist than for the philologist, historian or linguist.[20]

Morris may have answered some of the challenges put forth by Pounder and others, but she has led us back to the same old definitional dilemma: what do we mean when we say "black," "white," "European," "African"? What is the meaning of "Oriental"? The question involves more twists and turns when we review Said's notions of "Orientalism," and we ask ourselves who and what may be classified as "Oriental"? Is it permissible to use another nineteenth-century derivative (in much the same way as "black," "negro," or "African" is used), "Near East," to approximate this concept of the "Orient"/"Oriental"/"Orientalism"? Is this another example of "peculiarly perverse pedantry"? In using it do we affix the same or similar stigmas such as "racial consciousness" to cultures and peoples who might be characterized as "Oriental"? And by the usage of these definitions, is Egypt "Oriental," "African," "Oriental/African," "all of the above," or "none of the above"?[21]

Morris's use of Martin West to illustrate her position aptly demonstrates the case being made here. She quotes West: "It is hardly going too far to say that the whole picture of the gods in the *Iliad* is

19. Ibid, 9.

20. Sarah Morris, "Daidalos and Kadmos: Classicism and Orientalism," *Arethusa* (special issue, Fall 1989), 39–40.

21. The question is posed in light of what seem to be the historically understood definitions pertaining to the usage of "oriental" and "orientalist." It seems that the broadest pre-twentieth-century use would have included Greece as part of the "orientalist's" domain, though as Bernal has argued, the change that would have accommodated the need to rationalize "Westernness" and "otherness" may have been prevalent at least two centuries earlier. However, if scholars like Edward Wilmot Blyden are reflective of the tone and nuances of nineteenth-century scholarship, then his designation of "great" and "eminent" "orientalists" included scholars who saw not only Egypt as the provenance of their study but included Ethiopia as well. The logical extension of their inquiries should have then included substantial parts of Africa, if not all of it, as "oriental." "The Negro in Ancient History," in E. W. Blyden, Tayler Lewis, Theodore Dwight, et al., *The People of Africa* (New York: Anson D. F. Randolph and Co., 1871), 3–6. Extrapolation on the artistic record would also bear this out. See Hugh Honor, *The Image of the Black in Western Art*, vol. 4 (Cambridge: Harvard University Press, 1989), 82–136.

oriental."[22] Contrast and square this notion with Herodotus's observation:

> [T]he names of nearly all the gods came to Greece from Egypt . . . for the names of all the gods have been known in Egypt from the beginning of time. . . . It was the Egyptians too who originated, and taught the Greeks to use[,] ceremonial meetings, processions and liturgies. . . . The Egyptians were also the first to assign each month and each day to a particular deity, and to foretell the date of a man's birth, his character, his fortunes, and the day of his death. . . . The Egyptians, too[,] have made more use of omens and prognostics than any other nation.[23]

Then allow Diodorus his say:

> Now the Ethiopians [i.e., the black peoples], as historians relate, were the first of all men, and the proofs of this statement, they say, are manifest. For they did not come into their land as immigrants from abroad but were natives of it. . . .
>
> And they [the Greek historians relied upon by Diodorus] say that they [the black peoples] were the first to be taught to honor the gods and to hold sacrifices and processions and festivals and other rites by which men honor the deity; and that in consequence their piety has been published abroad among men, and it is generally held that the sacrifices practised among the Ethiopians [i.e., the black peoples] are those which are the most pleasing to heaven. . . .
>
> They say also that the Egyptians are colonists sent out by the Ethiopians [i.e., the black peoples], Osiris having been the leader of the colony. . . . And the larger part of the customs of the Egyptians are, they [the Greek historians] hold[,] Ethiopian, the colonists still preserving their ancient manners.[24]

This passage of Diodorus has much to say; however, it seems safe to speculate that among the customs that he claims have been bequeathed to the Egyptians are those of religious ritual and ceremony. It implies that it is through the Ethiopians that the gods themselves are known. If the gods of Homer's "blameless Ethiopians" are "oriental" as West asserts and Morris seconds, then how do we define Egypt and

22. Morris, "Daidalos," 45.
23. Herodotus, *The Histories*, 149–150, 152, 159.
24. *Diodorus of Sicily*, in Davidson, *African Civilization Revisited*, 61–62.

Ethiopia? What, again, does it mean to be "oriental"? Is the "oriental" "black"? Is the "black" "oriental"?

There are more questions that compound these. Morris introduces the phenomenon of the calque and Phoenicians as "Canaanites" or "Red (Purple) People."[25] "Red" or "purple" may be easily explained here as an association with the dyes and cloth over which the Phoenicians held monopoly. The Canaanite allusion merits more scrutiny in light of Edith Sanders's "Hamitic Hypothesis." Sanders opens with the biblical passages that curse Ham and his offspring, the Canaanites. She goes on to relate the text of a sixth century A.D. Babylonian Talmud that characterized the children of Ham as "black."[26] In an expansive variation their plight was described in this way by the Middle Ages:

[S]ince you have disabled me . . . doing ugly things in blackness of night, Canaan's children shall be borne ugly and black! Moreover, because you twisted your head around to see my nakedness, your grandchildren's hair shall be twisted into kinks, and their eyes red; again because your lips jested at my misfortune, theirs shall swell; and because you neglected my nakedness, they shall go naked, and their male members shall be shamefully elongated! Men of this race are called Negroes.[27]

While we may question the existence of the term "Negro" in the classical period, Sanders informs us that the oral traditions from which this exposition comes are thought by many scholars of Hebrew myth to be a justification for Israel's conquest of Canaan.[28] If we follow this with the conceptualization of "Eastern Ethiopians," "red Ethiopians," and Ethiopians of various mixture, we can see the ambiguity that presents itself if we stick to the rigidity of racial purity, that is, the "pure negroid" type.[29]

In this light, is Snowden's criticism, as Bernal notes, "misplaced pre-

25. Morris, "Daidolos," 43–44.

26. Sanders's work is historically grounded by the writings of scholars such as Blyden and George Washington Williams, who also challenged the "Hamitic Hypothesis" and its implications. Though they could not anticipate the changes that Hamitic descent would undergo in the twentieth century, they were clear on its vibrancy, its strength and creativity, and its *blackness*. See Blyden, "The Negro," 4–8. George Washington Williams, *History of the Negro Race in America 1619–1880*, (1883; reprinted New York: Arno Press, 1968), 3–4, 7–11.

27. From R. Graves and R. Patat, *Hebrew Myths* (1964), quoted in Sanders, "Hamitic Hypothesis," 522

28. Ibid., 522. Herbert G. May and Bruce Metzger, eds., *The New Oxford Annotated Bible* (New York: Oxford University Press, 1977), 12.

29. Herodotus, *The Histories*, 468. Snowden, *Blacks in Antiquity*, vii–viii, 101–103. Bernal, "Black Athena," 30.

cision"? As Snowden defines it, the "Ethiopian," the "Negro" or "Negroid" type, is an academic archetype that reflects a "purity" which has no reality. This conclusion can be reached through Snowden's own observations and those of writers of the classical period. I believe, however, that Snowden is correct in insisting that the classical era knew none of the racial categorization of the modern world, nor its implications. Yet similar physical types, their variations, and their mixture existed then as well as now. To borrow from another time and place, Elias Saad, in his *Social History of Timbuktu,* argues that there is a false dichotomy in the characterization of Africa as "black" or "white."[30] This seems quite true in the case of Egypt. To argue that certain physical types existed that correspond to modern equivalents is not to "impute contemporary color-based consciousness to classical sources." It is an attempt to explain certain phenomena through the use of comparison. As some of those who have objected to the "Egyptian" = "black" postulate point out, "[M]any people today who consider themselves Afro-American or 'black' . . . would have no trouble finding physical types resembling their own in contemporary Egypt."[31] Judging from the iconography, there is little difficulty in finding those physical types among ancient Egyptians either.

However, the point made by Snowden and others, and even Bernal, really does not argue that the Egyptians were not "black," "Negro," or African per se. It argues that they were not *Ethiopian*; and even that is done along the most tenuous of lines. Moving from Snowden's hypothesis and descriptions concerning racial categorization and variation among ancient Ethiopians to Bernal's argument on European variation and his observation that "there are many types of 'blacks' in Africa," other interpretations are possible. The "various Ethiopians" / "many blacks" motif characterizes the reality of the modern age: "black" is a literary and figurative device. And while the term "Ethiopian" signified real physical characteristics, those characteristics were by no means immutable.[32] The historiography of the modern age has been mutable as well. "Hamites" cursed as "blacks" now become "white" and therefore the just progenitors of civilization in Africa, beginning with Egypt.[33]

30. Elias Saad, *Social History of Timbuktu* (Cambridge: Cambridge University Press, 1983), 2, 8.

31. Frank Yurco, quoted in Levine, "Use and Abuse," 455.

32. Snowden, *Blacks in Antiquity,* vii–viii, 3, 112.

33. C. G. Seligman, *Races of Africa* (New York: Henry Holt, 1930). Basil Davidson, "The Ancient World and Africa: Whose Roots?" *Race and Class,* 29, 2 (1987), 7–8. Sanders, "Hamitic Hypothesis," 526–527.

"Mutability" suggests movement, transition, even ambiguity. It speaks to notions of relativity. It also points to options and alternative ways of explaining historical phenomena. But if we remove ourselves from such an oppositional construct in deciphering the role of various peoples in the formation of history, then options and alternative visions become ways of enriching the historical discourse and filling in its gaps. This view of history becomes a historiography in its own right.

In his criticism of Bernal, Frank Turner stresses the need to "critically demonstrate" the racism of nineteenth-century intellectuals rather than simply "carefully assert" such. I believe that everyone who writes on this issue holds the same view and in many ways believes that his or her own work constitutes such a critical demonstration. In that same regard, Turner would do well to address himself to Tilly's notion of history as a composite discipline. It is in those other disciplines and in the writing of history and Classical studies that the tangible evidence is found.[34]

It seems unnecessary to repeat the events and ideological consequences of the eighteenth, nineteenth, and twentieth centuries that concretely illustrate the dynamics of racism as they relate to the academy and the intellectual community in general. What does bear repetition, however, is a brief recital of the tomes and reams of material from Long to Gobineau to Glidden through Houston Stewart Chamberlain and Albert Beveridge to William Shockley that illustrate the sentiments, attitudes, concepts, and ideologies around which history, particularly racial history, is constructed.

For Turner, because his special interests lie in nineteenth-century British intellectual history, a reminder comes by way of Basil Davidson's brief, but effective list of British intellectuals who were the heirs of Victorian rationalization and who lent themselves to racialist discourse. For men like H. E. Egerton, Reginald Copeland, and Hugh Trevor Roper—who, as Davidson points out, mounted "a rearguard action"—their work simply reflected the "imperialist culture" of the times.[35] We need simply to ask now whether or not this exposition begins to address the need for a "critical demonstration" of tangible intellectual proofs of the ways in which racism might affect the historiography of the day in much the same way as Bernal and numerous others have pointed out.

By the same token, there has to be agreement with Turner that

---

34. Frank Turner, "Martin Bernal's *Black Athena*: A Dissent," *Arethusa* (special issue, Fall 1989), 104.

35. Davidson, "Whose Roots?" 8–9.

there are other forces attendant to racism that deserve serious consideration as well. Yet our purposes are not well served if we neglect or diminish the importance that racialist thinking has had in the construction of history.

Tamara Green, in her response to Bernal, provides another important element to this discussion when she asks,"[D]id the Greeks write History, at least in the way that we have come to understand the term?" Her question revolves around the critical historiographic question of what the Greeks wanted us to know about them. Relying on Peter Berger's notions of the construction of social reality, Green goes on to speak of the ways in which the ancient Greeks fashioned "conceptual machinery" to satisfy their notions of who they *wanted* us to believe they were. In relation to Bernal's thesis of modern revisionism from the "Ancient Model" to the "Aryan Model," Green offers the example of *Greek* revisionism in the Classical Age.[36]

As Green points out, recollection and memory are crucial to the development and maintenance of socially constructed reality. The conceptual machinery is imbued with "symbolic universes" or systems whose "most recurrent" forms "are myth, religion, philosophy, art and science." If we examine any one of these areas in the construction of Greek social reality, we are impressed with what we conventionally assumed to be an *anomaly*. Yet we should be forced to explore why the Greeks found these elements so significant that they would choose to include them within the very constructions that they felt defined the Greek identity.

One such construction is seen in the myth of Perseus. It needs to be underlined that the Perseus myth is not simply any Greek myth. It serves as the archetype for the Greek institutions of kingship and the ideal of the heroic character. Because of its importance, it seems to be highly significant that Herodotus would choose to relate the following about the myth by way of history and historiography:

> The common Greek tradition is, that the Dorian kings as far back as Perseus, the son of Danae (thus not including the god)[,] are as they stand in the accepted Greek lists, and are rightly considered as of Greek nationality, because even at this early date they ranked as such, I am justified in saying, 'as far back as Perseus. . . . [I]f we trace the ancestry of Danae, the daughter of Acrisius, we find that the Dorian Chieftains are genuine Egyptians. This is the accepted Greek version of the genealogy of the Spartan royal house. . . . *How it happened*

36. Tamara Green, *Black Athena* and "Classical Historiography: Other Approaches, Other Views," *Arethusa* (special issue, Fall 1989), 55–57.

that Egyptians came to the Peleponnese, and what they did to make them-
selves kings in that part of Greece, has been chronicled by other writers.[37]

"Thus," Green tells us, "we must recognize that the process of writing History means a determination of what events merit consideration in order to rationalize experience." Green goes on to assert that there was an "ambivalence" among ancient Greeks in terms of their regard for Egyptian and Near Eastern influence. That is, not all Greeks showed the same degree of appreciation for these outside influences; yet the majority recognized their impact and contribution to Greek culture and society.[38]

Following this assessment, in many ways the importance that we attach to the events that the Greeks record is not that they *actually* happened but that the Greeks chose to inform us that they happened. That fact—that historiographic choice—then sets the stage for modern assertion and denial of who and what the Egyptians were. The Greeks are the *first* to provide the epistemological construct to which Sanders refers.[39]

So our critical task in regard to criticism of Bernal and the reference to "blacks" is to examine earnestly the role the Greeks assigned to "blacks," "Africans," and so on, in the building and maintenance of their own "socially constructed reality." It is an assessment that cannot be bounded simply by a quantification of "positive" or "negative" renderings of "blacks." It must seek to understand the significance that both positive and negative presentations had on the reality that the Greeks constructed. It takes as its thesis the concept that the Greeks must have included these people in their history because they were important to the Greek understanding, and therefore our understanding, of who the Greeks were. Once we accept this premise, we can sincerely explore the importance of who these people ("Ethiopian," "Egyptian," "African," "black") were in their own right. The inclusion of this understanding would take us back to what Green assesses as the real nature of Greek historiography: the Greek "aim in inquiring about the past was to make sense of their present reality."[40] If this is the case, then we are obligated to ask where and how the "black" fits in.

If we think that history is a device used by people to tell us who they are, what they thought themselves to be, and what is important in

---

37. Herodotus, *The Histories*, 406; italics added.
38. Green, "Classical Historiography," 58–59.
39. Sanders, "Hamitic Hypothesis," 521.
40. Green, "Classical Historiography," 64.

their lives, then what the Greeks left suffices. By analysis and interpretation, what the Greeks left also tells us that they felt the Egyptians to be extremely important and believed that those same Egyptians had intimate cultural and physical relations with other parts of Africa—particularly "Ethiopia." The Greeks believed that these relations affected not only Egyptian civilization but Greek civilization as well. This is not a question of negative or positive influence, but a question of the power of being.

THREE

Historiography and Black Historians

[I]f all that Negroes of all generations have ever done were to be obliterated from recollection forever, the world would lose no great truth, no profitable art, no exemplary form of life. The loss of all that is African would offer no memorable deduction from anything but the earth's black catalogue of crimes.

Commander Foote,
"Africa and the American Flag"

It is all happening too soon.

Thomas Kuhn to Martin Bernal

Historiography is Newtonian

In chapter 10 of volume 1 of *Black Athena*, Martin Bernal writes of the "social, intellectual and academic forces" that when faced with works of "boldness and detailed scholarship" give those works little or no response. According to Bernal, "when reacting to a fundamental challenge, disciplines first of all ignore, then dismiss peremptorily, and only finally attack the challenge."[1] Bernal was speaking, at one point, of the reception the scholarly community gave to the 1969 publication of Siegfried Morenz's work *Europe's Encounter with Africa*. This work, along with Bernal's, argued that there was "significant cultural contact

1. Martin Bernal, *"Black Athena,"* 18.

between Greece and Egypt." Bernal then offers that this response by the "disciplines" has been received by the "only other group of scholars who believe that Egypt had a major cultural influence on Greece: black Americans."[2]

In this page of exposition Bernal acknowledges "the company he keeps" and the marginality of their ideas, particularly *their ideas*. Now we need to examine why those ideas have been marginalized. We need to know, as well, why they have not been resurrected and subjected to the kind of serious academic and intellectual scrutiny as *Black Athena*. We need to know why there has been no acknowledgment of their worth as ideas; no recognition of their contribution to the "sociology of knowledge."

As a formal exercise, black historiography is over a century old. George Washington Williams wrote his *History of the Negro People* in 1883. Yet prior to this there were certainly other notions of historical treatment within the African American community. A great number of these treatments existed within the framework of folklife and were dominated by the nuances of an oral tradition. Many of them were, however, published as seminal works that defined the African American condition. From an analysis of these works it is safe to assume that the historiography that Williams initiated owed much to this tradition though it marked an abrupt departure from it as well.

Molly Levine has written that Bernal's work is important in part because it is the "first to fully integrate [a] survey of theories . . . into a sociology of knowledge."[3] Levine may be correct, but it is important to remember that the works of the "company kept" by Bernal preceded him in an examination of the sociology of knowledge—of what knowledge says about society, how knowledge is constructed and structured, and what its uses are in the social arena. These works were in turn based on a folklife and literature that challenged conventional societal assumptions about African historical and social existence and the ways in which that existence might be evidenced in America under the most arduous of circumstances. Writers, orators, and polemicists like David Walker, Lydia Maria Child, J. W. C. Pennington, Frederick Douglass, and William Wells Brown initiated and sustained this tradition. As Walker wrote in his *Appeal*:

I would only mention that the Egyptians were Africans or coloured people, *such as we are*—some of them yellow and others dark—a mix-

2. Martin Bernal, *Black Athena:The Afroasiatic Roots of Classical Civilization*, vol. 1 (New Brunswick: Rutgers University Press, 1987), 434.

3. Molly Levine, "The Use and Abuse of *Black Athena*," *American Historical Review*, 97, 2 (April 1992), 444.

ture of Ethiopians and the natives of Egypt—about the same as you see the coloured people of the United States at the present day.[4]

Frederick Douglass, possibly the most celebrated mind of his era (again, in part given the "uniqueness" of *this type* of intellect in *this type* of body),[5] spoke directly to the sociology of knowledge in relation to the most "vital issue of the age. . . . The discussion of this point opens a *comprehensive* field of inquiry. It involves the question of the unity of the human race."[6] The "comprehensive" nature of the parameters of Douglass's discussion alludes directly to the claim that Levine makes for Bernal; it is also the opening salvo in my discussion of African American historiography and the silence attributed to those voices; or better yet, the "deafness" that afflicted certain ears. How is Douglass's grasp of this issue in all its complexity any less "important," or even less compelling, given his ability to "fully integrate [a] survey of theories . . . into a sociology of knowledge," than that of Bernal? The question is not a denigration of Bernal's immense talents or the profound service he has rendered to the scholarship and intellectual discourse of the late twentieth century. It is an inquiry into why scholarship and intellectual discourse in the late twentieth century are so remiss in recognizing, in part, as Bernal does, that there are intellectual precedents to his scholarship and many of them are lodged within the black community. These precedents and the intellectuals who set them, are the very historical basis for the discussions led by Afrocentrists, whatever their stripe. Within the context of this debate—that is, the debate concerning race, historiography, and the sociology of knowledge—it is the height of historical dereliction to entertain such a discussion, such a debate, such a discourse, without the inclusion and critical examination of the intellectuals of African descent who spoke

4. "David Walker's *Appeal*," in Sterling Stuckey, *The Ideological Origins of Black Nationalism* (Boston: Beacon Press, 1972), 47.

5. Douglass was well aware of the prevailing mode of thought and he addressed himself to the issue quite clearly: "[A]n intelligent black man is always supposed to have derived his intelligence from his connection with the white race. To be intelligent is to have one's Negro blood ignored. "The Claims of the Negro Ethnologically Considered," in Howard Brotz, ed., *Negro Social and Political Thought, 1850–1920* (New York: Basic Books, 1966), 235. Douglass's observation can be logically extended to the notion of history as well. We are referred to Hugh Trevor Roper, et al. See pages 1–3 in regard to blackness as an epistemology in the construction of history. Again, Douglass illustrates this by adding that

[t]he temptation therefore, to read the Negro out of the human family is exceedingly strong. . . . The desirableness of isolating the Negro race, and especially separating them from the various people of Northern Africa, is too plain to need remark. Such isolation would remove stupendous difficulties in the way of getting the Negro in a favourable attitude for the blows of scientific christendom. (232–233).

6. Frederick Douglass, "Claims," 227, 230; italics added.

to this very issue and who preceded Bernal by so many years and decades, if not a full century or more. The absence of recognition and analysis of their thought makes the exercise of deciphering the sociology of knowledge and its relation to race well nigh impossible, and certainly ahistorical.

The industry, intellect, and scholarship attributed to these earliest of writers on the African historical condition is epitomized in Edward Wilmot Blyden's *The People of Africa* (1871). Blyden opens with a chapter on "The Negro in Ancient History" in which he amasses an astounding array of facts and supporting evidence to illustrate his premise concerning the importance of the African (the "Ethiopian") in the formation of classical civilization. He throws down the gauntlet of race and historiography in his first paragraph:

> Presuming that no believer in the Bible will admit that the Negro had his origins at the headwaters of the Nile, on the banks of the Gambia, or in the neighborhood of the Zaire, we should like to inquire by what chasm is he separated from the other descendants of Noah, who originated the great works of antiquity, so that with any truth it can be said that "if all that Negroes of all generations have ever done were to be obliterated from recollection forever, the world would lose no great truth, no profitable art, no exemplary form of life. The loss of all that is African would offer no memorable deduction from anything but the earth's black catalogue of crimes."[7]

Blyden sets the tone for those who will follow in the way he uses classical material to make the point of an African presence in and contribution to the Classical Age documented in the classical sources themselves. His analysis and referencing of the Bible, Herodotus, Homer, and Diodorus, as well as the classicists of his time, serve to remind us that the issues posed by Bernal and *Black Athena* had currency in the African American community almost two centuries ago. And then they centered on race and the ways in which it was used to construct history in a manner that is remarkably similar to the way in which the debate is being carried on now. As an example of this, Blyden refers to what is now a quite dog-eared passage of Herodotus that has been used to debate the racial affinity of the Egyptians:

> The Colchians were evidently Egyptians, and I say this, *having observed it* before I heard it from others; and it was a matter of interest

7. E. W. Blyden, Tayler Lewis, Theodore Dwight, et al. *The People of Africa,* (New York: Anson D. F. Randolph and Co., 1871) "The Negro," 1–2.

to me; I *inquired* of both people, and the Colchians had more recollection of the Egyptians than the Egyptians had of the Colchians; yet the Egyptians said that they thought the Colchians had descended from the army of Sesostris; and I form my conjecture, *not only because they are black in complexion and wooly haired*, for this amounts to *nothing*, because *others are so likewise*, etc. etc.

Blyden's citation of Herodotus is included here because of what he chose to emphasize in this famous passage. His is a clear, and as we read further, strident declaration of the African in the Classical Age not as a limited actor, but a most prolific one. He uses Herodotus and similar interpretations to take on the "tottering criticism of such superficial inquirers as the Notts and Gliddons, *et id omne genus* who base their assertions on ingenious conjectures." He adds that "Pindar and AEschylus [*sic*] corroborate the assertions of Herodotus."[8] And with that, black historiography slams through a door. The room that it enters, however, is predominantly black, and that too, will have its repercussions on how such magnificent scholarship is received.[9]

As Dickson Bruce illustrates, black historiography was such a key component of the African American examination of the sociology of knowledge that almost a decade of student and faculty exhortation were devoted to it on black university campuses before Williams published *A History of the Negro in America*.[10] The earliest of black historiographic writings began with Egypt and Ethiopia in an attempt not so much to explain, the black position in a white world, but to offer an impetus for changing that position.

Black historiography, even before Williams, addressed these very questions, implicitly and explicitly. Since Williams, African American scholars and the various historiographies that they represent have had one generality: they have all spoken to the racist social and political forces that have framed their existence and the writing of history in the modern world.

Most of these scholars have been consistent in addressing the ways

8. Blyden et al., "The Negro," 10. Frederick Douglass also singled out Glidden, Nott, and Morton, noting that they wrote "evidently to degrade the Negro and support the then prevalent Calhoun doctrine of the rightfulness of slavery." *Life and Times of Frederick Douglass* (1892 revised ed.; New York: Collier Books, 1962), 375.

9. As Levine has put it, rather rhetorically: "Let *them* believe that Egyptians were black, that the Greeks stole their knowledge from Egypt—it doesn't really matter." Use and Abuse," 454.

10. Dickson D. Bruce, Jr., "Ancient Africa and the Early Black American Historians, 1883–1915," *American Quarterly*, 36 (Winter 1984), 692–693. Also see David McBride, "Africa's Elevation and Changing Racial Thought at Lincoln University, 1854–1886," *Journal of Negro History*, 62 (1977).

in which knowledge about them, their people, their history, and their culture has been constructed, interpreted, and disseminated. In fact, a crucial component of what has come to be called "Afrocentrist" thought is just that—the sociology of knowledge—and this, in fact, is one of the greatest sources of controversy centered on the general question of "blacks" in the Classical Age.

One of the central themes in the sociology of knowledge for black intellectuals is this question of construction, interpretation, and dissemination. Among the outstanding early contributions to this intellectual discussion were Carter G. Woodson's *Miseducation of the Negro* and W. E. B. Du Bois's *Education of Black People*. As Robert Harris has observed, the biases of "the academy as a qualification for membership in the historical profession" have been a method of gatekeeping which has marginalized black historiography in both the historical and contemporary sense.[11]

Yet the fact that a different sort of historiography (or several new historiographies) emerged among African American scholars from the mid-nineteenth century onward is implicitly acknowledged by August Meier and Elliot Rudwick in their *Black History and the Historical Profession*. They set as their charge a determination of the essential questions of historiography as they relate to black scholars:

> the relationship between scholarly values, ideologies and writings, the manner in which scholars' perspectives changed over time, the way that intellectual interaction influenced historical interpretation, and the role of philanthropies, publishers, history departments and professional organizations in advancing the field of inquiry.[12]

A determinant feature of these histories and historiographies is that the overwhelming majority focus on the African past with particular reference to classical Egypt and Ethiopia. So yes, as Levine complains, "ancient Egypt" does become a "metonym" for ancient Africa in much the same way Greece and Rome served that exact purpose for ancient Europe.[13]

Over time, the refinement of this aspect of African American historiography occurred with the emergence of African studies. African studies had a distinct impact on historical methodology. Beginning with William Leo Hansberry in roughly 1916, this methodological

11. Robert Harris, "The Flowering of Afro-American History," *American Historical Review*, 92, 5 (December 1987), 1151.

12. August Meier and Elliot Rudwick, *Black History and the Historical Profession* (Urbana: University of Illinois Press, 1986), xi. Harris, "Flowering," 1153.

13. Levine, "Use and Abuse," 452.

expansion, coupled with the broadened focus of African studies as a discipline, allowed for a reinterpretation of Africa and Africans that had begun with Williams in 1883. It was a reinterpretation of people, places, and events that in the conventional wisdom were assumed not to exist. A hallmark of this historiography and the histories that it created was a realization that "intellectual and political considerations are pervasively connective and interactive." This meant that the study of African-related histories did not reside exclusively in the academy. There was in all history related to the black experience a "new synthesis," much like that of which Nathan Huggins wrote regarding the African American heritage and its relation to American history. This becomes important because it was assumed that African Americans lacked history.[14] By extension, this notion had been transferred to Africa and to all peoples of African descent: because Africa had no history, it could make no contribution to the history of the world.

Black historiography began as a "counterbalance" to the prevailing historical notions of black inferiority. Early historical tendencies were revisionist in that they sought to champion racial pride while promoting integrationist sentiments as well.[15] Yet Ethiopia and Egypt remained key to "powerful arguments against . . . black inferiority."[16]

George Washington Williams

George Washington Williams's approach becomes a bellwether of prevailing trends and the ways in which black historians would seek to translate or to counter them. Williams's methodology of the historiography and history of black people began with an attempt to define race. In that regard, this "new" historiography was also defined by the scientific age that had invented the concept of race. Williams's attempt was clearly a response to the ideas expressed in degeneracy theory, eugenics, and social Darwinism. It was grounded in the positivist, objective, and scientific conceptualizations of the time. The historical context and the antecedents of the debate that Williams entered cannot be overemphasized. That it was a debate, well before Williams emerged, must be underlined. Again, Williams was heir to a historiographic tradition that was born of abolitionist/colonizationist sentiments. And while the two trends seemed at odds with one another, they were in agreement con-

14. *The William Leo Hansberry African History Notebook: Africa and Africans as Seen by Classical Writers*, Joseph E. Harris, ed. (Washington: Howard University Press, 1981), ix. Thomas Holt and Nathan Huggins, quoted in Harris, "Flowering," 1160.

15. Bruce, "Ancient Africa," 685. Harris, "Flowering," 1151.

16. Bruce, "Ancient Africa," 685.

cerning the glorious nature of the African past, particularly Egypt and Ethiopia (though a more recent African past of the medieval and Renaissance periods would be cited as well), and in their opposition to those who attempted to argue otherwise based on "scientific" premises and their social consequences. In other words, for the writers in publications such as the *African Repository* (1825) and the *Christian Examiner* (1848) the question of African slavery could not be justified or rationalized through biology or some explication of the African past. Egypt and Ethiopia were evidence of ancient African (black) genius and an indication of the potential of a black future outside the thralls of bondage.

It should also be understood that in this regard, Egypt was a historical and polemical symbol for the school of black historiography that George Washington Williams came to represent. Polemics notwithstanding, Williams and those who followed him also took a balanced methodological approach to their historiography and histories (in that they are indebted to the work of such scholars as Blyden). The favorable reviews that Williams received and the real need for histories that spoke to the experience of Africans, specifically in America, prepared the way for other histories devoted to African Americans. Joseph T. Wilson and William T. Alexander wrote in 1882 and 1887, respectively. While Wilson's book predates Williams's by a year and as Dickson Bruce writes, received "wide notice and respect," neither it nor Alexander's work reflected the scholarly acumen of Williams' volumes. Nor were they engaged in either the white or black communities in the way in which *A History of the Negro Race in America* was. The reviews that Williams's work received in the white press were an indication of this. As A. L. Chapin wrote in *The Dial* of March 1883:

> We welcome, as bringing timely and valuable light for the study of this problem, the work of Mr. Williams. . . . [I]n general . . . the work will well stand a comparison with books of history from the pens of white men. . . . [H]itherto almost all that has been written concerning that people is stamped with the prejudices of the dominant white race, and there is need that one should speak plainly and strongly for the other side.[17]

17. Ibid., 687–688. A. L. Chapin, "The Negro Race in America," *The Dial* (March 1883), 252. The irony of Chapin's celebration of Williams's work as one that "should speak plainly and strongly to the other side" of works that reflected the "prejudices of the dominant white race" was Chapin's observation that though "its author himself belongs to the colored race . . . his portrait seems to indicate, [he is] not quite a full-blooded African". Ibid. The issue of degeneracy, in its many forms, was prevalent. Chapin's comments implied that the strength of Williams's arguments could also be attributed to his biological makeup, which, as his picture indicated, was not "full-blooded African." Ibid.

Chapin makes it clear that the polemical tone of Williams's work was acceptable, and it is Williams's work that is regarded as a historiographical and methodological model based on its examination of both primary and secondary evidence. The Napoleonic expedition a century before produced archaeological evidence; biblical and classical sources were consulted; and writers spurred by Williams's example were not above analyzing the works of the most strident detractors of black achievement in the Classical Age or any other period to make their point. The French writers Volney, Denon, and Gregoire became textual favorites. As sources they seemed almost irreproachable; and their impact on the early development of the field of Egyptology was as far-reaching as it was significant. All three lent themselves to the racial debate in their pronouncement that "Egyptians were a Negro people," despite the declarations of scholars like W. G. Browne and A. H. L. Heeren that neither Egyptians nor Ethiopians were black, and at the very least, they lived in societies dominated by whites.[18]

The works that the Williams school inspired received little notice from the broader segment of American academia. This was in spite of their controversial stand that was illustrated by an espousal of a "positive view of ancient black civilization," and their important role in reframing "the traditional African motif" and reinvigorating its "historical and intellectual foundations." This neglect, too, must be attributed to a historical context that determined that the bulk of these works would be relegated to the halls of black primary schools and systems of higher education in the Jim Crow training of America's youth.[19] Jim Crow itself reduced the threat of these ideas to the conventional wisdom concerning the development of Western civilization by making the training of black children inconsequential. In spite of this, the glories of Egypt and Ethiopia and their contributions to the world permeated the day-to-day life of the African American community and its institutions. The poet and novelist Charles Chesnutt affirmed this permeation when he wrote in the popular *Alexander's Magazine* of May 1905:

> The Negro was here before the Anglo-Saxon, was evolved, and his thick lips and heavy-lidded eyes looked out from the inscrutable Sphynx cross the sands of Egypt while yet the ancestors of those who now oppress him were living in caves, practicing human sacrifices, and painting themselves with wood—and the Negro is here yet.[20]

Chesnutt's words illustrate that the conclusions of Volney, Denon, and Gregoire, and their disciples, received wide currency in the black

18. Bruce, "Ancient Africa," 689–690.
19. Bruce, "Ancient Africa," 692–693.
20. Bruce, "Ancient Africa," 699.

community. If these ideas were not mouthed by name, they were at least accepted by common folk as an essential element of who and what they were as people of African descent. They had entered the consciousness of the black community more than a quarter of a century earlier, if not before. And this became indicative of the fact that more than anything else, African Americans of the late nineteenth and early twentieth centuries charted and reveled in an African heritage that was ancient and took root in the historical, biblical, classical, and mythological soil of Egypt and Ethiopia. Their understanding of their heritage was formally presented in the school of historiography that epitomized the work of George Washington Williams and his followers.

As William Toll has indicated, Williams and those who followed him were compelled to write about blacks in antiquity to satisfy the demands of their audiences, which comprised a large body of youthful readers. Again, considerable effort was expended here to overcome the notions of race that stipulated that "Africans and their descendants were persons only fit for subjugation."[21]

This idea is fundamentally important in relation to the concepts of race and historiography as they are expressed here and illustrated in the writing and teaching of the history of the classical period. In particular, Woodson would refer to Grace Hadley Beardsley's *The Negro in Greek and Roman Civilization* as a prime case in point. Her reference to blacks within the context of classical Greece and Rome was for Woodson "a distortion of valuable facts."[22]

21. William Toll, *The Resurgence of Race* (Philadelphia: Temple University Press, 1979), 23–24. Toll goes on to state the ways in which this new school of black historiography differed from its predecessors:

> Prior scholars had focused primarily on individuals or events, but Williams sought to give form and purpose to the story of a *race* as it moved from isolation to modernization and self-confident participation in world politics. He was not so much concerned with demonstrating the ability of Black individuals to succeed in a modern setting as to demonstrate how Blacks as a people had a distinctive role in the evolution of a more humane world civilization. (23–24; italics added)

22. Woodson, *African Background*, 5. Du Bois was a bit more strident. He called Beardsley's work a "stupid combination of scholarship and race prejudice which Johns Hopkins University published." Du Bois was making a juxtaposition between the quality of Beardsley's research and the ease with which her conclusions were published and the prodigious difficulties that scholars such as William Leo Hansberry would experience. Du Bois was also contrasting Beardsley's work with the not yet published research of Frank W. Snowden and the difficulties he experienced because "classical journals in America have hitherto declined to publish his paper because it favored the Negro too much." *The World and Africa* (New York: International Publishers, 1946), x. Interestingly enough, Snowden is somewhat more charitable to Beardsley and her 1929 work. He is, however, quite unforgiving of Lloyd A. Thompson's *Romans and Blacks* (Norman: University of Oklahoma Press, 1989). Snowden, *Blacks in Antiquity*, viii–ix. Snowden, "*Romans and Blacks*: A Review Essay," *American Journal of Philology*, (Winter 1990), 111, 4.

FOUR

Carter G. Woodson

Within the framework of the sociology of knowledge, Charles H. Wesley and Thelma D. Perry wrote in the 1969 edition of Carter G. Woodson's *Miseducation of the Negro* that "Woodson's concept of *miseducation* hinged on the education system's failure to present authentic Negro history in schools and the bitter knowledge that there was a scarcity of literature available for such a purpose."[1]

Woodson's work had broader purpose, however. As an indictment of the entire American system of education, *Miseducation of the Negro* emphasized that the blatant and subtle applications of Jim Crow made an entire population, black and white, ignorant of the essential currents of historical progression. As Amos J. Beyan wrote of Woodson, study and travel "taught him that American historians ignored black contributions."[2]

---

1. Charles H. Wesley and Thelma D. Perry, Introduction to Carter G. Woodson, *The Miseducation of the Negro* (Washington, D.C.: Associated Publishers, 1969), v.

2. Amos J. Beyan, "Woodson, Carter Godwin," in Charles D. Lowery and John Marszulek, eds., *Encyclopedia of African-American Civil Rights* (New York: Greenwood Press, 1992), 591. Interestingly enough, August Meier and Elliott Rudwick write that "originally a Jim Crow specialty ignored by nearly the entire profession, [Afro-American history] became legitimated into one of the liveliest fields of study in American history." *Black History and the Historical Profession, 1915–1980* (Urbana: University of Illinois Press, 1986), xi–xii. Commenting on this, Arvarh Strickland writes, "The legitimacy of Afro-American history, if it needed legitimatizing, resulted from the work and dedication of Carter Godwin Woodson, who 'with his drive and vision was virtually singled-handedly responsible for establishing Afro-American history as a specialty.'" "Editor's Introduction," in Lorenzo J. Greene, *Working with Carter G. Woodson, the Father of Black History: A Diary, 1928–1930* (Baton Rouge: Louisiana State University Press, 1989), xvii.

To underline his point, Woodson wrote of these inadequacies as they were perceived in Negro colleges whose curricula centered on "ancient, medieval, and Modern Europe, but . . . [did] not offer courses in ancient, medieval, and modern Africa."[3] Working with the legacy of George Washington Williams, Woodson would help to refine black historiography from the early twentieth century onward, beginning with the establishment of the very important *Journal of Negro History* in 1916. In the works that flowed from this endeavor, Woodson aided in the creation a "historiographic shift" that firmly changed the focus of African American history from that of the master to that of the slave and former slave. This paradigm shift certainly foresaw the emergence of an Afrocentric model of historical writing, and it represented a new twist, an inversion of the epistemology of blackness. Yet within Woodson's mind, if Wesley and Perry are to be believed, this model was intended to have universal application as a historiographic and educational tool.[4]

The model and the institutions that Woodson helped to create to nurture it—the Association for the Study of Negro Life and History, the *Journal of Negro History*, and *Negro History Bulletin*—accomplished the very things that Rudwick and Meier set forth in their inquiry into the role of black historians in the historical profession.[5] Woodson provided the wherewithal for scholars of Africa and the African diaspora to study the African experience and its broad applications from a different vantage and then to have those researches receive their critical and scholarly due in a professional journal of history and before a body of professional peers.[6] It was within this newly created atmosphere that Egypt and Ethiopia, and the rest of Africa, and the African American experience itself might be seriously considered on the basis of the intellectual materials presented. Woodson provided the fora for an evaluation of ideas that could not be, and in many, many instances have not been, envisioned or entertained within mainstream academia until the advent of Bernal and *Black Athena*.[7]

3. Carter G. Woodson, "Miseducation of the Negro," *Crisis*, 40 (August 1931), 268.

4. Thomas D. Cockrell, "*Journal of Negro History*," in Charles D. Lowery and John Marszulek, eds., *Encyclopedia of African-American Civil Rights* (New York: Greenwood Press, 1992), 591. Woodson, *Miseducation of the Negro*, v–viii.

5. August Meier and Elliot Rudwick, *Black History and the Historical Profession* (Urbana: University of Illinois Press, 1986), xi.

6. Strickland, "Editor's Introduction," in Woodson, *Miseducation*, xviii.

7. Woodson's professional life is marked by numerous ironies. One irony that must be read as an implication of Jacqueline Goggin's "Countering White Racist Scholarship: Carter G. Woodson and the *Journal of Negro History*" is Goggin's analysis that the over 500 articles that Woodson reviewed in his 34 years as editor of the *Journal of Negro History* covered a chronological period of 400 years—the sixteenth through the twentieth centuries. The

In a brief, yet illuminating statement on the "New Program" of education presented in *Miseducation of the Negro*, Woodson links Africa with the classical world, and by implication espouses the teaching of a world history:

> We should not underrate the achievements of Mesopotamia, Greece and Rome; but we should give equally as much attention to the internal African kingdoms, the Songhay Empire, and Ethiopia, which through Egypt decidedly influenced the civilization of the Mediterranean world.[8]

We should also note the subtle shift of emphasis in Woodson's Ethiopian/Egyptian dichotomy: for Woodson it is *"through Egypt"* that the world receives the gifts of Ethiopia. He seems to posit primacy with Ethiopia over Egypt, and therefore over Greece and the rest of the Mediterranean world. By implication, the Ethiopians, "favored of the gods," were the only ones in a position to share such magnificence over such a long and enduring period with the rest of the classical world.

The Negro in Our History and
The African Background Outlined

Woodson wrote two works that dealt, in part, with the specifics of Egyptian-Ethiopian origins and their impact on the formation of classical Greece: *The Negro in Our History*, written with Charles Wesley and first published in 1922, and *The African Background Outlined*, which appeared in 1936. These works reflected the general historiographic themes of black scholarship of the period: they attempted to place the history of Africans within the larger framework of the world and, more particularly, within the context of a Western society that excluded them. Employing the schema that George Washington Williams made popular, Woodson opened both pieces with questions of historiography and race. As he would later note in *African Background* and elsewhere, Woodson stated forthrightly in *The Negro in Our*

---

implication is that in these early years it was thought that there was little else on which black scholars could write. They were restricted to the experience of Africans in the modern, "post-Columbian" era because it was perceived that that was the only history that blacks had: the history of their contacts with Europe following the Age of Discovery. In many ways, Woodson's own limited work in the premodern period belied this. *Journal of Negro History*, 68 (Fall 1983), 361–363.

8. Woodson, *Miseducation of the Negro*, 154.

History that the purpose of his writing was "correction to . . . the history and culture of the darker people . . . [in relation to] the neglects, innuendoes and omissions concerning the people of color [which] are disturbing to students of human relations." Through his efforts, black people were not to become "a negligible factor in the thought of the world," especially in an intellectual and academic milieu where "most historians know practically nothing about the Negroes in Africa prior to their enslavement."[9]

The inadequacies of race as a scientifically measureable determinant were particularly associated with discussion of the classical period. As I have noted above, Woodson chided those who believed that achievement could be awarded or denied on the basis of race. Yet within that context he maintained that the accepted racial construction of Africans was one that must be consistently applied to ancient Egyptians and Ethiopians. Any attempt to deny their "negroness" was met with the pithy and biting rejoinder that "if the Egyptians . . . were not Negroes, then, there are no Negroes in the United States."[10] The issues explored in statements of this type allowed Woodson to maintain the theme of Ethiopian-Egyptian cultural continuity, and the primacy of Ethiopia over Egypt.[11]

Woodson plays out this theme in *The African Background Outlined*. Relying on colonial authors such as Lady Flora Lugard and Maurice Delafosse, Woodson constructs the connection between Ethiopia and Egypt.[12] Woodson's real emphasis is the physical characterization of the Egyptian population and an attack on the notions of racial purity. The Egyptian population, according to Woodson, can only be defined as one that was mixed. The allusion was to a black population that "[a]mong the later Egyptians developed octoroons, quadroons, samboes and blacks, the same types which developed as the result of racial admixture in America."[13]

9. Carter G. Woodson and Charles H. Wesley, *The Negro in Our History* (1922; Washington, D.C.: Associated Publishers, 1962) preface by Carter G. Woodson, xiv, 4.

10. Ibid., 16. Woodson's was a familiar refrain to a familiar assertion: "[B]iased investigations . . . identify them [black peoples of note] as whites . . . even if such persons have a small percentage of Caucasian blood." Ibid.

11. Ibid., 14. This would also be the basis for his pre-Bernalian speculation that "the Greeks were thereby influenced to the extent that the investigators contend that the civilization of Greece had African rather than Asiatic origin."

12. In this light, not only are Woodson's notes valuable here, but particular insight is provided by Lorenzo Greene in his diary of his work with Woodson from 1928 to 1930. Greene records his own discovery of Lugard's work, her controversial theories and Woodson's discussion of her work and that of others in the course of staff briefings. The implications reflect the immense scholarship exercised by Woodson and his colleagues. Greene, *Working with Woodson*, 179–180, 256–258, 282.

13. Carter G. Woodson, *African Background*, 20–24, 25.

The blending of peoples in the Ethiopian/Egyptian confluence forces a comparison in racial terminology and its implications in a history of "perverse pedantry." In notes that anticipate the comments of Snowden and Levine on questions of racial purity and scholarly ambivalence, Woodson remarks:

> The European idea of designating a man as a Negro only when he has one hundred per cent Negro blood must be borne in mind as contrast to the American attitude for considering a man white only when he has one hundred per cent white blood.[14]

Woodson goes on to state: "Most of these . . . authors, however, show the usual bias. They classify as white every progressive African who has not one hundred per cent Negro blood."[15] The last comment made an inclusive argument for both American and European scholars' views of African antiquity in relation to Egypt. Woodson's statement only mirrored the past century of general historiography. Frederick Douglass (see chapter 3, note 5) had expressed the same sentiments in 1854; they were views that were long held, and they served to counter the very explicit notions guarded by the white population, both scholarly and lay.

Woodson was clear that these ideas of exclusion as they related to Africans in the Classical Age were modern in their origin. Employing the archaeological and literary material of the period, Woodson concluded that the "most ancient Greeks" considered Africans "a remarkably beautiful people." The frescoes of Minos, the sculpture of Greece attested to an African presence that spoke not only of "parity," but of intimacy as well. As Woodson related, "[S]everal authorities have taken this to mean that the early Mediterraneans were what we in America designate today as *colored* people, the inevitable result of a melting pot."[16]

Using many of the same sources, in a chapter entitled "The Negro in the European Mind," Woodson charts the same historiographic development as does Bernal and provides an analysis that preceded, and is complemented by, George Fredrickson's *Black Image in the White Mind*.[17] Woodson's articulation of the black as depicted in numerous

14. Woodson, *African Background* 24–25, n. 9.
15. Ibid., 189, n. 14.
16. Woodson, *African Background*, 217–218.
17. Ibid., 217–255. There is a bit of historical irony here too, when an account is taken of the similarities between Woodson's "The Negro in the European Mind" (1936) and Fredrickson's *The Black Image in the White Mind* (1971). Frederickson makes no mention of Woodson in this work.

ancient sources, literary and graphic, was one that was quite favorable. He emphasized this point in contradiction to one of the most prominent pieces of research of the time, Grace Beardsley's, *The Negro in Greek and Roman Civilization* (1929).[18]

In the chapters "Informants on Africa" and "Ethiopia and Egypt," Woodson goes directly to primary sources and their interpretations in order to support his premises about African and Ethiopian antiquity. Here he begins to develop the thesis of Ethiopian and Egyptian cultural and institutional formation over the Greeks as well as other North African peoples. In this he allows Lady Flora Lugard and Maurice Delafosse to speak:

> [W]hile they [Ethiopians] are described as the most powerful, the most just, the most beautiful and long-lived of the human race they are constantly spoken of as black, and there seems to be no other conclusion to be drawn than that at that remote period of history the leading race of the *Western World* was a black race. . . . In Nubia and Ethiopia stupendous, numerous and primeval monuments proclaim so loudly a civilization contemporary to, aye earlier than that of Egypt, that it may be conjectured with the greatest confidence that the arts, sciences and religion descended from Nubia to the lower country of Misraim [Egypt]; that civilization descended the Nile, built Memphis, and finally, sometime later, wrested by colonization the Delta from the sea.[19]

> Many facts corroborate the hypothesis which tends to relate the first formation of the Sudanese populations known as Negroid to an epoch far more remote than that which is generally assigned to it and to attribute to the prehistoric peoples who preceded the Egyptians, the Libyan Berbers and the Semites in North Africa, the influence which has often been accorded to these latter.[20]

18. Ibid., 217–219. Woodson took exception to Beardsley's notion that the only position held by the African in Greek society was a servile one. Ironically, he argued that within the Roman sphere "the Romans . . . had little or no contact with ancient Africans." This clearly was not the case if the research of authors such as G. L. Cheesman (*The Auxilia of the Roman Imperial Army* [Chicago: Ares Publishers, 1914]) and Frank W. Snowden has any credence. In fairness, however, Woodson's reference used Ethiopian-Roman relations as the example juxtaposed with Greek sentiments concerning the Ethiopians.

19. Woodson, *African Background*, 5, 21. Lady Flora Lugard, *A Tropical Dependency* (London: James Nisbet & Co., Limited, 1912), 220–221; italics added.

20. Woodson, *African Background*, 20. Maurice Delafosse, *Negroes of Africa: History and Culture* (Washington, D.C.: Associated Publishers, 1931), 18–19. It is interesting to note that some 130 years later, Delafosse, probably unwittingly, helped to salvage the reputation of his countryman, Constantin de Volney, who had been forced by a hostile intellectual community to recant any notions that the Egyptians might have sprung from a "Negroid" population.

With these modern interpretations and primary sources such as Herodotus and Homer, Woodson began to hammer out the theme of the authenticity of Ethiopian/Egyptian culture that would later become a key feature of Afrocentric scholarship:

[S]ome *later* observers, like biased Europeans and Americans of our times, have tried to prove that these ideas were borrowed, but they themselves, after spinning out their legends and theories, have to admit that their assertions are only conjectures. They have no more proof that what the Africans knew at the time was borrowed from foreigners than that the latter have borrowed such ideas from *blacks of the interior*.[21]

This must have been one of the earliest times that the precursor of modern Afrocentrist thought was articulated. Woodson had presaged the arguments of Afrocentrists, in particular the adherents of the "Nile Valley School,"[22] and the concepts associated with Cheikh Anta Diop's *Nations negres et culture* and *Anteriorite des civilizations negres*, sections of which appeared in English as *The African Origins of Civilization*, translated by Mercer Cook.[23]

For Woodson, the physical characteristics of the Egyptians were the consequential illustration of Egypt's link to the world at large. Egypt's greatness drew the world and the physical ramification was that "Egypt the land of Negroid mixed breeds, became the link between black Africa of the Nile and the other parts of the ancient world."[24]

Again, Woodson calls on Lugard to buttress his thesis:

[W]hen the history of Negroland comes to be written in detail, it may be found that the kingdoms lying toward the eastern end of the

21. Woodson, *African Background*, 21; italics added.

22. The "Nile Valley School" has been a very important component in the development of the Afrocentric discourse. This intellectual grouping is primarily identified by more conventional scholars on the basis of the "amateur" Egyptology associated with its members. The scholars of this group represent academics from various disciplines, as well as other professionals, who have had considerable impact on the debate. They are made up of, in many ways, the "angry radical Afrocentrists" to which so many refer. In their number are luminaries such as John Henrik Clarke, Yosef Ben Jochannon, Asa Hilliard, Ivan Van Sertima, and Jacob Carruthers.

23. While there remains considerable tension around Diop's assertions, methodology, and credentials—in that order (very much in accord with Bernal's observations concerning the ways in which ideas that do not conform to convention are received. See p. 46 and Bernal, *Black Athena;* 18)—it is important to recognize that Woodson saw the same types of implications in 1936, three decades before scholars chose to attack Diop. The political convergences of Third World insurgency, African independence, and the struggles of African Americans may have created the necessary climate in which Diop's translated writings might be seen as a threat.

24. Woodson, *African Background*, 22.

Sudan were the homes of races who inspired, rather than races who received the traditions of civilization associated for us with the name of ancient Egypt. . . . If this should prove to be the case, and the civilized world be forced to recognize in a black people the fount of its original enlightenment, it may happen that we shall have to revise entirely our view of the black races, and regard those who now exist as the decadent representations of an almost forgotten era, rather than the embryonic possibility of an era yet to come.[25]

In much the same way as Delafosse would do a few years later, Lugard had resurrected the letter and spirit of Volney. She had also begun to explore the epistemology of blackness, again through inversion, by implying the need to revise the conventional historical treatment of Egypt. In many ways, Woodson's life is replete with ironies. One is found no less in the notion that he may have derived some particular humor, if not satisfaction, from the fact that one of his key sources in his crusade that the history of Africa and Africans not be misrepresented or misstated was a woman granted peerage for her husband's role in advancing British imperialism in Africa. We could also speculate whether or not Sir Hugh Trevor Roper had ever had the pleasure of engaging Lady Lugard in person or in print.[26]

In a play on colonial theorists and the manufacture of Hamitic/Semitic mythologies for African ruling genealogies at the close of the pre-Christian era, Woodson accepted the conjectures of successive Semitic migrations only to have the Semitic peoples diluted—or as Long, Gobineau, and others would have put it, only to have them "degenerate" into "a fusion of races that Americans would segregate for being black Negroes." The result was a mélange that characterized the "rich, invincible and feared Ethiopian Empire which eventually brought Egypt under its control." For Woodson, Ethiopia was both conqueror and source of wide cultural dissemination. The properties by which the Ethiopians were identified were, as Flinders Petrie put it, indications of the cultural and racial oneness of Egypt and Lower

25. Ibid., 23. Lugard, *Tropical Dependency*, 17–18.
26. Woodson wrote in the October 1932 issue of the *Journal of Negro History*, vol.17, that peoples of African descent, and in particular educated Africans had

a great opportunity which they cannot afford to neglect, since they will be misrepresented to the world if they permit to go unchallenged the misstatements of fact made by numerous writers who do not understand Africa.

"Notes: The Director's Survey of Research in Europe," *Journal of Negro History*, 17 (October 1932), 505–506. Lorenzo Greene also notes that both he and Woodson were somewhat surprised and in awe of their "discovery" of Lady Lugard's work. Greene, *Working with Woodson*, 178–180, 256–258, 282.

Nubia.[27] The African/Semitic/Hamitic mixture was proof of the "Negro as an enduring factor in Northeast Africa." The existence of this mixture reflected a larger "problem of ethnology and ethnography. Were the Negroes in North Africa absorbed or did they absorb others?"[28]

The questions that absorbed Woodson moved him from Africa to Euro-America and the creation of African America. The questions spanned the ancient to the present. In the area of physical characteristics they focused on one central issue: how can people who are so markedly alike be deemed so dissimilar on the basis of "scientific" premise? What were the social, political, and economic dynamics that made the dark Egyptian a paragon and the dark American a pariah? What could erase the accomplishments of an entire civilization if the dark Egyptian and the dark American were thought to be related? Here Woodson suggests the implicit difficulties in racial definition while simultaneously working within them.

The notes that Woodson provides as a study guide to *The African Background Outlined* are a prime example of the intellectual and the epistemological utility of the work. They help chart the historiography and the trends of the time. In that regard, the book is a tool created by Woodson to aid future scholars in countering conventional historiography and in creating new ones.

These are the circumstances into which Woodson was immersed as the second black to receive a doctoral degree from Harvard University. The world and, more important, America were dominated by racist and racialist notions that sought to justify the recent demise of slavery and to rationalize late nineteenth- and early twentieth-century imperialism. The key to this justification and rationalization was the academy.[29]

27. Woodson, *African Background*, 24–25.

28. Ibid., 190.

29. Woodson and Wesley, *The Negro in Our History*, xv, xix–xx, xxiv; Woodson, *Miseducation of the Negro*. Du Bois, *The Education of Black People*. Fredrickson, *Black Image in the White Mind: The Debate on Afro-American Character and Destiny, 1817–1914* (New York: Harper and Row, 1971), 71–96. Bernal, *Black Athena*, 1–73, 189–336. The European effort was bold-faced in the rationalization of imperialism. Only Cecil Rhodes needs to be called upon to make the point. Rhodes foresaw that the need to train the young administrators of the realm fell to the dons of schools such as Oxford and Cambridge. From their midst emerged not only those who would serve in the colonies but those who would become home and foreign secretaries and prime minister, as well. Entire new educational institutions were erected: the London School of Economics' School of Oriental—and, later, African—Studies, is probably the most marked example.

For the United States, the schools were "lowercased" in that they represented schools of intellectual thought and historiography. They were certainly influenced by the global competition of imperialism, but they also had to contend with the unique American dilemmas

For black Americans, this era—from the close of the Civil War through the 1940s—like many others, had its own precarious particulars. In response to white power paternalism there emerged at least two schools of thought and action in the black community. In their shorthand, for better or worse, they have been labeled "accommodationist" and "radical." Associated with the accommodationis school were figures such as Booker T. Washington, founder and principal of Tuskegee Institute, confidant to presidents and captains of industry, and a veritable power in his own right. A dominant figure of the radical school was W. E. B. Du Bois, professor of economics, history, and sociology; founding member of the National Association for the Advancement of Colored People; and editor of both *The Crisis* and *Phylon*. Washington has been conventionally pigeon-holed as conservative and Du Bois as his exact opposite and nemesis.[30] The importance of Woodson's work and the obstacles that he faced would suffer from similar attempts at categorization.

In the social and historical context in which Woodson worked, it was held that there was no such thing as "African antiquity." The work of black intellectuals was to be directed to the solution of the "Negro problem";[31] and to the practical application of their skills and training to the achievement of that solution as outlined primarily by the major philanthropic organization of the time. Prominent white scholars had already illustrated that "Negroes," blacks, and, therefore, Africans had no antebellum history, no history before their association with Europeans. And the brief history that they had acquired in post-Emancipation America, particular that of Reconstruction, was illustrative of the history that they lacked as a whole. In this regard, historiographic boundaries were preordained.

that race, racism, and slavery posed in defining the emergent American hegemony. Here fit the arguments of the Dunning-Burgess school, of disciples of Ulrich B. Phillips, and of the many others who saw in the lost cause of American slaveocracy the justification for the past and the rationale for contemporary actions. Goggin, "Countering White Racist Scholarship," 356.

30. August Meier, *Negro Thought in America, 1880–1915* (Ann Arbor: University of Michigan Press, 1963), 171–184. Robert C. Twombly, *Blacks in White America Since 1865: Issues and Interpretations* (New York: David McKay, 1971), 76–78, 108–121.

31. Du Bois movingly summarized the position in 1903 in his *Souls of Black Folk*: "Between me and the other world there is ever an unasked question: . . . How does it feel to be a problem?" His response, along with that of Woodson and others, was quite similar to, if not exactly the same as, that dictated by institutions of higher education, foundations, and government agencies. The response was very possibly what the black community dictated as well: solve the problem. The difference in approach to this solution was based on *how* Du Bois, Woodson, and others might choose to solve their problem and, more specifically, how they might choose to define it. (Greenwich: Fawcett Publications, 1961), 15–22.

Woodson's professional life seems to have had its share of contradictions. In many circles, he was regarded as one of the "darlings" of American philanthropic foundations, yet he functioned constantly under the perception of their intention to restrict his research. His perceptions were exemplary of the complex relations that existed for him and other black scholars among themselves and their institutions; with white scholars and white institutions; and with the foundations themselves. There was, in many ways, a palpable air of "academic racism."[32] Woodson was aware of this, even if he chose to call it by another name. Charles Wesley, in his preface to the 1962 edition of *The Negro in Our History*, spoke of the ways in which Woodson attempted to resist the efforts of "the foundation to direct or modify the work of the Association." Woodson recognized that these efforts cut across a wide swath of institutional America: "The Negro faces another stone wall when he presents such scientific productions to the publishing houses. They may not be prejudiced, but they are not interested in the Negro." He went on to say:

This is a most unfortunate situation in the modern world where wealth is boundless, but those who have been favored with fortunes are not usually interested in the promotion of the truth. Often when financial support is given, such strings are attached as to prevent the research into matters which may prove prejudicial to economic interests. In the case of the Negro there appears also the added handicap from those opposing the teaching of doctrines which may interfere with white supremacy. What is desired in such quarters is to suppress the whole truth and to publish such a portion of it as will not change the present way of thinking.'[33]

In spite of these revelations, Woodson was still affected by a profound sense of conservatism, and yet he still remained a champion of the history of African peoples. Again, this was in an era when the history of African peoples, and in particular, the Negro, was doubted, even among those who would become Woodson's staunchest supporters. Lorenzo J. Greene, a Woodson protégé, recalled how he in his initial meeting with Woodson, after receiving an autographed copy of *The Negro in Our History*, left the appointment "pitying the man for devoting his life to something which Greene did not believe existed, Negro history."[34]

As Rudwick and Meier noted, "Afro-American historical scholarship

32. Goggin, "Countering White Racist Scholarship," 358.
33. Woodson and Wesley, *The Negro in Our History*, xx, xxii–xxiv.
34. Greene, *Working with Woodson*, xxii.

was scarcely a major consideration" for America's dominant foundations. Their assertion was based on Woodson's own observation that

> the average philanthropist is not interested in the the study of Negro life and history for the reason that he does not believe it worthwhile and even if it is of value he seriously doubts that Negroes are qualified to do the work scientifically.'[35]

In 1937, Lawrence Reddick in his essay "Some Real Research Barriers in the South" supported this notion as it pertained to the learned societies:

> [T]he American Historical Association has on occasion allowed such men as Professor Monroe Work of Tuskegee to appear. On the other hand, when one member of the committee on programs and arrangements suggested the names of Carter G. Woodson and Dr. Charles Wesley (both Harvard Ph.D.'s and authors of several volumes), who happen to stem from a more aggressive tradition, the committee was immediately reshuffled and this member was promptly dropped.[36]

The "aggressive" nature of Woodson's scholarship is as important as the issue of his being black. Coupled, aggressiveness and blackness become a potent force that is repellent for conventional thinkers and the organizations they represent.

Faced with a black intellectualism that was increasingly characterized as aggressive (more so because of the issues it sought to pursue and popular assumptions concerning black scholars' abilities to pursue them), publishing houses, philanthropies, professional societies, and, of course, the academy all proved themselves to be archly conservative on the question of black history. Their views amounted to historiographic prescriptions to which most of the established academic and intellectual community subscribed.

The implication was that the study of history was not for black people. This harkened back to the days when the writing of history itself could be only a "gentlemanly pursuit." Its removal from the pragmatic and the mundane meant it could not satisfy the needs of the black masses, or the nation at large, as determined by the philanthropies of the country; philanthropies that were in large part endowed by the fortunes of America's corporate giants. In this sense, Booker T. Washington, the Tuskegee Machine, and the compulsion for practical education seem to have triumphed at the board tables of corporate foundations

---

35. Meier and Rudwick, *Black History*, 26, 49.
36. Quoted in Goggin, "Countering White Racist Scholarship," 356.

(though some analysts will prefer to read this the other way round). The attempt to exclude black scholarship from the writing of history was historiographical. It presupposed that the problems of black America (or black America as the problem) were too immense for its best minds to be concerned with a frivolity termed history and that the writing of history was in any case beyond these minds. Hence, U. B. Phillips's characterization of Woodson's work as "amateurish."[37]

Woodson's position on his role as a promoter of black scholarship was reflective of this dismissive attitude and another telling fact: from 1895–1980 only fourteen pieces of scholarship authored by black intellectuals had been accepted in the "leading white" journals; and, of those, only five dealt with black themes. Benjamin Quarles pointedly noted that his work was calculated to be conservative and not provocative so that it could be published: "[T]o some degree my having been published in white historical journals can be attributed to the blandness of my writings, their non-upsetting tone, their avoidance of pain tenor."[38]

Here, Woodson was involved in institutional development designed to combat an exclusionary and "racist historiography." As Charles Wesley put it, given the evidence, Woodson "was interested in the difficulties which Negro scholars faced in the publication of their works of scholarship."[39]

In his own words, Woodson said:

What is the use of knowing things if they cannot be published to the world? If the Negro is to settle down to publishing what others permit him to bring out, the world will never know what the race has thought and felt and attempted and accomplished and the story of the Negro will perish with him.[40]

Yet for all of his activities and pronouncements, Woodson was not overly critical of philanthropic foundations. One wonders if he could afford to be. As Horace Mann Bond pointed out in a critique of Woodson's *Miseducation of the Negro*, the major foundations received "singularly gentle treatment."[41]

37. Ibid., 52.
38. Goggin, "Countering White Racist Scholarship," 359.
39. Woodson and Wesley, *The Negro in Our History*, xix–xx.
40. Ibid., xx.
41. Horace Mann Bond, "Dr. Woodson Goes Wool-Gathering," *Journal of Negro Education*, 2 (April 1933), 211. Bond sharply remarked that "one might expect a scathing criticism of white philanthropy from Dr. Woodson's general attitude," but that was not the case. Bond's criticism was directed to Woodson's tactic of showing his displeasure with the foundations by castigating (and sometimes justifiably critiquing) the work of black

In spite of the maneuvering, Woodson was still forced to acquiesce to the general research agenda of the foundations as it related to the "Negro problem." On three separate occasions (1925, 1926, and 1929) Woodson let it be known that his organization was modifying its research interests: "[I]n the future the Association will not prosecute any further study of the Negro prior to the Civil War." Research was to be directed "largely to a study of the social and economic conditions since their emancipation." Woodson spoke directly about the ways in which the agenda was being dictated:

> I should make it clear . . . that this program of studying the social and economic conditions of Negroes in the United States since the Civil War is not exactly our program. It was suggested to us by the representative of the Memorial. That board was very much interested in such studies, and believed that the Association should pay more attention to matters of this sort. We agreed to do so. The Memorial gave us the money for the purpose, and we spent it as suggested. You will remember that our special interest is in history rather than things purely social or economic.[42]

The Legacy of George Washington Williams et al.

Without contrition, echoing Booker T. Washington, Woodson attempted to espouse an oxymoronic program: a nonpropagandic, race-lifting history and historiography. In this notion alone, he may have been at odds with very many of his contemporaries and with the man who was believed to have made the most "outstanding contribution" to the history of black people "until the rise of Woodson"—George Washington Williams. Woodson himself argued that Williams's work had "not [been] surpassed." It in fact had set the "scientific and objective high standard of historiography." In spite of Williams's meticulous and pathbreaking work, blacks in history and the history of blacks still experienced "difficulty in securing a hearing."[43]

---

colleagues and the black institutions that they represented. These became direct and indirect attacks on philanthropic decisions to support black colleges and universities, the foundations' attempts to direct research, *and* their not too gentle insistence that Woodson affiliate with one of these chosen institutions. Woodson's characterization of black colleges and universities as "undeveloped" seemed both real and contrived as he attempted to maintain autonomy over his own intellectual property.

42. Meier and Rudwick, *Black History*, 50.

43. Carter G. Woodson, "Negro Historians of Our Times," *Negro History Bulletin*, 8 (April 1945), 155. "Ten Years of Collecting and Publishing the Records of the Negro," *Journal of Negro History*, 10 (October 1925), 599.

Woodson was gravely aware of the prevailing sentiment that blacks not be encouraged to pursue history. He had faced it in the board-rooms of corporate philanthropies; it was seen in the letters of rejection from publishers; it was on the lips of white intellectual and aca-demics. Yet Woodson understood that the study of history was critical; it was "key to the development of racial pride and self respect."[44]

However, Woodson and his contemporaries—as well as those who still toil in the light of his legacy—faced a real dilemma in light of the "Negro problem": what bearing did "digging up the ancient past . . . have on disfranchisement [sic], segregation, lynching and the massacre of the innocent?" This was essentially the dynamic described by Meier and Rudwick concerning the direction of black scholarship at the turn of the twentieth century and its relation to the solution of the Negro problem.[45]

The theoretical and methodological approaches to the solutions were more sociological than historical. They were rooted in post-Reconstruction rather than antebellum historicity. Again they rested on the assumption that blacks were without history, so it was only proper to concentrate on their present and future. Theirs was an an-thropological and social being, in essence a state without change.

Even in the face of these assumptions, where the generation of black historians who preceded him might be openly polemic, Wood-son showed a certain degree of ambivalence to black history as polemics. He adamantly professed that the history of black people was not to be put to propagandic purposes. History was not for agitation—at least not as he defined it. He certainly would not overtly embrace Du Bois's notions of art and history as propaganda, though in the main the two men were more similar than dissonant.[46] Even in the cel-ebration of the "scientific" no opportunity could be lost to correct or challenge "misrepresentations" of the race. This vigilance often led to accusations that the *Journal of Negro History* had an editorial policy that was uncritical of pro-black work and overly "critical of historians who have not taken a pro-Negro slant." Melville Herskovits's review of *The African Background Outlined* asserted in the same fashion, according to Woodson, that the work was "lacking [in] objectivity and charged with a strong anti-white prejudice." Of course, Woodson, in good polemi-

44. Meier and Rudwick, *Black History*, 3.
45. Woodson, "Negro Historians," 156. Meier and Rudwick, *Black History*, 49–51.
46. W. E. B. Du Bois, "The Propaganda of History," in *W. E. B. Du Bois: Writings* (New York: Literary Classics of the United States, 1986), 1026–1047. "Thus all Art is propaganda, and ever must be despite the wailings of the purists. . . . I do not care a damn for any art that is not used for propaganda." "Criteria of Negro Art," *The Crisis*, 32, 6 (October 1926), reprinted in *The Seventh Son*, ed. Julius Lester (New York: Vintage Books, 1971), 319.

cal fashion, responded that "the book claims for the Negro what the reviewer and most persons of his circle would deny as justly belonging to the record of the Negro."[47]

This background is presented because it helps to contextualize over a century of black historiography. It gives a certain graphic historical relief to the fears of modern critics such as Levine as they relate to the "radical" Afrocentrists. Levine's abuse of *Black Athena* is simply an echo of the historiographic past. Herskovits termed it "anti-white" in 1937, but it certainly had been similarly characterized long before that. In Woodson's professional life and those of his contemporaries, this was another real irony given the very genuine limitations to access in the scholarly press that black authors faced. *The African Background Outlined* was published by Woodson's own press.

All this comes in striking contrast to Woodson's studied opposition to the position, attitude, and demeanor of so many of his contemporaries such as Du Bois. Woodson was certifiably "conservative"; the investigations of the Rosenwald Foundation proved this, and he went out of his way to cultivate this persona at every opportunity. As Meier and Rudwick point out, Woodson disavowed radicalism; it had no place and could be counterproductive in his desire to attract important black and white conservative support. Conservatism was the mantle that might "advance the legitimacy of his work."[48] It appears that then, as now, it was not enough. Here again, within the spaces of black conservatism lay the basis for Afrocentrism, radical or otherwise—a basis for intellectual rebellion and historiographic revision along the very same lines that Bernal would propose in *Black Athena*.

"A New Picture of Africa"

Woodson clearly acknowledged his historiographical past.[49] His work was in keeping with the greatest historical minds, "Negroes of vision" who "had endeavored to record the salient facts of Negro History." In 1925, he would write that "ten years of collecting and publishing the records of the Negro" under the auspices of the *Journal of Negro History* "has made the world see the Negro as a participant rather than a lay figure in history." For Woodson, one of the earliest recollections of

47. Carter G. Woodson, "Notes: Dr. Melville J. Herskovits' Method Examined," *Journal of Negro History*, 22 (April 1937), 293. Goggin, "Countering White Racist Scholarship," 365. Meier and Rudwick, *Black History*, 52.

48. Meier and Rudwick, *Black History*, 12, 21, 25, 42.

49. The phrase "a new picture of Africa" comes from Sr. Anthony Scally, *Carter G. Woodson: A Bio-Bibliography* (Westport: Greenwood Press, 1985), 19.

making the world see must have been in his assertion of the African contribution to the formation of the "ancient Mediterranean region" expressed in *The Negro in Our History*.[50]

Having announced in 1917 (the draft had to wait out the Great War in order to be published) that a major intent of *The Negro in Our History* was to explore "how the Negro has been influenced by contact with the Caucasian," Woodson came to see that another tack was altogether possible as well. By 1932, he thought it necessary to undertake research into gauging the effects of Africans on the lives of Europeans from the ancient period to the present to ascertain "the influence of their life [the life of Africans] on these creators of modern thought." Interestingly enough, his quest implied the need to acquaint Europeans (and of course those of European descent) with their own African past. Woodson's mission was patently historiographic: he was "in Europe to find out what the scholars know about Africans and how they know it, what they do not know about these natives and why they do not know it."[51]

Woodson reported on this research in his "Director's Survey of Research in Europe." Spending the summer in Europe, Woodson met with a number of people, including the scholars Henri Labouret and Diedrich Westermann, to discuss ideas that would serve as the basis for his *African Background*. Woodson wrote that his inquiries and those into the study of the Negro were greeted with some enthusiasm; however, most of the researches followed the "usual program of Americans and Europeans" who were content "to study the Negro without the aid of Negro scholarship." However, Woodson went on, "the religious element seems to be especially anxious to see the record of the Negroes of Africa scientifically treated . . . in . . . more extensive study of the African background."[52]

Woodson's historiographic bent had its own ambiguities as well. The "Negro scholarship" of which he spoke was that of Western trained blacks whose training provided them with "a scientific objective" and who were yet able to escape "bias against [their] race." For these researchers of African descent, this type of exploration offered "a great opportunity which they [could] not afford to neglect."[53] Here, Woodson was merely rearticulating the major theme—the raison d'etre—of the black historians of his era and well before. This theme could be traced to the history and historiography of George Washing-

50. Ibid., 15–19. Woodson, "Ten Years," 598. Woodson and Wesley, *The Negro In Our History*, 8.

51. Carter G. Woodson, "Notes: The Director's Survey of Research in Europe," 504.

52. Ibid., 504-505.

53. Ibid., 505.

ton Williams, and it had been passed on to Woodson and his peers and their protégés. This clearly became a governing facet of black historiography at the close of the twentieth century.

Woodson's European researches were clearly preparation for *The African Background Outlined,* a work that he felt, early on in 1932, would enhance the *overall* intellectual and scholastic discourse as a key feature of the sociology of knowledge and the reconfiguration of the epistemology of blackness. The work became suggestive of how one might "study blackness" across the historical spectrums of time and space.

As Wesley pointed out, Woodson's work was indicative of the resurgence of an older tradition—the "resurgence of the historical truth about Africa", a challenge to the "old tradition of Africa's history." That old record, epitomized by the works of Toynbee and Trevor Roper, was characterized by the eleventh edition of the *Encyclopedia Britannica*:

> Africa with the exception of the Nile Valley and what is known as Roman Africa is . . . a continent practically without history and possessing no records from which history might be constructed. The Negro is essentially a child of the moment and his memory, both tribal and individual, is very short. If ancient Egypt and Ethiopia be excluded the story of Africa is largely a record of Asiatic and European conquerors and colonizers.[54]

This tradition was an indispensable ingredient of works such as Toynbee's *Study of the World.* In so many words, Africa was not of this world, at least not in the historical sense:

> The black races alone have not contributed positively to any civilization—as yet. . . . [W]ithin the first six thousand years the black race has not helped to create any civilization. . . . [I]t is to be remembered that there are many white peoples that are as innocent of having made any contribution to serve any civilization as the blacks themselves. . . . If anything positive emerges from this classification it is that half our civilizations are based on contributions from more than one race.[55]

For Woodson and Wesley the only counter that might be made to someone of Toynbee's stature was one that was direct and resounding: "Africa has a definite historical claim to be the cradle of civilization."[56]

---

54. Charles Wesley, "Resurgence in Africa's Historical Tradition and the American Reaction," *Negro History Bulletin* 24, 4 (January 1961), 81–82.

55. Ibid., 82.

56. Ibid., 85

These kinds of injunctions came from the pens of Harvard-trained historians; yet they were assertions which led to the

> settled policy of philanthropic foundations and of academic circles to intimate that Carter Woodson was altogether too self-centered and self-assertive to receive any great encouragement.[57]

In view of the circumstances, the conservative Woodson could become precursor and hero for future Afrocentrists even though he might not be regarded as "genuinely" Afrocentric by some in the fold. Woodson championed the notion that "there were certain neglected aspects [of history] which only the Negro himself can develop," and he regarded this as the essence of his own work. To that end he attempted to institutionalize the intellectual and scholarly pursuits of black researchers in both academic and popular veins.

Both these pursuits meant corporate courtship and intervention which in the end Woodson perceived as placing restrictions on his work. Ironically, one of the most caustic elements of Woodson's disagreement with the foundations concerned their desire that he, the association, and his publications affiliate with a black college or university. One of the best arguments on Woodson's behalf centers on his desire to safeguard his intellectual property. His response and that of his allies was to mount a defense based on his conservative credentials. It was a strategy that left many in philanthropic circles "impressed by evidences of Woodson's conservatism," but in the end left Woodson with the distinct impression that those he had sought to acquiesce to were attempting to "destroy the work of the Association." Du Bois reminded him to "remember . . . the enemy has the money and they are going to use it." Later, on another occasion which seemed to signal a real break with his benefactors, Woodson stated that "it is rare that the management seeks any sort of assistance from members of the oppressing race."[58]

Woodson's intellectual life was representative of the many intersections of race and historiography. Race clearly shaped his life and his life's work, and it came to dictate their product. As a historical figure to be studied by other historians, Woodson offers a clear example of the fuel that racism provides Levine's "radical Afrocentrists."

57. Meier, *Black History*, 70.

58. Herbert Aptheker, ed., *The Correspondence of W.E.B. Du Bois: Volume I* (University of Massachusetts Press, 1973), 448–449; also cited in Meier, *Black History*, 59. Ibid., 41–62.

FIVE

William Edward Burghardt Du Bois

I am challenging Authority.

W. E. B. Du Bois, *The World and Africa*

[T]he race idea, the race spirit, the race ideal . . . [is] . . .
the most ingenious invention for human progress.

W. E. B. Du Bois, "The Conservation of Races"

Seule des continents l'Afrique n'a pas d'histoire.

Maurice Guernier, quoted in W. E. B. Du Bois,
The World and Africa

The current definition of the word "Negro" was narrowed
again and again . . . [N]evertheless in the usage of many
distinguished writers there really emerged from their thinking two groups of men: *Human Beings and Negroes.*

W. E. B. Du Bois, *The World and Africa*

William Edward Burghardt Du Bois was contextually bound to proceed
like those before him. He recognized that "the greatest historian of the
race appeared when George Washington Williams issued his two-
volume *History of the Negro Race in America.*"[1] He also recognized that
as a result of the works of scholars such as Williams and Joseph T.

---

1. Du Bois, "The Negro in Literature and Art," in Nathan Huggins, ed., *W. E. B. Du Bois: Writings* (New York: Literary Classics of the United States, 1986), 865.

Wilson, a "new school of historians . . . led by Carter G. Woodson" was created.[2] The contextual boundaries of their space and his were articulated by the tangible qualities of race. Yet for Du Bois, the tangible nature of race was marked by fundamental differences and nuances.[3]

Like his predecessors and peers, Du Bois was well aware of the inadequacies of Western historiography as it related to Africa in general and to Egypt and Ethiopia in particular. Du Bois explicitly understood the importance of race in the construction of history. This understanding led him to begin his historical work with expositions on the nature of race—or its lack thereof. In path-breaking analysis, he also argued the role of history in the construction of race.

The differences and nuances in Du Bois's work are first witnessed in "The Conservation of Races." It is here that we see the beginnings of a change in the conceptualization, definition, and centrality of race for Du Bois. And it is here that Du Bois's "new" definition of race seems to create the most problems for analysts. Du Bois sets the stage in "The Conservation of Races" for his subsequent writings as a historian of African peoples. Again, that Du Bois should begin with interpretations of race is in keeping with the school of historiography set down by Williams and with the "new" school inaugurated by Woodson. However, Du Bois's departure from the two is in his directly ambivalent way of addressing the conceptualization, definition, centrality, and utility of race. This "direct ambivalence" comes from Du Bois's need to use the term and concept (his concept) of race as "an instrument of progress."[4] For Du Bois, the fact that race might be construed as an "instrument of progress" is indicative of the "ingenious" nature of the concept and its ubiquitousness.

My argument here is illustrated by three major points. First, Du Bois does not begin by arguing the "reality" of race. He argues the "idea," the "spirit," and the "ideal" of race. He does this because he understands race to be an *invention*—a social construction. Second, he is able to draw this conclusion because he is clear that a *physical definition of*

2. Du Bois, "The Propaganda of History," from *Black Reconstruction*, in *Writings*, 1047.

3. For me, the "fundamental" nature of Du Bois's articulation is seen in the number of scholarly pieces that address Du Bois's conceptualization of race as it appears in "Conservation of Races." Among the most prominent are Kwame Anthony Appiah's "The Uncomplete Argument: Du Bois and the Illusion of Race," in Henry Louis Gates, *"Race," Writing, and Difference* (Chicago: University of Chicago Press, 1986); Tommy Lott, "Du Bois on the Invention of Race," *Philosophical Forum*, 24, 1–3 (Fall–Spring 1992–1993); and Lucius Outlaw's forthcoming essay "On W. E. B. Du Bois's "The Conservation of Races." Appiah's contested and award-winning *In My Father's House* probably caps the list of works that center on Du Bois's conceptualization of race and the problems and opportunities it presents in the attempts to understand the construction of race.

4. Du Bois, "The Conservation of Races," 485.

race is well nigh impossible. The final product, even for the biological enthusiast, is a generalization so broad that speculation leads us to infer that there are "at least two, perhaps three great families of human beings,"[5] or possibly many more if we accept the determinations of Blumenbach and others.

So finally, Du Bois, moving from the idea of "invention" through the weaknesses of an inherent biological characterization, constructs a definition that acknowledges the instrumentality of race, or, more precisely, the instrumentality of the "idea," "spirit," and "ideal" of the "invention" of race:

> What then, is a race? It is a *vast* family of human beings, *generally* of common blood and language, *always* of *common history*, tradition and impulses, who are both voluntarily and involuntarily striving together for the accomplishment of certain more or less vividly conceived ideals of life.[6]

Du Bois's language speaks to the direct ambivalence that characterizes his definition. The "vast" nature of his race invites allusions to its diversity. The generality of "common blood and language" suggests that these can be just as easily invented/constructed as any other attribute. One need only look to history, linguistics, and genealogy to support this conclusion. The phrase "always of common history" becomes the crux, however. Du Bois is not arguing that there is simply a specific set of events, dates, and circumstances that this family of human beings shares that designates it as a race. Rather, Du Bois is arguing that it is the way in which events, dates, circumstances—facts—are interpreted, shaped, *constructed*, that creates this common history and its traditions. In this regard, moving beyond his peers and predecessors, Du Bois makes the case for history as key in the construction of race.

George Shepperson, Vincent Harding,[7] and Tommy Lott concur on

5. Ibid., 484. This theme is followed up in the three successive works on Africa. Du Bois also argues that the definition of the "Negro," in particular, was drawn so narrowly that it was useless. He concluded in *The Negro* that "no scientific definition of race is possible" (7). In *Black Folk Then and Now: An Essay in the History and Sociology of the Negro Race* (1939, New York: Octagon Books, 1970), Du Bois offers the same dictum, almost verbatim, 1. In 1946 he would write: The theory of absolutely definite racial groups was therefore abandoned and 'pure' racial types can be regarded as merely abstractions which never or rarely existed." *World*, 116.

6. Ibid., 485; italics added.

7. George Shepperson, Introduction to W. E. B. Du Bois, *The Negro* (1915; New York: Oxford University Press, 1970). Harding is referenced by Shepperson in his depiction of Du Bois's "Black Messianic vision," a conceptualization that alluded to the role of African Americans as "transformers and redeemers of the world" (xxi).

this point, if only by inference, from Du Bois's sense of his own mission and that of African Americans. Lott goes on to call Du Bois's construction a "socio-historical definition of race."[8] The construction of history is a construction of consciousness. It is Du Bois's "conscious striving together for certain ideals of life." Those "ideals of life" become the differentiating factors of race in this definition. They must be embraced consciously; there is no inherent or biological principle to Du Bois's conceptualization. In this case, race is an active and a deliberate consciousness.

With this definition Du Bois accomplishes two things. First, he debunks the notion that race is powered by biological determinism. The rejection of this idea is a resounding theme from "The Conservation of Races" through *The World and Africa*. The biological is not excluded, it is simply not dominant. The range of physical variation precludes its dominance.

Second, because of the emphasis on consciousness and the historical construction of identity—the way in which peoples use history to construct identity, that is, race—Du Bois posits great weight on the ways in which he believes people perceive/perceived themselves. So, beginning as his predecessors and peers would, he offers this: "Egyptians . . . regarded themselves as Africans."[9]

Du Bois invokes the metonym that Levine deplores: Egypt is Africa. Du Bois's move is a deliberate historiographical choice. He says as much when he reminds us that Egyptology is a child of prejudice and racialized thinking:

> One must remember that Egyptology, starting in 1821, grew up during the African slave trade, the Sugar Empire and the Cotton Kingdom. Few scholars during the period dared to associate the Negro race with humanity, much less with civilization.[10]

Bearing this in mind, Du Bois's mission was in part to focus attention on the ways in which white scholars constructed black identity and to imply, conversely, that blacks were capable of constructing iden-

8. Du Bois, in fact, makes this statement himself when he says that "the function of race up to the present time" has been "sociological and historical." "Conservation," 487. Vincent Harding, "W. E. B. Du Bois and the Black Messianic Vision," *Freedomways*, 9, 1 (1969), 45, cited in Shepperson, introduction to Du Bois, *The Negro*, xxi. Lott, "Du Bois," 170.

9. Du Bois, *World*, 99. Quoting Palgrave in *The Negro* (8) and *Black Folk Then and Now* (4), Du Bois reinforces his case and his reliance on Egyptian perception through the use of myriad sources, placing great emphasis on archaeology. The artwork of temples and tombs, the sculpture and the obelisks represent undeniable proof of an African, even "Negroid," Egypt.

10. Du Bois, *Black Folk Then and Now*, 25.

tities themselves.[11] This was a historiographic mission in keeping with the realization of the impact of race on the construction of history. As important, however, was the appreciation that history also could be used in the construction of race.

Du Bois's treatment of race is more than just the assertion of the unreliability of pseudoscientific conjectures about biological determinism or sociohistorical pronouncements on who and what the ancient Egyptians were. Du Bois makes his case by concentrating on the peoples who were central to his history and the ways in which they were depicted in conventional history. The historiographic nature of this approach places emphasis on the choices that the writers of conventional histories made and the reasons they made them. In some ways the questions generated by this approach were moot; they did, however, allow Du Bois to make his case by incisively analyzing the definitions and images that white writers constructed of black people and by using those definitions and images against the arguments that had become America's conventional wisdom. Here, Du Bois also begins a construction, or reconstruction of the epistemology of blackness. He offers, through inversion and juxtaposition, a new way of looking at black people and of having black people look at themselves. Du Bois's work argues, in effect, that black folk can invent themselves.

It is the juxtaposition of image and history that was Du Bois's strongest weapon in the construction of race. And it was here, particularly with the question of *image* and history, that Du Bois used the examples of Egypt and Ethiopia and the newly created discipline of Egyptology. This is interesting. Having recognized the racist roots of Egyptology in the political economy of slavery, sugar, and cotton, Du Bois was quick to realize how the seemingly irrefutable truths of the "science" could be used against it in the juxtaposition of image and history. In his treatment of Egypt and Ethiopia, Du Bois relied heavily

---

11. In the forefront of the black construction of race were the intellectuals of the African Methodist Episcopal Church (A.M.E.). In 1888, C. A. A. Taylor, writing in the *A.M.E. Democrat*, took up the definition and development of "The Negro Race." In 1892, William Walroud Moe offered the provocative essay "The Boasted Inherent Superiority of the Anglo-Saxon Race on Trial, With the Universally Authoritative Acknowledgment of the Unique Ethiopian Race." Moe's work appeared in the A.M.E. *Church Review*. Between 1892 and 1895, Bishop Benjamin Tucker Tanner wrote several pieces that examined the invention of race from a decidedly black standpoint. To illustrate the case, Tanner moved his readers from biblical chronology through an examination of Darwinian theories. Tanner's work included several essays and correspondence in the A.M.E. *Church Review* and the monograph, *The Color of Solomon—What?* (Philadelphia: A.M.E. Book Concerns, 1895). In 1895, George Wilson Brent wrote on "The Ancient Glory of the Hamitic Race" in the *Church Review*. There is little doubt that Du Bois and his contemporaries were aware of these views and others. From 1894 to 1896, Du Bois may have been directly exposed to the authors and their writings from his short tenure at Wilberforce University, an A.M.E. school.

on the work of Egyptologists. His most effective tour de force was the way in which he used their images to construct his history.

Images and History

Egyptology, as a discipline, was based, in overwhelming measure, on the examination and analysis of Egyptian artifact. The biblical record and the myths and histories of the ancient period provided images that alluded, both explicitly and implicitly, to the blackness of Egypt. The scholars who preceded Du Bois, particularly those of African descent, emphasized the *imagery* of these accounts over and again. It took, however, the Napoleonic expedition into Egypt to bring the hard, stony fact of the Egyptian image to life and to situate it squarely in the center of the debate that Du Bois argued shaped the modern age: the "color line"—race.

Du Bois understood why white scholars clung [cling] so tenaciously to Egypt as a white, or at least nonblack, paradigm. Egypt, within the construction of the racial "possibilities" of whiteness, has extreme importance in the social *and* historical construction of whiteness, and the apportionment of tangible and intangible resources in the modern age. Because of the various constructions of identity and, more importantly, because of the two diametric racial constructions of the modern Western world, black and white, Egypt has become a preeminent ground of contention. Its prominence and the intensity of the contention are, as Du Bois put it, "because . . . the valley of the Nile . . . led to the European civilization of which the world boasts today."[12] In the ironies of historiography, here is Bernal's thesis well before Bernal; the pity is that Bernal could not do Du Bois, his predecessors, and his peers more justice than three pages in a multivolume work. From Du Bois's pen to Bernal's page:

> African colonists passed over to Greece by way of the islands beginning with Crete. From Numidia they crossed into Sicily, Italy and southern France; by Gilbraltar into Spain. There is evidence of Negro blood in Asia Minor as far as the Black Sea and the Caucasus Mountains.[13]

The emphatic nature of Du Bois's declarations were in direct opposition to the observations he recorded in *The World and Africa*: [I]t is

12. Du Bois, *World*, 99, 123; *Black Folk Then and Now*, 15.
13. Du Bois, *World*, 123. For Bernal's treatment, see *Black Athena*, vol. 1, 21–22; 38–62; 75–120.

one of the astonishing results of the history of Africa, that almost unanimously in the nineteenth century Egypt was not regarded as part of Africa."[14] Du Bois's assertion that Egyptians were Africans[15] works in direct contradiction to the images whites created of black folk and the needs those images satisfy, images "colored almost entirely by their attitude toward modern Negro slavery" and the reduction of the world's population to "Human Beings and Negroes."[16]

In light of these images and the histories that they produced, Du Bois was compelled to "challenge authority"—the authority of scholars such as G. Maspero, A. H. Sayce, George Reisner, J. H. Breasted, Guernier, and others, who "studiously ignored the Negro on the Nile and in the world and talked as though black folk were nonexistent and unimportant."[17] It was a challenge to "those who would deny the presence of Negro blood to any great extent in Egypt." Du Bois acknowledged that their numbers were large.[18]

These were the "personalities and prejudices" who were and are the beneficiaries of capitalism, early industrialization, and modern slavery. Their benefits and comfort were and are the key to the "false writing on Africa" that was the crux of Du Bois's mission. These personalities and prejudices "would deny this interpretation of history," an interpretation that defined Egyptians as African and therefore "Negroid" and black within the context of existing convention. Their interpretation meant that "Ethiopia" (e.g., Nubia/Kush; Meroe/Napata) because of its civilization was not black. As Du Bois noted, "[E]fforts . . . made to separate the history of Egypt from Africa and the Negro race [make] a similar determination with regard to Ethiopia . . . even more contradictory."[19]

In spite of the blatant contradiction, the most prominent white minds of the age would argue that along with the Egyptians, "Ethiopians were not Negroes!"[20] Under this prescription modern Ethiopians and Somalis, among others, could be stripped of their "Negroness" and hence their "Africanness" and their "blackness." Du Bois recognized what Edith Sanders perceptively explores in her "Hamitic Hypothesis" (See Chapter One): the "term 'Hamite' under which millions of Negroids have been characteristically transferred to the white race by some eager scientists" has been one of the tools employed to deny

14. Ibid., 99.
15. More emphatically, "the Egyptians were Negroids." World, 106.
16. Ibid., 116, 118.
17. Ibid., viii.
18. Du Bois, Black Folk Then and Now, 25.
19. Du Bois, World, 115.
20. Ibid., 117. Du Bois, Black Folk Then and Now, 15, 17.

the interpretation of history that would challenge the "false writing on Africa."[21]

As Du Bois pointed out, "according to such definition, most of the black people of Africa and the world are not Negroes and never were."[22] Then again, this was exactly the analysis that Woodson attacked when he argued that "if the Egyptians . . . were not Negroes, then there are no Negroes in the United States"

The images that Du Bois criticized contradicted the theses and conclusions of those who employed them regarding the humanity and civilizations of black folk. It was a case of Egyptology against itself. A. Weigall's amazement at that "astonishing epoch of nigger domination" and the ejaculation of World War I troops from Australia and New Zealand on leave in Cairo: "My god! We didn't know Egyptians was niggers!" rank as two of Du Bois's most poignant and ironic citations. It is exactly their poignance and irony that allow for the linkage that Du Bois sought—a linkage of Africa to Egypt, and Egypt to Ethiopia, spanning time and encompassing the physical and cultural dynamics of the African continent. It is the linkage that W. G. Palgrave suggested when he observed that

"among the statues of the Egyptian rooms of the British museum . . . is the genuine African model."

It is this "genuine African model" that Du Bois embraced as decidedly and definitively Negroid: "the large gentle eye, the full but not over-protruding lips, the rounded contour, and the good-natured, easy sensuous expression." He asserts that to this race Africa in the main and parts of Asia have belonged since prehistoric times."[23]

So beginning with Volney and Denon and moving through the work of David Randall-McIver, Du Bois was able to substantiate his claims, explore their implications, and construct a racial paradigm that supported his construction of history. All the while he was quite clear that the history that he constructed would also lend itself to the construction of race. He contended that "in the eyes of the Greeks a thousand years B.C. and even in the age of Pericles, black Africans were considered equal to though different from Greeks and superior to European and Asiatic barbarians." For the Greeks, he continued, "Africa . . . was . . . a land of ideals."[24] Reference to the Perseus cycle serves as an illustration of Du Bois's assertion of the impact of Africa on Greek

21. Du Bois, *The Negro*, 7, 9; *Black Folk Then and Now*, 6.
22. Du Bois, *Black Folk Then and Now*, viii, 17; *World*, 118.
23. Du Bois, *The Negro*, 8. *Black Folk Then and Now*, 4.
24. Du Bois, *World*, 119.

racial consciousness.[25] Here, the implied greatness of Africa as an ancient legacy by way of Ethiopia and Egypt, and Africa as "a land of ideals," dovetails with Du Bois's conceptualization of racial consciousness. The "land of ideals" is the generator of the "race idea," the "race spirit," and the "race ideal" in their most positive forms.

The twists and turns of racialist thinking are made apparent and transparent by Du Bois's analysis of the works of people such as George Reisner. The proclivity of "some eager scientists" to transform Africans and African achievements into white men and white accomplishments was as clear to Du Bois as it was to Frederick Douglass and the black intellectuals who followed him. Reisner's denial of the Ethiopian's blackness was literally a changing of the leopard's spots. In the end, even Reisner himself could not justify the notion: he conceded that "Egyptian civilization was from the south and from the black tribes of Punt" and that Egypt and Lower Nubia were "culturally and racially one land."[26] Reisner and Saya later argued that the Ethiopians were indeed of Negro stock; they had simply been dominated by the Libyans, and this domination explained Ethiopia's monumental achievements.[27]

The question implicit in Reisner's about-face is who were the Libyans? The answer is better served in Du Bois's questions: Who were the Ethiopians? Who were the Egyptians? What is an African? The answer to those questions certainly provides a better understanding of Libyans as African peoples. Du Bois asks, if the Ethiopians were not Negroes,

what then are Negroes? Who are Africans? Why has the whole history of Ethiopia been neglected or ascribed to white "Hamites"? And why does every historian and encyclopedist, whatever he writes of the history of the Upper Nile, feel compelled to reiterate that these black people were "not Negroes"?[28]

In *Black Folk Then and Now*, after reviewing the evidence, Du Bois broached the issue in relation to the Egyptians: "[W]hat race, then, were the Egyptians? *They certainly were not white* in any modern sense of the word—neither in color or physical measurement."[29]

He had taken his cue for all these from his answer to the query

25. Maghan Keita, "Deconstructing the Classical Age: Africa and the Unity of the Mediterranean World," *Journal of Negro History*, 79, 2, 150–151.

26. Du Bois, *The Negro*, 21; *Black Folk Then and Now*, 21.

27. Du Bois, *Black Folk Then and Now*, 17.

28. Du Bois, *World*, 118.

29. Du Bois, *Black Folk Then and Now*, 22.

"what is a Negro?" There was no agreement on this categorization, simply "the most extraordinary confusion of thought and difference of opinion." The physical attributes of Negroes and Negroid peoples varied greatly over the broad range of physical geography and cultural and biological space known as Africa and its adjoining areas.[30]

The question of racial definition was political; and the political issues had been expressed, directly and inadvertently, in the words of the many scholars that Du Bois referenced for his work. Volney had come to the conclusion at the close of the eighteenth century that those people who were held in slavery in the western hemisphere were indeed the same people as those who had been masters of the earth in antiquity. Randall-McIver could echo the amazement of others that "an African pharaoh should have been able . . . to style himself as Emperor of the World." Chamberlain's observations on Nefertari were reflections on a "great beauty" and a great mind. The intellectual capacities of these Africans who made up a considerable proportion of the Egyptian population was, again, expressive of Du Bois's notion of the "race ideal." Flinders Petrie capitalized the concept when he said that the southern focus of Taharqa's temple at Thebes was indicative that the south was the "center of thought" for Egypt.[31] It is only fitting that Taharqa's temple should face south; this was the direction from which came Egypt's intellectual and moral authority. As Flinders Petrie observed again, "[I]t was remarkable that renewed vitality came to Egypt from the south."[32] Edward Wilmot Blyden noted that as the Sphinx should face the great plain of Memphis, her face told the tale of centuries:

> Her features are decidedly of the African or Negro type with "expanded nostrils." If the Sphinx was placed here—looking out in majestic and mysterious silence over the empty plain where once stood the great city of Memphis in all its pride and glory, as an *"emblematic representation of the king"*—is not the inference clear as to the particular type or race to which that king belonged?[33]

Du Bois's argument on the nature of Africans, Ethiopians, Egyptians, Libyans, and the like illustrates the contention between ideology (racism) and image. Reisner's affirmations are useful models here. They were made in the face of evidence that, if not irrefutable, made a striking case for the Africanness of Egypt, an Africanness that sup-

30. Du Bois, *The Negro*, 7, 12–13.
31. Du Bois, *Black Folk Then and Now*, 27–31.
32. Du Bois, *World*, 107.
33. Du Bois, *The Negro*, 19; italics added.

ported the statistical analysis of Randall-McIver and his colleagues. Their analysis placed the percentages of "Negroes" in the Fifth through Eighteenth Dynasties at between 15 and 24% of a population that was already decidedly Negroid. Analysis like this forced scholars such as like F. L. Griffith to conclude that blacks were integrated at all levels of Egyptian society. Du Bois would have accepted this conclusion and taken it a step further: if modern racial categorization was the mean, then Egypt was black in all its variation.[34]

All this evidence flies in the face of the Robert Pounders of the world who would argue that there was no appreciable Negro/black/ African presence in Egypt, as if Egypt were not a part of Africa. Du Bois recognized the need to "treat Egyptian history as an integral part of African history." This was the history that others sought to deny.[35]

Du Bois, Criticism, and Bernal

An essential purpose of this book is to gauge the academic and intellectual response accorded Martin Bernal and *Black Athena*, and to assess that in relation to African American scholars who are his predecessors and peers. These would be the forerunners of the "radical Afrocentrists" and the "radical Afrocentrists" themselves.

In this context, gauging the response to the work of Du Bois encompasses at least three minds here. In the circle of some of his contemporaries, most of Du Bois's work was received with a positive, if nonchalant, acceptance. There was also, however, a response from other quarters that was quite negative and dismissive. In other circles, the nonchalant and dismissive coalesced. Works such as *The Negro, Black Folk Then and Now,* and *The World and Africa* were seen, as Francis Broderick put it, to "possess some information, but nothing which indicates the mind or hand of an original scholar." Broderick, it seems, wished to diminish the larger-than-life qualities attached to Du Bois's scholarship, and it is certainly justifiable that some critics exhibit a greater desire for empiricism in terms of documentation and the citation of sources than Du Bois allows in these works.[36]

However, Du Bois was clear on the limitations of his work on Africa. In *The Negro,* he acknowledged that the short length of the volume precluded any extensive or in-depth coverage of the material. There

34. Du Bois, *Black Folk Then and Now,* 23–24; *World,* 108.

35. Du Bois, *World,* 99, 117.

36. Francis L. Broderick, *W. E. B. Du Bois: Negro Scholar in a Time of Crisis* (Palo Alto: Stanford University Press, 1959), 228. Quoted in Shepperson, introduction to Du Bois, *The Negro,* xii.

could be only "mainly conclusions and generalization with but meager indications of authorities and underlying arguments"—more analytical coverage would lie in the public's request for a "later and larger book" (*Black Folk Then and Now* and *The World and Africa*).[37] In *Black Folk Then and Now*, Du Bois opened by saying, "this is not a work of exact scholarship; far too few studies in history and sociology are."[38] From the vantage of *The World and Africa*, Du Bois wrote concerning *The Negro*, of "evidence of a certain naive astonishment on my part at the wealth of fact and material concerning the Negro peoples, the existence of which I had myself known little despite a varied university career."[39]

Du Bois was certainly conscious of his shortcomings, but he was not so apologetic as to let the entire academic profession off the hook. Du Bois's consciousness on the subject is underscored in his revelations of the impact that Franz Boas had on him at an Atlantic University commencement address where Du Bois recalled that Boas told the black student body that "you need not be ashamed of your African past."[40]

The criticism of the empiricists and those like Broderick, who found nothing new, has been answered in part by Shepperson's assertion that

the originality of W.E.B. Du Bois in *The Negro*, was that he tried to pull together into one succinct but comprehensive whole the different elements of African history, at home and abroad, as they were known by the first decade of the twentieth century.[41]

Shepperson went on to note that Du Bois was not afforded the luxury of the researches of post–World War II and post–African independence scholars, which his work in many ways pioneered.

Yet Broderick's assessment falls short in another way. He did not entertain the various analytical angles from which the subject (Africa) might be approached. As a Du Bois biographer, he had lost sight of one of Du Bois's missions: the reciprocal and dialectical relation between the construction of history and race, and the instrumentality of the two. This escapes Broderick's criticism of Du Bois's three major African works, as does the essential historiography of the pieces. As David Levering Lewis notes of the criticism of Du Bois's *John Brown*, "nothing was said about *the point of view* of his history." This critical element is an indispensable feature of the three African works. In *John*

37. Du Bois, preface to *The Negro*.
38. Du Bois, *The Negro*, 3; *Black Folk Then and Now*, vii.
39. Du Bois, *World*, vii.
40. Ibid., vii.
41. Ibid., xiv.

Brown, Du Bois made assertions that the community of conventional scholars dismissed without hearing only to have them proven on the basis of later research. Professor William E. Dodd's criticism of the "fanciful" in Du Bois's work was a portent and an illustration of the biases of the academy. It was an indication of the difficulties that existed, and still exist, for ideas that counter the given convention. In this case, we might refer to Du Bois's contention that Egyptians were "blacks."[42]

As Lewis has pointed out, *The Negro* was not a well-written piece. In attitude and fact, it would have been regarded "as invidious if propounded by a European scholar." However, Lewis continues, it was a

> pioneering synthesis of the latest scholarship, brilliantly beamed through a revisionist lens. . . .
>
> *The Negro* was a large building block in an Afrocentric historiography that has achieved credibility through the writings of scholars such as Basil Davidson, Martin Bernal and Cheikh Anta Diop.[43]

In this regard, the angles of analysis that Du Bois offered extrapolated on the latest researches and reconstructed those researches within the contexts of historical imagination and historiography. The result was a unique philosophy of history that made historical actors of peoples who were assumed to be without history.

If Du Bois's work was treated with nonchalance in some circles, in spite of the lapses in documentation, its acceptance, even among critics, was based on the fact that there was a general acknowledgment that what Du Bois left undocumented was, in most instances, regarded as true and correct. Yes, the Egyptian was plausibly African, and therefore Negro. The critics had eyes and they could see. With the image of Du Bois beside that of Ramses, what adjustment could be made to make the other less black in the conceptualization of twentieth-century America? Of course, some of the coarser critics would refer to "mixture," but even this would not make Du Bois any more than what he was—a black American.

When Du Bois began *The Negro*, the engine of modern imperialism was in high gear. Du Bois and the world could not help but be influenced by it. Du Bois's career up to this point was marked by that influence. The first Pan African Congress took place in 1900; World War I was on the horizon; and Africa's place in the world was underscored,

---

42. David Levering Lewis, *W. E. B. Du Bois: Biography of a Race, 1868–1919* (New York: Henry Holt and Company, 1993), 359–360; italics added.

43. Ibid., 461–462.

in Du Bois's eyes, by the impending conflict. Du Bois dated the preface of *The Negro* February 1, 1915; in May of the same year *The Atlantic Monthly* published "The African Roots of War," in which he offered a political economic analysis of Africa's central role in World War I. It should be noted that Du Bois contextualized his analysis historically and ended with the metaphor of a black, African Egypt.[44]

Du Bois's analysis had to be tempered by the American age of James K. Vardaman. Vardaman, building on Hegel, argued on the floor of the United States Senate that Africa had no civilization or history other than that bequeathed by the "white man"; and without the white man, the African "has universally gone back to the barbarism of the jungle."[45] The utterances of philosopher and politician also provide the context that would drive conventional criticism of Du Bois's work for the next half century. The use of Hegel and Vardaman illustrates the difficulty, if not the impossibility, of separating scholarship from politics.

The 1939 reception of *Black Folk Then and Now* referred to the utility of *The Negro*. Melville Herskovits noted that in approximately a quarter of a century, *The Negro* had "grown in usefulness and [had] become a standard reference."[46] There is some discussion as to whether *Black Folk* was simply an enlargement of *The Negro* or a new book in its own right;[47] Du Bois had forecast its appearance as early as 1915 in the preface of *The Negro*. Correspondence between Du Bois and his publisher acknowledged that the format used for *The Negro* would benefit the production of *Black Folk*.[48]

Judging from the reviews and correspondence, *Black Folk* was well received. It can be assumed that an article in the *New York Times Book Review*, which commanded almost the entire page, spoke to the significance of Du Bois's stature and the importance of his work. Interestingly enough, the reviewer also went on to contextualize the climate in which both *The Negro* and *Black Folk* were written: "a moment when the struggle for colonies is likely to become a strategic factor in the precarious balance of peace."[49]

44. Du Bois, "The African Roots of War," in Julius Lester, ed., *The Seventh Son: The Thought and Writings of W. E. B. Du Bois*, vol. 1, (New York: Vintage Books, 1971), 452–463.

45. Quoted in Shepperson, introduction to Du Bois, *The Negro*, xi.

46. Melville Herskovits, "Negro History" rev. of *Black Folk—Then and Now*, *The New Republic*, 100 (August 10, 1939), 55.

47. Ibid., 55. J. T. G., rev. of *Black Folk, Then and Now*, *Catholic World*, 123. August Meier and Elliot Rudwick, *Black History and the Historical Profession* (Urbana: University of Illinois Press, 1986), 68.

48. Du Bois Papers, R44/00335/1935H.

49. William Shands Meacham, "Where Slave Traders Blazed the Trail of Civilization: A Cultural and Economic History of Africa, the 'Tragic Continent,' rev. of *Black Folk Then and Now*," *New York Times Book Review* (July 2, 1939), 3.

Domestic racism and international imperialism suffused a general climate of conservatism for both black and white America. The significance of stature and importance notwithstanding, Du Bois and his work were not readily accepted in all academic circles. The reasons for this, in part, go back to the very beginning of Du Bois's career as an intellectual and to, as Lewis and many others write, the legacy of Booker T. Washington and the attitudes that he engendered. These attitudes shaped Du Bois's reception in broader academic, philanthropic, and publishing spheres. As Lewis writes, in the early years, through 1919, Du Bois's lack of access to funds became "more stifling month by month." Writing specifically of Du Bois's Atlanta years, Lewis says that "admired by visitors, Du Bois remained isolated and ignored by the white people of the city that his labors were putting on the map of social science."[50]

As he sought a broader venue for his ideas, it became clear that it was not simply the whites of Atlanta who shunned him but also conservative blacks molded in the crucible of the Tuskegee Machine and the national white structure associated with its well-tuned maintenance. Among the most scathing critics of his work was none other than Woodson.[51]

Du Bois seemed unable to acquiesce. His penchant for activism and the infusion of history and Marxist analysis into his sociology, as well as his historiographical bent, was clear early on. He could not "help saying and writing things—repeatedly and with what seemed perverse arrogance—that only poisoned further the well of white beneficence."[52] Du Bois was clear on what this "perverse arrogance"—this independence—meant in relation to funding when he wrote to Woodson in 1932 of "the enemy," "money," and the enemy's ability to use it.[53]

Ironically, Du Bois's observations to Woodson implied that Woodson was cut from the same cloth in many respects. Du Bois underscored this point in a eulogy for Woodson published in *Masses and Mainstream*, in which he noted that

50. Lewis, *Du Bois*, 343–334.

51. Carter G. Woodson, rev. of *Black Folk Then and Now*, *Journal of Negro History*, 24, 4 (October 1939), 460–463. While it is not the subject of this work, Meier and Rudwick highlight the difficult and contentious relationship that existed between Du Bois and Woodson, and one can only assume the vast network of associates that Woodson developed and nurtured. They counter by offering that Du Bois's response, in particular, "was always scrupulously fair in dealing with Woodson." Meier and Rudwick, *Black History*, 13, 68.

52. Lewis, *Du Bois*, 352.

53. Aptheker, *Correspondence*, 1, 448–449.

Woodson did not prove the ideal recipient of philanthropy. . . . [H]is independence of thought and action was exaggerated. . . . After a while it became the settled policy of philanthropic circles to intimate that Carter Woodson was altogether too self-centered and self assertive to receive any great encouragement."[54]

Even within this atmosphere there was a widespread reception for *Black Folk*. The review in the *New Yorker* emphasized the necessity of Du Bois's work in an ignorant and racially charged America: "Dr. Du Bois's material will be new to most whites, and his viewpoint (he is black) a needed corrective."[55] It was this kind of "corrective" that Lewis most certainly saw as part of Du Bois's perceived "perverse arrogance"; yet, as this and other reviews and correspondence indicate, there were quarters in which the work was received as an overwhelming success.

In private correspondence, Joseph Jenkins, Jr., writing from Lynchburg, Virginia, and Wirt Faust from Bowling Green, Ohio, showed the geographic breadth over which the work was broadcast in that first year. Jenkins apparently had tuned into a Chicago radio station, WBBM, and picked up University of Chicago professor T. V. Smith's "philosopher-politician debates with himself" in which *Black Folk* was featured and the "review was favorable."[56] We can only wonder how many other Americans across the country—and particularly African Americans—tuned in to catch Smith's comments.

Faust's comments were glowing for the "comprehensive and thorough study" that Du Bois had compiled. Faust did his part in getting out the word by informing Du Bois that his and Mrs. Faust's copy of *Black Folk* would be "circulating amongst my various friends."[57]

Du Bois was also quite pleased with the work. In a letter to Lillie Maie Hubbard in May of 1939, he wrote that *Black Folk* was the "climax" of "an excellent year." It was in his opinion, a work of "priceless contents."[58]

As should be expected, there was also real and substantive criticism; much of which was a sign of the times and much of which alluded to the position that scholars such as Du Bois were expected to occupy within the American intellectual establishment. Some of this criticism was political in spite of its "factual" orientation. All of it is subject to

54. Du Bois, "Portrait," 21–22. Meier and Rudwick, *Black History*, 70.
55. Seligman, rev. of *Black Folk Then and Now*, *The New Yorker*, 15 (January 17, 1939), 91.
56. Du Bois Papers, R50/360/1939I.
57. Du Bois Papers, R50/00094/1939F, 2–3.
58. Du Bois Papers, R50/00315/1939H.

political and social interpretation given the American and the international climate.

William Shands Meacham of the *New York Review of Books* registered "dissent." He was particularly concerned with Du Bois's assessment of the current state of affairs in America as it related to the Negro and race progress. He did not share Du Bois's view that America had "surrendered" to racial prejudice; nor did he believe that the degree of racial prejudice was as Du Bois maintained. Meacham also took issue with Du Bois's contention that the "liberal elements of the nation" were under southern domination. In sum, as a counter to Du Bois's general thesis on the state of the Negro in contemporary America, Meacham asserted that America had "encouraged . . . Negro genius . . . and that has flowered" here. Meacham might have added that Du Bois himself was the most striking example of this. However, we might surmise that Du Bois might have added a twist to Meacham's observation: it was the Negro who had encouraged and nurtured the genius of America and was excluded from the harvest of her blooms.[59]

Herskovits's praise early on in his review was tempered by a familiar refrain that was acknowledged by J. T. G. in the *Catholic World* review. J. T. G. wrote that not only was Du Bois incorrect in statements concerning Catholicism, but in the more general sense, the failure to provide adequate documentation was a characteristic endemic to the work of "too many Negro writers" and an act "which the Negro so rightly deprecates in white authors dealing with the Negro."[60]

The political and social implications of "generalizations difficult of proof" and Herskovits's criticism that Du Bois did not take "greater advantage of the most recent work" or take a more "critical point of view" of the materials may have supported the argument that blacks were incapable of doing historical studies. Such an inference can be drawn from Herskovits's assertion that Du Bois was "incomparably better" in his discussion of "present day problems."[61] Here, as in the case of Woodson, the foundations were given voice through the opinions of scholars, and some scholars responded to the willing ear.

Molly Levine's concerns were raised over half a century ago, as well. Herskovits attacked what might be called the "proto-radical Afrocentrist" position: "Negro chauvinism is no less defensible than any other brand; *and it is* as inadvisable to insist that Egypt for instance, had a Negro culture as it is to rule out the participation of Negroid folk in the making of that civilization."[62]

59. Meacham, "Where Slave Traders Blazed the Trail," 3.
60. J. T. G., rev. of *Black Folk*, 123.
61. Herskovits, "Negro History," 56.
62. Ibid., 56; italics added.

Here, we might wish to revisit Herskovits's criticism of *The African Background Outlined*. Herskovits asserted that *African Background* was "lacking [in] objectivity and charged with a strong anti-white prejudice". In this sense, his charge of "Negro chauvinism" in regard to Du Bois's work is consistent, in spite of the fact of Du Bois's consultation and correspondence with him on the work.[63]

Herskovits's comments in both instances might be interpreted as evenhanded, honest, and judicious scholarly assessments of the works at hand. However, others might allude to J. T. G.'s aphorism concerning "generalizations" as "fact without bothering to check them carefully."[64] Both instances might provide the basis for dismissing Du Bois's work over the key issue of contention, then and now: the "blackness" of the Egyptians.

Even within that context, what are the alternatives that Herskovits's comments provide? If there is "negroid participation" yet the culture is not "Negro," what is the oppositional conceptualization? Are we to assume, as we read Pounder, that because there was, as he believes, no "significant role for blacks in Egyptian society," that society is therefore a "Caucasian culture"? The issue is the implications of the conceptualization on both sides; the context out of which such conceptualization is born; and, as Woodson put it, the double standard of critical analysis.

Again, we need to consider Lewis's observations on Du Bois's *John Brown* as historiographic and historical, and theoretical and factual, in light of William E. Dodds's comments on the work as a "sensational . . . [and] somewhat inaccurate story."[65] The grudging commendations of the reviewers of Du Bois's African works, and in particular *Black Folk*, were overshadowed by what Herskovits considered "minor points" that in "aggregate . . . lessen the usefulness of the first half of the book." Herskovits's description of the marginalized "usefulness" of the first half of *Black Folk* diminishes the book's historiographic and historical arguments. These "minor points," as Lewis recalls of *John Brown*, obscure the real value of *Black Folk* as Du Bois's reconceptualization of Africa and African peoples in the history of the world. These

63. Du Bois Papers, R50/00263/1939H. Woodson's reply to Herskovits is telling. In a rejoinder written in the *Journal of Negro History*, 22 (April 1937), Woodson launches into a six-page critique of Herskovits's review under the title "Dr. Melville Herskovits' Method Examined." Woodson began by declaring that Herskovits's review "contains so many misinterpretations and misstatements" that he was compelled to reply. Then through the six pages, Woodson excoriates Herskovits on the biases of social science, the injection of race into history, and the double standard of white scholastic criticism. Woodson ends by stating that it was a "mistake...to ask an anthropologist to review a work which is chiefly historical" (293–294).

64. J. T. G., rev. of *Black Folk*, 122.

65. Lewis, *Du Bois*, 359.

are the same historiographic and historic considerations that Lewis found present in *John Brown* and to which both he and Shepperson refer in *The Negro*.[66]

In spite of Du Bois's intention "to focus for a time the attention of intelligent white readers and historians . . . the reception of his John Brown biography was typical" not only of his Atlanta years but those that would follow for a long time to come.[67] This is borne out in the reception of his "Reconstruction and Its Benefits," read at the 1909 meeting of the American Historical Association, and its publication a year later in the *American Historical Review*. As Lewis points out, "virtually nothing more was ever said among white historians about its *heterodox interpretation*."[68]

Indeed, as Bernal noted of "heterodox interpretation," it was ignored or dismissed, or virtually so. That was the case until Herskovits resurrected it by way of his offhand reference to *Black Reconstruction* in his review of *Black Folk*. With clear distaste for the Marxist interpretation that undergirded the book's theoretical premise and a genuine disbelief that "certain" peoples could "consciously" promote actions that would forge their identity, Herskovits attacked both *Black Reconstruction* and *Black Folk* for Du Bois's interpretive and conceptual supposition that "read into slave revolts something analogous to a self conscious modern labor movement."[69]

Du Bois was not to be outdone by such criticism—criticism that was double-edged in its critique of his theoretical premises and in its allusions to the inabilities of peoples of African descent to function on the most creative and critical intellectual planes in constructing and taking advantage of life's opportunities. In a 1940 response to H. A. Noyes's criticism of Du Bois's "slavery to the dictums of Carl [sic] Marx," and his tendency to "overestimate the ability of colored races," Du Bois was emphatic:

Karl Marx has repeatedly been refuted by persons who have never read his works. As to the "ability of the colored races" I think I am

66. Herskovits, "Negro History," 56. Lewis, *Du Bois*, 357, 359–360, 462. Shepperson, introduction to Du Bois, *The Negro*, xii, xiv.

67. Lewis, *Du Bois*, 357, 362.

68. Ibid., 384. italics added. Though Lewis is correct technically, Du Bois noted that the paper did "greatly exercise" some parties, including the likes of Ulrich B. Phillips, at the time of its presentation. It is also interesting to note that in the *American Historical Review* there seems to be no record of any review of Du Bois's three African pieces. Du Bois, *Dusk of Dawn*, in Huggins, *W.E.B. Du Bois: Writings*, 786. Also see Jacqueline Goggin, "Countering White Racist Scholarship: Carter G. Woodson and the Journal of Negro History," *Journal of Negro History*, 68 (Fall 1983), 356.

69. Herskovits, "Negro History," 56.

possibly in a better position to judge that. I have been in Europe, Asia and Africa and have sat in the school room with representatives of nearly all the principal races. Moreover, just now is hardly the time to boast of the mental capacity of Europeans.[70]

This was correspondence that we can safely assume Herskovits and others never saw, yet it answers their declarations and their innuendos.

Here, from 1909 or before through 1939 and beyond, we can speculate that most of Du Bois's work garnered a similar reception. It was

a reinterpretation incompatible with the contemporary historiography, advancing facts and arguing positions diverging so radically from what the gentlemen listening to Du Bois knew that it could find no meaningful place in their tradition of inquiry.[71]

Du Bois's work was, in many ways, as Bernal noted, "dismissed." This may also account for the ease, for lack of a better term, with which Bernal afforded Du Bois and his fellow travelers so little space in his own work.

Herskovits's criticism may not have been as damning as these pages imply, and Du Bois and his publishers made the most of it. In part, Herskovits's remarks became the central portion of at least one magazine advertisement for *Black Folk*. In bold relief Herskovits is quoted: "The most important contribution of this book is the breadth of the treatment of its subject."[72] However, Herskovits's review comments pointed to the key elements of Du Bois's "mission" that Herskovits's conceptualizations of history and academic dispassion and objectivity seemingly could not square: Du Bois's attribution of consciousness to Africans and their descendants, slaves or not, was part of his equation where the equivalencies were history = race = identity = consciousness. The sum could only be realized in conscious embrace. The realization of one's history, one's race, one's identity, was not a passive phenomenon.

Du Bois was consistent on this point and so were his critics. When *The World and Africa* appeared in 1946, Robert Perl, reviewing for the *Christian Science Monitor*, showed the type of ambivalence that was witnessed in the commentary on Du Bois's earlier works. Du Bois's brilliance could not be overlooked, and his candor was powerfully unsettling:

70. Aptheker, *Correspondence*, 2, 253–254.
71. Lewis, *Du Bois*, 383–384.
72. Du Bois Papers: R50/00303/1934H, 1.

Though Dr. Du Bois is a distinguished scholar and his book is based on extensive research, the result is not sober anthropology and history, but poetry and legend. It is full of corroded passion, of anger opening into illumination, of logic dwindling to nostalgia. It moves proudly like a pageant. It is history as Herodotus understood it. It is also special pleading which will antagonize as much as it convinces.[73]

The disconcerting nature of Du Bois and his work, the "arrogance" to which Lewis speaks by way of Mary White Ovington ("he insists on making them [white folk] angry or miserable"),[74] was tersely summarized in *Foreign Affairs*. In one sentence—all that was required—the journal pinpointed the manner in which Du Bois made the established order ill at ease: "The noted American Negro sociologist *continues* his exposition of the *Pan-African anti-imperialist interpretation of history* expounded in *previous* works."[75] Begrudgingly or not, reviewers concluded that this was what the white world required; it was prescriptive—"a sharply needed service." It was "the corrective" of which the *New Yorker* reviewer had written eight years before.[76]

The medicine has always proved difficult to take. The doctors and their cures have always been distasteful to the American public. Again, the words of the reviewer in *Foreign Affairs* point up the contradictions inherent in Du Bois as human and in his words as ideas for this public. To be a "noted American Negro sociologist" was an oxymoron for many. To be one who challenged political economic convention with a "Pan-African anti-imperialist interpretation" simply compounded matters. How dare he?

How dare those who followed Du Bois? As Lewis notes, it was recognized in 1915, again in 1939, and then in 1946 as well that Du Bois was consistent in arguing that there was at least one other way of looking at Africa and analyzing its history. This "Pan-African anti-imperialist" perspective was a way of centering the argument. It was the bedrock for the future arguments of the Afrocentrists, and it too rested on a foundation that preceded Du Bois's work by at least a century or better.

Du Bois's active embrace of a polemical yet factually driven discourse—an activist discourse—and his insistence on the existence of a conscious, if even downtrodden, population of African descent had its liabilities. As the editor of *Harper's Magazine* noted, the subject of

73. Robert Perl, "Africa Talks Back," *Christian Science Monitor*, (June 21, 1939), 18.

74. Lewis, *Du Bois*, 352–353.

75. Anonymous rev. of *The World and Africa*, by W. E. Burghardt Du Bois. *Foreign Affairs*, 25, 3 (April 1947), 708; italics added.

76. Robert Perl, "Africa Talks Back,". Seligman, rev. of *Black Folk*, 91.

"Negro" could only be broached so often. "I am reluctant to turn again to the Negro question at this time."[77] The possibilities for publication and funding were circumscribed in spite of brilliance and in contrast to a spectacularly prolific record of research and scholarly publication.

Lewis informs us that the early years of Du Bois's career were marked by the lack of substantial funding for the projects he engaged. This lack of funding derived as much from the choice of projects as from Du Bois's approach to and defense of those projects. This first example was clearly illustrated in a November 1927 reply Du Bois received from John D. Rockefeller's personal secretary, Thomas B. Appleget, concerning Du Bois's request for funding for a project on black servicemen in World War I. Writing on behalf of Rockefeller, Appleget made Rockefeller's views on the issue known:

> As far as Mr. Rockefeller is concerned, although the considerations which you raise are appreciated, it is regretted that he is not inclined to contribute in accordance with your suggestion. Mr. Rockefeller is necessarily limited by principle which experience has shown him to be wise. . . . [I]t is regretted that the project represents one in which Mr. Rockefeller, in accordance with his principles, does not feel he can participate.[78]

The limitations of Rockefeller's principles could make things difficult for Du Bois, though on other occasions the foundation was particularly encouraging for a project that never reached fruition, the *Encyclopedia Africana*.[79]

---

77. Du Bois Papers, R44/00295/1935H. To a large degree, this is the argument of the critics of Afrocentrism, diversity, and multiculturalism—they have heard too much of it, and enough is enough. The essence of Du Bois's "preoccupation" with things Africana would be characterized in 1991 as the vanguard of an ideology set on "discrediting broader cultural ideas." Of course, there is little analysis of what gives these "broader cultural ideas" their currency—at least not in the realm of mainstream debate. And where that does occur, as the lives of Woodson, Du Bois, and others instruct us, the results of such analyses are dismissed. Robert Reinhold, "Class Struggle," *New York Times Magazine* (September 29, 1991), 27. David Nicholson, "'Afrocentrism' and the Tribalization of America," *Washington Post* (September 23, 1990): These are also the ideas inherent in the works of former United States secretary of education William J. Bennett, in his conceptualization of the "cultural wars." Arthur M. Schlesinger, Jr.'s *The Disuniting of America: Reflections on a Multicultural Society* (New York: Norton, 1992) and Dinesh D'Souza's *Illiberal Education: The Politics of Race and Sex on Campus* (New York: Free Press, 1991) are two of the most prominent examples of the assault on the historiographic suppositions that are the basis for the work of Du Bois and those who follow him.

78. Aptheker, *Correspondence*, 1, 367–368.

79. Ibid., vol. 2, 145, 151–152.

While Du Bois did not *seem* to lack venues for publication, publishers, like funders, attempted to control the content of his work. The earliest indication of this could be seen in George W. Jacobs and Company's request in 1904 that Du Bois reconsider their offer concerning a biography of Frederick Douglass. The publisher had demurred to Booker T. Washington's interest to write on the same subject. Du Bois then chose Nat Turner as an indicator of the power of slaves and slave insurrections—the same issue to which Herskovits would object. As Lewis indicates, "this may have been a great deal more than the editor bargained for." The publisher's counterproposal was for a biography of John Brown.[80]

Du Bois's career is replete with instances like these. Understanding that compromises sometimes had to made, Du Bois proved himself a master at circumventing proscriptions. His *John Brown* is a prime illustration of this.

Although the attitudes of funders and publishers may have eased later in his career, Du Bois was still plagued by their "reluctance" to overindulge the "Negro question" in the face of his determination to remain a partisan of it as a historian and sociologist. Du Bois was clear in his correspondence to Woodson that he understood only too well how money would be used to control ideas and even to pit potential collaborators against one another.

In fact, one of the most remarkable cases centers on Du Bois's notions of consciousness, race, and history. This is seen in the 1897 essay "The Conservation of Races," as well as in the editorial discussions of 1904 concerning Frederick Douglass, Nat Turner, Toussaint L'Ouverture, or John Brown as a biographical subject. And the publication of *Black Reconstruction, Black Folk Then and Now,* and *The World and Africa* serves as a conclusion for Du Bois's treatment of the construction of race and history and the critics' response to it. In the early days, given the consistency of Du Bois's theme, he could be denied on the basis of discomfort and "principle." Later, as a "red" hysteria swept the country, the consciousness he ascribed to black people from 1897 onward would be linked to Marxist analysis and from there, of course, to Communism.

Du Bois's slave insurrections and his black reconstruction required an a priori consciousness, a sense of identity and history from which race could be constructed. These ideas were clear, consistent, and indelible. Du Bois's promotion and defense of them did not sit well with philanthropists, publishers, critics, or the United States government. Particularly later, these ideas could be discredited when they were

80. Lewis, *Du Bois,* 355–357.

linked to Marxism and this, too, could be used to undermine Du Bois's work. In fact, what better way to discredit the history than to discredit the historian?

On the best of days, in academic circles, Du Bois's African work might be relegated to three pages in the most prominent contemporary book on Africa and the ancient world written at the close of the twentieth century. On the worst of days, his work is dismissed and ignored. In those spaces, as Herskovits and others have implied, like Herodotus, he was no historian.

SIX

William Leo Hansberry

"I swear, as Re loves me, as my father Amon (who fashioned me) favors me, this shall befall it, according to the command of Amon . . . I will take it like a flood of water." . . . Then Memphis was taken as (by) a flood of water.

Piankhi at Memphis
from the stela at Jebel Barkal

And when the king [of Assyria] heard concerning Tirha'kah king of Ethiopia, "Behold, he has set out to fight against you," he sent messengers again to Hezeki'ah, saying . . . "Do not let your God on whom you rely deceive you by promising that Jerusalem will not be given into the hand of the king of Assyria."

2 Kings 19: 9–10 (*The New Oxford Annotated Bible*)

They also say that the Egyptians are colonists sent out by the Ethiopians [i. e., the black peoples], Osiris having been the leader of the colony.

Diodorus Siculus

In 1944, William Leo Hansberry wrote of the "necessity to alter profoundly many of the older and widely received concepts" concerning Africa and its relation to the world. Hansberry's article in *Phylon*, one of the nation's oldest and most prestigious black academic journals, was entitled "African Studies."[1] Hansberry's mission and his advocacy of African studies was the culmination of a cumulative process that had begun well before his first year at Atlanta University. It was a process that would take him from Atlanta University to Harvard, from the halls of America's historically black colleges and universities to the halls of power in Ghana, Nigeria, and Ethiopia.

Hansberry might have argued that his mission began in earnest the summer following his first year in college when he read Du Bois's *Negro*. With that reading, he said "Dr. Du Bois . . . rescued me from the horns of . . . academic and psychological dilemmas," from the notion that Africa was without history and culture before the advent of the "Christian slave trade from 'enlightened' European lands."[2]

Du Bois's impact on Hansberry was profound:

Inasmuch as most of the agents of Western inculturation—geographers, missionaries, colleges, public schools and the press at large— had always pictured Africa "south of the Sahara" as gigantic jungles which then and always had been hardly more than the haunts of "savage beasts and still more savage men"—it is easy to understand how it was not altogether easy for me to accept at the very first all of Dr. Du Bois' iconoclastic observations at first face value. After a little reflection, however, on Du Bois' long demonstrated ability to utilize social and historical evidence and testimony with the caution of a true scholar, I concluded that he must be basically right, despite the Western world's prevailing notions to the contrary.[3]

As Hansberry's own work matured, Du Bois's influence became manifested in a relationship of mutual admiration. Du Bois would indicate as much when he wrote in the foreword of *The World and Africa*:

[B]ut of the greatest help to me has been Leo Hansberry. Mr. Hansberry, a professor at Howard University, is the one modern scholar who has tried to study the Negro in Egypt and Ethiopia. I regret that he has not published more of his work. The overwhelming weight of conventional scientific opinion has overawed him, but his work in manuscript is outstanding.[4]

1. William Leo Hansberry, "African Studies," *Phylon*, 5 (1944), 62.
2. William Leo Hansberry, "W. E. B. Du Bois' Influence on African History," *Freedomways*, 5 (Winter 1965), 74–75.
3. Ibid., 78.
4. Du Bois, *World*, x.

Du Bois's praise of 1946 was part of an ongoing dialogue of shared information and encouragement between him and Hansberry. From 1933 onward, Du Bois and Hansberry exchanged correspondence with some frequency concerning their various works. The importance of Hansberry's work is highlighted, not only by Du Bois' praise for him in *The World and Africa* but in the letters that preceded its publication as well. In 1935, as Du Bois was negotiating the possibility of a new edition of *The Negro*, he wrote to Hansberry: "[Y]our work has always been of great help to me." And then as a mentor, as he had done before and would continue to do, he encouraged Hansberry to publish his very important work.[5]

Professor Hansberry was, in many ways, fueled by his relationship with Du Bois; and as Du Bois implied, Hansberry was also a source of energy and enlightenment to him on the questions of ancient Africa. In that regard, Hansberry was almost apologetic. In commentary on Du Bois's outline for the *Encyclopedia Africana*, Hansberry wrote to Du Bois, explaining, "[M]y professional interests center mainly around Africa in Antiquity and the Middle Ages. . . . I am aware that I might be inclined to place too much stress on topics belonging to the earlier periods of African history."[6] Apology aside, Hansberry did not miss the opportunity to ask, "[H]ow much attention is to be given to items appertaining to the earlier periods of African history?"[7] This query can be regarded as a signature of Hansberry's career. Yet even in this Hansberry surely felt some obligation to Du Bois. As Williston Lofton indicated, "Du Bois . . . opened [Hansberry's] eyes to the historical heritage of the black man." As Hansberry himself put it, Du Bois could be charged with "shaping and giving direction to my own somewhat unusual career as a devotee of Clio's Art."[8]

Du Bois's praise for Hansberry was well placed. This seems especially to be the case if any credence is given to the observations of the men who trained him at Harvard, among them Ernest A. Hooten, who implied that Hansberry had not received a doctorate from Harvard not through any shortcoming of his own, but because the university had no one on the faculty who could match his competencies, let alone exceed them. In a 1946 letter to the Rosenwald Fund, Hooten wrote:

> Mr. Hansberry has pursued studies in this field for more than twenty-five years with unquenchable enthusiasm and prodigious industry. He

5. Du Bois Papers, R44/00235/1935A. Aptheker, *Correspondence, 2,* 467.
6. Du Bois Papers, R50/00209/1939H.
7. Ibid.
8. Williston H. Lofton, "The Man and His Mission," *Freedomways,* 6, 2 (1966), 159. Hansberry, "Du Bois," 73.

has received little assistance or encouragement from any source and has made himself certainly the most competent authority upon this subject, which involves the use of widely scattered multifarious sources. I am quite confident that no present day scholar has anything like the knowledge of this field that Hansberry has developed. *He has been unable to take the Ph.D. degree in his chosen subject here or anywhere else because there is no university or institution, so far as I know, that has manifested a really profound interest in this subject.*[9]

In January 1947, Professor W. F. Albright wrote to Mordecai Johnson, president of Howard University. An anthropologist who had studied Northern and Eastern Africa, Albright indicated that when he was first introduced to Hansberry's work he was

prepared to be disappointed. . . . [O]ver a long period of years I had not seen a single publication by a Negro in this general field . . . which reached what I considered even a minimal scholarly standard. What was my pleasure, therefore, was to find that Mr. Hansberry had covered the ground with extraordinary thoroughness and competence. . . . Mr. Hansberry has missed virtually nothing of any relevance to his wide field. . . . His judgement with regard to many highly controversial subjects proved excellent, and his knowledge of contemporary workers in the field is so thorough that he seems almost invariably able to pick out just the scholar, American or foreign, to advise him on any point. Last, but not least, he shows considerable skill in writing, where he joins a vivid style with clearness and cogency.[10]

These observations on the life's work of Hansberry are made to illustrate the central theme of this work. They focus on the questions of professional neglect and intellectual dereliction by the larger academic community. In spite of the praise of scholars like Du Bois, Hooten, and Albright, Hansberry was never fully appreciated by his peers, black or white. Woodson, Snowden, and many of his colleagues at Howard seemed unable to grasp the magnitude of his work, its scope, or its potential. Contemporary Africanists and Afrocentrists, in large measure, have yet to embrace him. His career poses at least one serious question to African studies as a field—a field that he pioneered.

9. Ernest A. Hooten to the Rosenwald Fund, September 17, 1946. Hansberry Papers, Moorland-Spingarn Collection, Howard University. Cited in James G. Spady, "Dr. William Leo Hansberry: The Legacy of an African Hunter," *A Current Bibliography on African Affairs* (1970), 33; italics added.

10. Dr. W. F. Albright to Dr. Mordecai Johnson, January 6, 1947 (Hansberry Papers). Cited in Spady, "Dr. William Leo Hansberry," 33–34.

Why are African studies almost solely relegated to the modern era? The question speaks to the exact questions that Woodson posed in his rebuttal of Herskovits's review of his work. For Woodson, the issue was that there were no historians of African history. For Hansberry, it seemed that whatever historians there might be, there was no commitment to the African nature of this particular historical enterprise. The implications of Hansberry's work for the Afrocentric discourse are large and will be taken up at a later point.

The response of Hansberry's colleagues to his work and the fact that institutional and extrauniversity support was always in short supply were analytically summarized by Hansberry himself. He observed that his ideas were "clearly at odds with the prevailing notions about Africa's past" and the ways in which black institutional structures, especially universities, could be engaged to rewrite the past through challenging and then revolutionizing historiographic and epistemological constructions. In short, in many ways, Hansberry posed a major threat to the conventions of academic life as they related to Africa on both sides of the colorline.[11]

Du Bois's observations and encouragement notwithstanding, it is quite difficult to accept the conclusion of many who would lionize Hansberry. They have argued that his "problems" within academia could be attributed to the "lack of published materials," as the editor of *A Current Bibliography in African Affairs* surmised.[12] This conclusion is much too facile, and it overlooks the fact that Hansberry, while not

11. Joseph Harris, ed., *Pillars in Ethiopian History: The William Leo Hansberry African History Notebook*, vol. 1 (Washington, D.C.: Howard University Press, 1974), 11. Hereafter referred to as the *Hansberry Notebook* 1. A comment on the limitations and the immense value of these notebooks is in order here. The limitation seems to me to be singular. As Hansberry's edited lectures they lack, for the most part, the kind of documentation that most scholars would like to make them beyond reproach. Harris attempts to address this by indicating that Hansberry wrote in a time when citation seemed optional. He offers that "Hansberry seldom used them [citations]," operating in the professional context that granted the qualified scholar the privilege of reaching "individual conclusions without extensive documentation" (xi). Harris argues that some of the ideas that Hansberry espoused were accepted as givens. Even in that light, and in spite of it, Hansberry's lack of "documentation" is mollified by the textual references he makes to the wide variety of works and authors at his disposal. This makes the researcher's task somewhat more difficult in terms of verification, but not impossible.

The value of these notebooks, however, is illustrated in the clarity, ingenuity, and richness of Hansberry's thought. Hansberry clearly posits for us a new way of looking at the question at hand and grappling further with its historiographic and epistemological import. The facts combined with his interpretation argue that in no way can his materials be dismissed with the specious assertion that they are "undocumented."

12. See Spady, "Dr. William Leo Hansberry," 25. Also see Raymond J. Smyke, "Pioneer Africanist," *West Africa* (November 20, 1965) B, 1299. Smyke goes so far as to cast Hansberry as a "true victim of the adage 'publish or perish.'" B.

as prolific as Woodson or Du Bois, was published. As important, if not more so, was the regard in which scholars such as Du Bois, Hooten, Albright, K. O. Dike, Nnamda Azikiwe, and others held that work. On the same plane, possibly even higher, may have been Hansberry's impact on his students. His words and ideas were not simply "fondly" remembered by heads of state, but were credited with inciting a new way of looking at Africa and the world, and themselves. Hansberry very pointedly challenged the old order, so much so that early on in his intellectual career he felt the wrath of the "greats" of the academy. Reisner, "infuriated" with Hansberry, thundered at him one day in class: "I do not believe that Negroes founded these great civilizations. You are a brilliant student Hansberry, but you are a product of our civilization."[13]

Reisner's position was historiographic and epistemological. It reflected a political economic temperament. As Hansberry argued, in many ways the academic world was not ready for his interpretation of Africa in history. No place did this seem truer, ironically, than at Howard University, where politics and race intersected with great vehemence. As Joseph Harris relates, almost from the outset of his tenure at Howard in the early to mid 1920s, some of Hansberry's colleagues attempted to "discredit him personally and professionally." They argued that Hansberry's work on Africa, his interpretations, and his teaching were "endangering the standards and reputation of the university by teaching matters for which there is no foundation in fact."[14]

Their protests must be contextualized with some reference to Howard University as a federally funded black institution, the pressures of race in early twentieth-century America and their institutionalization, and the ways in which race impacts our ways of knowing. As the intellectual lives of Woodson and Du Bois illustrate, the notion of new ways of doing history, and therefore knowing, were not to be taken lightly. In some ways, they were not to be tolerated. Foundations, institutions, and the faculties they supported were charged with finding ways to bring the prodigals back into the fold or to excommunicate them completely.

In Howard's case, faculty concern over Hansberry's "unfounded" scholarship and teaching meant that his endeavors in African studies were under siege from almost the very beginning. In light of questions concerning teaching and scholarship, Hansberry's "ability to coordinate the African Studies program" was questioned. Under Stanley

13. From the Charles C. Seifert Papers, Arthur C. Schomburg Collection, New York Public Library. Cited in Spady, "Dr. William Leo Hansberry," 28–29.
14. *Hansberry Notebook* 1, 8.

Durkee, Howard's last white president, the board of trustees "voted to discontinue" the course of study. The move was short-lived, but when the program was reinstituted it was without moral or financial support. The program was run, virtually, out of Hansberry's pocket.[15]

If irony becomes a focus, then again the comments and complaints of Hansberry's critics are answered by the fact that so much of what they castigated proved their own ignorance. As Harris points out, an overwhelming portion of Hansberry's analyses is now accepted as fact. Politics coupled with ignorance, however, assured that Hansberry would be excluded from the institutional inauguration of the very program he had spent his life developing. In 1954, with funding from the Ford Foundation, Howard began its formal African studies program without even consulting Hansberry. The most facile excuse of those involved in the program's planning and initiation was that Hansberry was on a Fulbright sabbatical. In any case, it appears that upon his return, his expertise was used only sparingly; he "did not play a major role."[16]

Added to these slights was the fact that, in spite of his role in the formulation of African studies and the acclaim for his work, both domestically and abroad, Howard never saw fit to acknowledge its debt to him in the conceptualization and realization of the university's role in the vanguard of the African studies movement. Among his accolades were honorary degrees from universities in both Ghana and Nigeria; the establishment by the University of Nigeria of the Hansberry College of African Studies in his name, to which he was appointed "Distinguished Visiting Professor and Adviser to the College of African Studies"; and his distinction as the first recipient of the African Research Award from the Emperor Haile Selassie Prize Trust.[17]

We can only speculate on the role that racism played here. After all, for the most part, what has been described are the dynamics of internal politics at a *black* institution of higher education. Such an approach, however, begs the question of how black institutions such as Howard garner support and the politics of that support. It must also be noted that foundations have always been critical to the well-being of these institutions and their individual faculty members. Neither Howard nor Hansberry was an exception to this rule.

In that regard, we may also speculate on the reasons for the denial of research funds for Hansberry from the Rosenwald and Carnegie foundations, given the glowing letters of recommendation from scholars such as Hooten and Albright. If the example of Woodson is of any

15. Ibid., 8–9.
16. Ibid., 16–18.
17. Spady, 37; Smyke, "Pioneer Africanist," 29.

relevance here, in the case of the Rosenwald Fund one issue becomes quite clear: Hansberry was not of the conservative stripe that the fund's executors deemed acceptable.[18] He was also, at the same time, engaged in a professional pursuit that was ultimately the calling of "gentlemen"—history. There appears nowhere in the record attempts by Hansberry, unlike Woodson, to moderate his position by addressing himself to *the* problem as defined by the foundations.

In the course of speculation, however, there are spaces where race and Hansberry's historiographic and epistemological mission intersect. In 1937–1938, while he was at Oxford University, an opportunity to join the Kirwan Nubian expedition presented itself. Hansberry articulated his thesis quite succinctly: he wanted to pursue a historical *reinterpretation* of archeological work in Ethiopia and Nubia between the eighth century B.C. and the sixth century A.D.[19] Hansberry saw his thesis as a rebuttal to the work of authors such as Hermann Junker, who had argued in 1921 that "Egyptians and the neighboring peoples of the Sudan were not Negroes but Hamites." Hansberry's request was rejected.[20]

Prior to this, however, Hansberry himself had speculated on the possible reactions such requests might receive. In the late 1920s and early 1930s he had made inquiries into participation on a number of digs. His requests all seemed to be sensitively redirected. In order to check the reality of the situation, as it were, he wrote to his old and "trusted advisor," Dows Dunham of the Museum of Fine Arts in Boston. In a letter of February 2, 1932, Dunham replied forthrightly:

> To be perfectly frank with you, if I were in charge of such an expedition, I should hesitate long before taking an American Negro on my staff. . . . I should fear the mere fact of you being a member of staff would seriously affect the prestige of other members and the respect which the native employees would have for them. . . . I feel sure that you know me well enough to realize that I do not say this out of any feeling of race prejudice.[21]

If Dunham's reply was not reflective of personal "race prejudice," it did reflect the biases of the time as far as the scholarly proclivities of black people were concerned. Hansberry's ideas would have no hear-

18. August Meier and Elliot Rudwick, *Black History and the Historical Profession* (Urbana: University of Illinois Press, 1986), 12, 21, 25, 42.

19. *Hansberry Notebook 1*, 14; italics added.

20. Hermann Junker, "The First Appearance of Negroes in History," *Journal of Egyptian Archaeology*, 7 (1921). *Hansberry Notebook 1*, 14.

21. Ibid., 13.

ing because Hansberry could not and would not be seen (at least not on an archeological dig). And, the logic might have been, if Hansberry could not be seen—if he were invisible—then for all intents and purposes, he was inaudible as well.

We are forced to realize how prescient Hansberry was. The most recent findings on Nubia over the past ten years and the exhibitions that have accompanied them illustrate the centrality of his thesis. Hansberry's published works and lectures show theoretical and conceptual refinement that place his thinking on Africa in the classical and medieval ages ahead of that of Woodson and Du Bois. In part, this can be attributed to his willingness to engage new technology and fields of study to make his case. His embrace of archeology while the field was quite young was part of his realization of its use in making the case for Africa during the periods in question. Hansberry argued, implicitly and explicitly, that the physical evidence of the field would prove him correct. His approach to his singleness of vision was multidisciplinary.[22]

Of course, his expertise in these areas is also characteristic of the single-minded nature of his focus. As he indicated to Du Bois in 1939, his worked centered on, and would continue to center on, Africa in antiquity and the Middle Ages. As important in this regard, however, was his willingness to move from the "disputed" [Egypt] to the virtually "unknown" [Ethiopia] and to use this connection very forcibly to make his case.

Hansberry's argument was as supremely unpretentious as it was forceful: if one wished to know Egypt, one must study Ethiopia. Egypt, like Greece and the "Europe" built upon it, were "out of Africa." Here, again, one of Bernal's predecessors comes to the fore.[23]

Race

While race was a real and tangible factor in Hansberry's professional life, his concern for race as a subject of intellectual inquiry was lukewarm. He was certainly aware of the controversy engendered in questions of race; after all, that was central to his thesis of history. He was ultimately concerned about the role of *black* people in the world during the ancient and medieval periods. However, he showed little, if any, interest in the debates over their characterization or whether "race" in it-

---

22. Joseph E. Harris, ed., *Africa and Africans as Seen by Classical Writers: The William Leo Hansberry African History Notebook*, Vol. 2 (Washington, D.C.: Howard University Press, 1981), 84. Hereafter referred to as the *Hansberry Notebook 2.*

23. Ibid., 117.

self was "scientific." That ground had been covered by others, most notably Du Bois and Woodson. In that regard, much of Hansberry's approach to race can be described as an acceptance of the conventional in that race could be regarded, in the main, as biologically essential. That biology, however, alluded to physical characteristics only as descriptors. It said nothing of intellectual or spiritual capacities, or the ability to build culture. One of the most telling pieces of information on Hansberry's engagement of "race" is in his review, "A Negro in Anthropology." Here, he took Sir Harry Johnston's assertions concerning the Negro as "'a fine animal . . . [who might] revert by degrees "to a condition" no longer human'" as a point of departure. Hansberry noted that Johnston was a "distinguished Nordic anthropologist—and imperialist." In that, he encapsulated Johnston's historiographic notions and their intent, and he indicated as well why there has been suspicion among black peoples of anthropology and its uses.[24] Possibly the most interesting conclusion that Hansberry draws in relation to this project is the fact that "many individuals whose external features would seem to indicate that they are predominately white may nevertheless have a considerable portion of Negro blood."[25] This, of course, could be a useful segue to observations on the "Ethiopian nature" of the ancient (and contemporary) Egyptian population.

Theories of race are largely suggestive in Hansberry's major works. The key to his emphasis on Ethiopia is all that it implies in the classical, medieval, and early modern usage of the terminology. That terminology refers, specifically to black folk:

> "Aethiopia" is . . . the collective designation of practically the whole of the then known parts of Africa which bordered Egypt and the Great Sahara on the south. That is to say, the designation included not only modern Nubia and present-day Ethiopia but vast regions in Central and western Africa as well. The central African area was called simply *Aethiopia Interior* while the westernmost regions which bordered on the Atlantic Ocean were regarded as the homeland of the *Hesperii Aethiopes* or the Western Ethiopians.[26]

Hansberry has done one extremely interesting thing here in providing what he believed to be the accepted determination for the terms Ethiopia and Ethiopian for the periods in question. He reiterates what

24. William Leo Hansberry, "A Negro in Anthropology," *Opportunity*, 11 (1933), 147–148.
25. Ibid.
26. William Leo Hansberry, "Ancient Kush, Old Aethiopia, and the Balad [sic] es Sudan," *Journal of Human Relations*, 8 (1960), 357.

his contemporaries have said all along but adds new emphasis to it with Latin citation and the broadest of geographic designation. Ethiopia is all of Africa south and west of Egypt.

Relying on the "new sciences"—anthropology and archaeology— Hansberry employed scholars such as Sir Arthur Evans to make the point. For Evans "Ethiopian" was synonymous with "Negroid" and was characterized by terms such as "prognathous," and "swarthy," and having "abdominal prominence," and a "steatopygous rump."[27]

This designation of Ethiopia and the Ethiopian was central to Hansberry's thesis on Africa and its role in world history. Egypt was not enough. Hansberry was not content with the prospect of a begrudgingly black and Africanized Egypt as the fundamental representative of African achievement for the ancient and medieval periods. Northern, Nilotic Africa did not make his case forcefully enough. Hansberry's Africa needed to be genuinely "Ethiopian"; and "Ethiopia" needed to be recognized as representative of the heart of Africa and its whole. For Hansberry, the artifacts that turned up over and again in ancient treasure houses and medieval vaults—the trade goods, the ivory objets d'art, the ostrich eggs, the gold—all showed the grandest possibilities of "Central African origin" and the organization of the polities that collected and distributed these things globally. Evans, again, provided Hansberry with clues to this organization in his discussion of overland trade routes into the African interior during antiquity and the notoriety of the "Ethiopian type."[28] Flinders Petrie linked the "early dynastic Egyptian culture" of pyramid construction with similar activity in Central Africa (an assertion that would also be carried to the tomb culture of early Mycenaen Greece). Leo Froebenius argued a relationship between the "Ethiopian or Nubian god Bes" and worship in some West African cultures.[29]

If these assertions had "racial" meaning, it was this: they illustrated the "ancient African beginnings" of the American Negro and cultural and civilizing characteristics that were "in most respects the equal and in some respects the superior of anything to be found in the other sections of the world."[30] These cultural and civilizing characteristics underlined the ability of the Negro to become an "integral part of

27. *Hansberry Notebook 1*, 37. Also see Frank M. Snowden, *Black in Antiquity* (Cambridge: Belknap-Harvard University Press, 1970).

28. Ibid., 39; Smyke, "Pioneer Africanist," B.

29. William Leo Hansberry, "The Material Culture of Ancient Nigeria," *The Journal of Negro History*, 6, 3 (July 1921), 271, 273, 281–283.

30. William Leo Hansberry, "The Social History of the American Negro," *Opportunity*, 1, 6 (June 1923), 21.

American civilization . . . in spite of the contact with, and the attitude of white society." This ability was due, in large measure, to the "reflexes and complexes elaborated and refined and handed down" through the "age-old civilizations of the Negro African," civilizations that were the inspiration not only for Greek, Roman, and Arab civilization but for Western civilization as a whole.

Hansberry's treatment of race does several things: first, it supports Du Bois's concept, as argued in "The Conservation of Races," that race and culture have an equivalency. In Hansberry's argument on the "refinement" and "handing down" of that culture and civilization, he implies no biological agency, but a mechanical one in the construction and maintenance of African culture and civilization and its promise for Negro Americans. The mechanical apparatus is education, and the education of the Negro on this issue is Hansberry's mission.

Second, Hansberry moves the primacy of Africa's impact on the construction of world culture and civilization from Egypt to Ethiopia. We no longer have to contend with the question of Egypt's blackness and the consequences of that blackness on our civilization.

The "blackness" of Athena becomes moot. Hansberry's third point makes this so. His argument is that Ethiopia is Egypt's fount, and at the same time, Ethiopia is all of Africa with the exception of Egypt. Yet Egypt is undeniably African at its source.

In his fourth point, Athena's "blackness" is underscored by the assertion that Ethiopia's legacy in the construction of civilization is witnessed from the ancient through the modern period—from Greek and Roman through Arab and Western civilizations. Finally, he concludes, this can be seen in the power of the American Negro as the builder of and participant in civilization.

Hansberry's conclusion offers an implicit recognition of the pseudoscientific nature of race, if in no other way than that the attributes assigned to black peoples were ahistorical. In this lay the germ of Hansberry's thought: the denial of the truths of Africa and African history are the very core of modern thought. Recognition of this would wreak a "very tremendous change" in what we think we know and why we think we know it.[31]

As Hansberry observed,

"the thoughtful . . . ask how, by whom, and why peoples of the great continent were so grievously traduced in the eyes of the world."[32]

31. Hansberry, "Material Culture," 261.
32. William Leo Hansberry, "Africa and the Western World," *Midwest Journal*, 7 (1955), 137.

Historiographer/Africanist/Epistemologist

Key to understanding African Americans who chose to write their own history and to write that history in the context of the world is the historiographic bent of their task. Most are quite conscious of this. Certainly, that is the case of those discussed thus far. They are also conscious of the potential of that history and their ability to expand and shape it. Hansberry noted this consciousness when he wrote of the need to replace the "ethnic literature" of his time—a literature that excluded Africa, Africans, and those of African descent—with "terms and concepts which will characterize the Africans, their cultures and their institutions as they really are." This is an early call for Afrocentrism. Yet it comes with an important caveat: the necessity to guard against being "tricked by [our] own ethnocentric impulses."[33]

Hansberry was quite aware that the history of Africans in America [the Americas] was lacking without a history of Africa and Africans before the Americas. He had a clear understanding of the limitations of "contemporary European chronicles." Where most of his predecessors and contemporaries were comfortable with the glories of an ancient past, Hansberry saw history as a cumulative process; something upon which one built. Africans did not simply leapfrog from the ancient to the modern; there was history in between. Egypt did not spring full-blown; there was Ethiopia before it.[34]

The path to Hansberry's historiography was charted by a methodological shift. Hansberry was as dedicated to the attempt to write history from the field as he was in love with archival work. History from the field entailed methodological shifts and the employment of disciplines such as anthropology, archaeology, and sociology. In this, Hansberry was committed to writing social history, a history that, as Peter Gran writes, is a distinct departure from the conventional narrative in its attempt to let those who have not been heard make their voices known.[35]

In this vein, Hansberry argued that the role of the social historian was the recognition and interpretation of the nuances of the historical record. This stood in stark contrast to the somewhat stilted empiricism of political and economic history. In the case of African history, Hans-

33. Ibid., 157. Hansberry, "Du Bois' Influence,"74.

34. Hansberry, "Ancient Kush," 376.

35. This notion of work from the field can be seen in Hansberry's preoccupation with the archaeological dig. In this, Hansberry set one of the standards of methodology in African studies. Hansberry, "Material Culture," 262, 271, 279–281. Spady, "Dr. William Leo Hansberry," 29. Smyke, "Pioneer Africanist," B. Peter Gran, *Beyond Eurocentrism: A New View of Modern World History* (Syracuse: Syracuse University Press, 1996), 2–6.

berry saw no other choice than marshaling these various disciplines to the disposal of his task. Convention, he wrote, is

> totally at variance with historical fact. . . . [W]hile this information bears very definitely upon the history of Africa in the prehistoric ages, in historical antiquity and in medieval times, it, for the most part has been neither garnered by professional historians nor reported in the traditional manner; but has been assembled in the main by professional archeologists, palaeontologists, and historical geologists.[36]

Hansberry's embrace of social history was also a recognition of the sociology of knowledge, and the role of the social historian and her or his historiography. Again, his mentor, Du Bois, might be heard here. "Those intangible and illusive, nevertheless real forces which we call temperament, psychology, the spirit of a folk" were to be measured against and alongside of the empirical. The essentialist threads in such a task are grounded and debated in the questions Du Bois raised in "The Conservation of Races." For Hansberry, they were played out in the question of the temperament, the psychology, and the spirit of Ethiopians, generally and particularly, and with great specificity for the ancient and the medieval.

Hansberry's insistence on the exploration of Africa's medieval existence was both historiographic and epistemological. It was also his way of maintaining Africa's presence on the stage of world history. He emphasized the activities of real persons and their actions in trade, statecraft, religion, and diplomacy, and the ways in which these actions gave substance to the myth and history of this period from the medieval through the early modern ages. The representations of and search for Prester John and his court at every turn through the end of the fifteenth century exemplifies this emphasis.

It is also in this work that Hansberry makes one of his most critical declarations concerning the conceptualization of knowledge in the modern age and how the construction of that knowledge has been based on the denial of Africa. In building the linkages between Africa of the ancient and Africa of the medieval periods, Hansberry noted that the materials that emerged from these two periods were crucial to the Renaissance revival. Hansberry argued that the African presence in Renaissance thought and literature is palpable. Hansberry's assertion was not characterized by one of the central questions of the Enlightenment that focused on the African's fitness for slavery. His position was much more fundamental. Hansberry declared that the very notions that characterized the Renaissance and were key to its cele-

36. Hansberry, "African Studies," 64.

bration—specifically humanism—were the elements that figured so largely in the Greek texts of the period. Those, not coincidentally, were classical works that centered on Ethiopia.

> [T]he revival of interest in classical learning made available to the generality of European scholars of the period that vast body of historical and geographical information contained in the writings of ancient Greek and Roman authors about *Africa Antiqua* which had been almost wholly unknown to all but a few cloistered monks for nearly a thousand years.[37]

The main issues of this historiography and the discourse it prompted were those of production, maintenance, and dissemination. Like Woodson, Hansberry realized that this knowledge was of no use unless it could be shared. Unlike Woodson, however, Hansberry felt that the strongest institutional base for the research, study, and teaching of this material was America's historically black universities and colleges.

In 1921, after receiving his bachelor's degree from Harvard, Hansberry declared his mission in a broadside that he mailed to black educational institutions across the country. In the "Effort to Promote the Study and Facilitate the Teaching of the Fundamentals of NEGRO LIFE AND HISTORY," he cited a twofold objective. The first of these was to "prepare black leaders" with the knowledge of the role of Africans and peoples of African descent in the "past and world affairs." Second was the building of "black pride and confidence."[38]

He initiated his pioneer project, through correspondence, at Howard University in 1922. A year later he joined the faculty and increased the size of the African civilization complement to three courses. In this particular endeavor, his historiographic acumen was revealed again in his collection of sources and the construction of archives in an area rarely explored in conventional scholarship and clearly beyond the pale for black schools.

By 1925, the success of Hansberry's work in teaching and the promotion of research and scholarship was clearly evident. This success was institutionalized in the 1925 symposium on the "Cultures and Civilization of Negro Peoples in Africa." This endeavor was a forerunner to the Africa Studies Association, yet is hardly recognized as such. The quality of the research resulted in the presentation of twenty-eight papers by Hansberry's students.[39]

By 1925, Hansberry's three courses boasted a combined enrollment

37. Hansberry, "Ancient Kush," 376–377.
38. *Hansberry Notebook 1,* 5.
39. Ibid., 7. Smyke, "Pioneer Africanist," 28.

of 814 students, probably one-third to one-half of the Howard student body at the time. By extension, by the close of his career, Hansberry had affected literally tens of thousands of students. As a former Hansberry student, Dr. Nnamdi Azikiwe, later the prime minister of Nigeria, wrote: "His deep and abiding interest in ancient and Medieval Africa was a source of inspiration. Indeed, his researches in this vast untapped source of historical scholarship have been an original contribution to human knowledge."[40]

Hansberry's historiographic intent in the institutionalization of the study of Africa was clear. In his vision, Howard University's role was in the initiation and guardianship of African studies. Hansberry's analysis and almost prophetic view of Howard's potential for seizing the "Supreme Opportunity," was summarized in 1923:

> In the revision of history which is now underway, this travesty on truth will be corrected and the Negro will be restored. . . . How long . . . will depend mainly upon the position and attitude the Negro assumes in academic matters in which he is of primary concern. If he continues to sit by and let French and German and English and Japanese scholars take the lead and give him the cue in such matters he will have to wait many years. . . . There is little or no immediate gain to them or their fellow-countrymen in the furtherance of the real truth about Africa, its people and their past. As a matter of fact too enthusiastic efforts of this nature tend to bring down the opprobrium of their fellowmen. Under these circumstances it is not reasonable for the Negro to expect European or American scholars to take the proper lead in these matters. . . . [T]here is no reason why the Negro should depend upon others to take the lead and set the standards in these investigations.[41]

The black university was key to the promotion of these aims. "There is no reason why Howard University cannot become in a few years after, the premier tribunal of the world in matters of Negro life and history."[42]

This institutionalization of African historiography appears to be the earliest attempt at the establishment of African studies in the United States. Hansberry's admirers argue that this is one of his most important, yet least celebrated achievements, and they ask "why?" If this

40. Spady, "Dr. William Leo Hansberry," 31. Smyke, "Pioneer Africanist," B. Lofton, "Man and His Mission," 160.

41. William Leo Hansberry, "Howard Supreme Opportunity," *Howard University Record*, 17, 8 (1923), 417. Quoted in Spady, "Dr. William Leo Hansberry," 30.

42. Ibid.

were acknowledged, the preeminent organization for the study of Africa in the United States might see fit to honor him *along* with Melville Herskovits. Slighted even more than Bernal's "fellow travelers," Hansberry remains invisible within the ranks of the African Studies Association. His invisibility angers the not-so-radical Afrocentrists, who, as Joseph Harris writes, found him to be clearly in the "vanguard of African Studies in this country."[43]

Along the same lines, one of the keys to Hansberry's historiography and a characteristic that separated him from both Woodson and Du Bois is his admirers' definition of him as an "Africanist"—an Africanist when there were virtually none; when the study of history was denied to blacks; when the history of black peoples was defined as a postbellum, colonial phenomenon, overshadowed by the dictates of addressing "the problem."

Hansberry's historical dedication was acutely focused, if not singular, in his regard for Africa. His absorption with Africa in historical toto surpasses the efforts of current Africanists. In fact, his focus, work, and hypotheses should be regarded as standard for serious, modern Afrocentric scholarship.

Hansberry's work regarding medieval Africa illustrates this paradigm and its historiographic repercussions. The insights gained from the social and political economic reconstruction of medieval Africa will rewrite the history of early modern, precolonial, and colonial Africa. The questions that will arise from considerations of medieval Africa's interaction with the world will rewrite world history. The simple recognition of an Africa in the medieval and Renaissance periods will play a huge role in such a historiographic reconstruction, aside from the fact of what the consequences of such an existence will mean. Hansberry, more than anyone else, insisted that such a time and place existed *and* that it spanned the world at large.

So Hansberry is cited as an Africanist when there were virtually none; as an Africanist who was of African descent and a historian, when the field and the discipline had little room for either. He is also characterized by the uniqueness of his work as an Africanist: his dedication to the construction of an ancient and medieval African past in a field dominated by modernists. This dedication is compounded by his willingness to take his Africanist historiography a step further by insisting that one of the fundamental motivations for the Age of Discovery and the Enlightenment was the reinforcement of Renaissance, medieval, and classical literature that centered on Africa by way of Ethiopia and "the Ethiopian."

43. *Hansberry Notebook 1*, x.

Providing a voice that Bernal would echo, Hansberry postulated that the Renaissance discovery of the works of Homer, Herodotus, Heliodorus, Diodorus, Pliny, and others in regard to their Ethiopian notices was "primarily responsible for the modern European revival of the ancient Greek notion that no ancient people . . . were more humane and compassionate in spirit than was Aethiopia's high souled folk."[44] According to Hansberry, the editions of these works from the late Renaissance through the early modern period were proof of ancient Africa's impact on Enlightenment thought. These texts meant that "Renaissance thought [was] influenced profoundly . . . [by] the early history of the eastern and western parts of Africa."[45]

As important is the fact that Hansberry's Ethiopia-centered historiography was also epistemological. More than rewriting history and historiography, more than opening the field of African Studies, for Hansberry the proper understanding of Africa and peoples of African descent would bring about fundamental epistemological change.

Along the lines of the *Oxford English Dictionary*'s definition of epistemology, Hansberry wanted to reinitiate the question "what is knowing and the known?" As Ferrer would ask in 1836, "what is knowledge?"[46] Hansberry was particularly interested in these questions as they related to the construction of knowledge in a modern world built on the principle of race and the exclusionary practices of racism. The essential question was what is the knowledge of this world, as we know it, without a proper knowledge of Africa?

The proper knowledge of Africa would result in one of the "most important revolution[s] in the world of *modern* thought."[47] Its consequences would aid the refinement of Enlightenment and post-Enlightenment intellectualism. It would reshape the very thought that celebrated human capacity and rationalism, yet apologized for slavery and the pseudoscientific construction of race.

In this revolution spurred by the knowledge of Africa the most crucial issue of our modern lives would be revealed. For Hansberry, the centrality of how we know what we think we know revolved around the truth of Africa and African history, and the systematic denial of Africa and Africans that is at the very core of modern thought. The truth of Africa would wreak a "very tremendous change" on what we think we know and why we think we know it. Hansberry's knowledge of Africa and its history would "alter profoundly" not simply our vision of Africa but our vision of the world as a whole.

44. Hansberry, "Ancient Kush," 379.
45. Ibid., 376–381.
46. *Oxford English Dictionary* (compact edition), 884.
47. Hansberry, "Material Culture," 261; italics added.

Here was the vocation and the gift of African studies. In fundamental epistemological change, Hansberry sought to educate (reeducate) and enlighten (reenlighten) the Western world where the "existence of . . . African culture was still unknown."[48] The historical and historiographic facts stressed one solid epistemological conclusion: Africa was "not the *terra incognita* that modern ignorance has imagined."[49]

In fact, the data of Hansberrys day even revealed information that when

> properly assembled and disseminated would be capable of revolutionizing completely . . . the inherited and traditional, and generally erroneous opinions now almost universally held regarding the position of inner Africa and its peoples in the outline of world history.[50]

Hansberry's notions of epistemological change, like everything else that revolved around his charge for the historical restoration of Africa, was tied, in large part, to institutional commitment and structures. He felt that his work, in particular the "Varia Africana" (a work quite similar to Du Bois's and Woodson's concepts of an encyclopedia Africana), would institutionally position Howard and the field of African studies with the capacity for "revolutionizing the old and deeply ingrained misconceptions about Africa, Africans, and black people generally."[51]

He went on to say:

> "No institution is more obligated and no Negro school is in a better position to develop such a program as Howard. . . . This is the area in which Howard has the most promising and immediate opportunity to distinguish itself as a leader in the general cause of public enlightenment."[52]

Yet Howard and an important group of Hansberry's colleagues were reticent, and even adamant, in their opposition to accepting that obligation. Hansberry's work was not only out of line with convention, it was "to use his own words . . . 'clearly at odds with prevailing notions about Africa's past'" and the ways in which black academic structures could rewrite that past through challenging and then revolutionizing historiographic and epistemological constructions.[53] Such a

48. George W. Carpenter, quoted in Hansberry, "Africa and the Western World," 136.
49. Hansberry, "Ancient Kush," 376.
50. Hansberry, "African Studies," 63.
51. *Hansberry Notebook 2*, 10.
52. Ibid., 10–11.
53. Ibid., 11.

project could be deemed as dangerous to the very interests of the "Negro school" and its scholastics.

For Hansberry, Egypt was important, but Ethiopia was the key. Ethiopia, in all of its forms, was decidedly and undeniably black, in spite of attempts to cast it otherwise.

> [T]he primeval antiquity of Ethiopian civilization and its alleged ancestral relation to Egyptian civilization were among the most widely received and the most enduring of all historical traditions about non-Hellenic peoples that ever took root in the classical world; for it is true that long after the "glory that was Greece" and the "grandeur that was Rome" were no more, it was still widely believed in learned circles that it was the Ethiopians of remote antiquity who laid the foundations upon which all subsequent civilizations were built.[54]

Here was the tool "necessary to alter profoundly many of the older and widely received concepts concerning the whole course of human affairs."[55]

In all of its forms Ethiopia was universal. It was specificity and generality. It was Kush, Nubia, and Axum. It was indigenous, Judaic, Christian, and Muslim. Its presence was ancient, medieval, and modern. It was all of Africa. It epitomized "black" and blackness. From antiquity through the Middle Ages, "Aethiopia" was the "collective designation" for Africa and within this

> we know . . . that a thousand years ago there was in Africa Negro civilizations that were already thousands of years old and what is of more importance—that these civilizations were essentially the creations of the brain and brawn of Negro Africa's own black sons.[56]

Ethiopia

If "ancient Egypt did indeed derive a substantial part of its population and many if not most of the basic elements of its early civilizations from the regions represented today not only by Nubian Sudan and Ethiopia *senso stricto*," then the question of the African roots of classical civilization, Hansberry would have argued, lay not exclusively or primarily with the study of Egypt but with the study of Ethiopia.[57]

54. Hansberry, "Ancient Kush," 365.
55. Hansberry, "African Studies," 62.
56. Hansberry, "Social History," 21.
57. Hansberry, "Ancient Kush," 387.

And while Hansberry has indicated that the Nubian Sudan and Ethiopia *senso stricto* may accommodate the needs of conventional scholars, his real desire is to expand the understanding of what it means to be "Ethiopian" by allowing that definition to encompass "many other regions in the south and west of Africa as well."[58]

This Nubia/Kush/Ethiopia, according to Hoskins's 1835 *Travels in Ethiopia*, "was the land whence the art and learning of Egypt, and ultimately Greece and Rome derived their origin. In this remarkable country we behold the earliest efforts of human science and ingenuity." Hoskins thought that his observations were supported by eminent scholars, including the likes of A. H. L. Heeren, J. F. Champollion and Ippolito Rosellini, among others.[59] This commentary necessitates critical examination in spite of the fact, or very well because of it, that Heeren and W. G. Browne would argue that the remarkable level of art and learning witnessed in Ethiopia were simply manifestations of its "whiteness." Here again we are treated to Edith Sanders's analysis of the "Hamitic Hypothesis," of which these conclusions are the core. However, for Hansberry, obviously, another statement was being made: The cradle of African civilization by way of Ethiopia was central Africa. "Ethiopia" was "Central Africa."[60]

Relying on classical authors, Hansberry began in his lectures to outline the antiquity of the classical world's intimacy with Ethiopia. His basic argument was that there was clearly contact and interaction between Ethiopians and the peoples of the eastern Mediterranean basin hundreds of years prior to the first notations and the earliest usage of the term "Ethiopian" by Homer in the ninth century B.C. Clearly, an "important part of the populations of Arabia, Mesopotamia, Persia, and India" were of Ethiopian descent. This conclusion was further substantiated by Herodotus's comments concerning the "Eastern Ethiopians."[61]

Hansberry spoke of Ethiopian northward migrations from the second millennium onward. This gave the Ethiopians a highly conspicuous position in Egyptian records: "With the exception of Kush, no ancient land figured more prominently in the historical and religious writing of the ancient Egyptians than did the often mentioned region of Punt."[62] Hansberry went on to note that

58. Ibid.
59. Ibid., 385.
60. Smyke, "Pioneer Africanist," 28.
61. *Hansberry Notebook 2*, 5–6.
62. Ibid., 11.

[i]n the beginnings of European literature, few names are better known and older than that of Ethiopia. . . . [B]efore the geographical and historical terms Babylon and Assyria . . . or for that matter the terms Greece and Rome themselves...Ethiopia was already an old and familiar expression. . . . [T]he very oldest literate communities of Europe were evidently "Ethiopia conscious."[63]

Ethiopia and its derivatives were "among the oldest living terms known to the geographical historical literature of Europe."[64]

Hansberry takes his listener or reader through this historical lexiconical preparation because it is essential in the necessity to counter the "orthodox conservative view" of Africa in general, Ethiopia and Egypt in particular, and their role in the history of the world. This approach was to contradict Budge's assertion that Homer and his contemporaries had no "exact" knowledge of Ethiopia. Hansberry assembles his information to illustrate that Budge and others were not to be taken "too literally." It was clear that the "influence of Ethiopian culture" on "Egyptian tradition" could not be overlooked or ignored."[65]

Hansberry attributed disregard for the Ethiopian presence to the Wolfian school, Leopold Ranke and his supporters. Hansberry's observations are quite interesting given Bernal's assertions concerning the historiography of the nineteenth century and Tamara Green's evocation of Ranke in terms of what he implied was the immutable nature of historical fact in telling what "really happened."[66]

As much as Hansberry regarded his work as a rejoinder to scholars such as B. H. Junker, the clarity of his historiographic and epistemological concern was most evident in relation to Wolfe, Ranke and others. For Hansberry, the classics under their influence were subject to "so many doubts and reservations that few historians dared to make serious use of them." In this vein, "Ethiopian civilization [was] hardly more than bits of poetic extravaganza and graceless fictions."[67]

This approach to the classics and Ethiopia reiterated Budge's conclusion that the early Aegeans knew nothing "trustworthy" of Ethiopia and the Ethiopians. This was justification for George R. Glidden and Josiah Nott of the new American School of Ethnology to vigorously pursue taking ancient history "out of the hands of the Greeks."[68] The

63. Ibid.,19–21.
64. Ibid.
65. Ibid., 25.
66. Bernal, *Black Athena,* vol 1, 1–35. Tamara Green, *"Black Athena* and Classical Historiography: Other Approaches, Other Views," *Arethusa* (special issue, Fall 1989), 57–59, 64.
67. *Hansberry Notebook 2,* 27.
68. Horsley-Meacham, "Bull of the Nile: Symbol, History, and Racial Myth in 'Benito Cereno,'" *New England Quarterly,* 64, 2 (June 1991), 237–238.

thrust of their argument was that "there were no channels through which such information could reach them [the ancient Aegeans]." Therefore there could be no Aegean acquaintance with Ethiopia and Ethiopians prior to the fifth century B.C. with the invasions of the imperial armies of Xerxes in 480. Their contention posited that Ethiopia was terra incognita for the ancients. Acceptance of this thesis became, Hansberry observed, the "general practice of [modern] scholars." Hansberry's observations mirror Bernal's criticism, predating it by several decades.[69]

Hansberry countered these positions by marshaling an argument that reviewed the work of the late nineteenth century that enhanced the historical credibility of the classics. This was primarily seen in the archaeological discoveries of scholars such as Heinrich Schliemann and Arthur Evans. These discoveries proved more ancient and direct Ethiopian contact with early Aegean civilizations than had ever been speculated previously. Crete became a prime example of this thesis, providing proofs that would make it the basis for contending that Ethiopians had asserted "a profound influence on the material and literary aspects of Greek civilization. . . . Archeological synchronisms made it possible to establish links between prehistoric Crete and ancient Egypt."[70]

Diodorus's relatively late statement that Ethiopians sent "great forces abroad into other countries where they succeeded in bringing many parts of the world under their dominion . . . long before the Trojan war" is weighted and reinforced by Herodotus's writings on the Colchians, and both are supported by the Minoan findings of an early Ethiopian presence that precedes them.[71]

Hansberry acquaints us with the implications of all this research. The notices tied to the archaeological discoveries show a long history of Minoan contact with "black" and African cultures "from the very beginnings of early Minoan civilization." As Evans noted, the "beehive" tombs of the Aegean bear a "striking resemblance to a type of very ancient tomb that had a wide distribution throughout Africa." Evans believed that these architectural structures might have been "introduced into the Aegean area by emigrants from Africa," which led him to "attribute the foundation of Early Minoan culture to an actual settlement of colonists from North Africa in Crete."[72]

For Hansberry, the research showed "that there was a large black or Negroid element in North Africa in the proto dynastic period of Egypt." The implications of this conclusion are fairly clear. Here lay

69. *Hansberry Notebook 2*, 27–28.
70. Ibid., 32.
71. Ibid., 29–32.
72. Ibid., 35–36.

Egypt's African roots exposed; and those roots indicated that Minoan culture knew the "Ethiopian type from the beginning of the Minoan age," and for a period of time considerably longer than the critics of the classics or those who argued against an African presence in the classical world were willing to concede.[73]

The archaeology of the Minoan ruins revealed the most important evidence of "Aegean and African contacts" and the possibilities of the "Central African" origins of some of that contact. The goods of the tombs themselves allow Evans to speculate on the classical testimony of overland routes into the African interior.

One of the most striking attestants to an African presence in Minoan Crete is the "Minoan Captain of the blacks." Evans argued that the presence of this fresco was a clear indication that "Minoan commanders, like the Egyptian pharaohs in their imperial endeavors, 'made use of black regiments for the final conquest of a large part of the Peleponnese and mainland Greece.'"[74] In this, Hansberry refers to one of Herodotus's and Bernal's most enduring themes: the "Return of the Heraclidae." He indicates that the "oldest literary references" speak of them as a "southern people." To the notions of these "children of Heracles" must be added Herodotus's remarks on the origins of Heracles and the genealogy of the ruling house of Sparta. Here too, Frank Snowden weighs in with insight on the Danaans, reminding us as well that there were considerable numbers of Ethiopians in the Egyptian population from the early portions of the third millennium on.[75]

Hansberry illustrates the ways in which archaeology undergirds the classical literature. He does so with great effectiveness, using Ethiopia as the example. Through the archaeological data there is the indication "that there was a relatively large black population in the Greek world throughout these ages." This conclusion was supported by a significant number of scholars, including Rene Vernean, William Sollas, and Marcellin Boule.[76]

However, Hansberry was also among the first to admit that the old traditions die hard. In spite of archaeological, artistic, literary, mythic, and historical evidence,

---

73. Ibid., 35–36.

74. Ibid., 39–40.

75. Herodotus, *The Histories* 406. Bernal, *Black Athena*, 53, 109–110. Frank M. Snowden, Jr., "Asclepiades' Didyme," *Greek, Roman and Byzantine Studies*, 32 (Autumn 1991), 240–241, 244–245.

76. *Hansberry Notebooks* 1, 42–43. Chester Chand, "Implications of Migrations from Africa to Europe," *Man*, 63 (August 1963), 152.

few . . . secondary works find it convenient to include, or allude to the fact that the same discoveries which have confirmed the traditional connection between the early civilizations of Europe and ancient Crete have also revealed certain evidence which seems to connect Ethiopia and black Africa with ancient Crete.[77]

He goes on to assert that "it was with the aid of Ethiopians that Cretan culture was first carried to the coast of Europe and then inland."[78]

This view was confirmed by the Evans excavation at Phaeton in 1894, and supported by the subsequent works of MacIver and Seligman. Here, archaeological finds such as the Kames papyrus, the stele of Amonrenas, and Ethiopian pottery found in Egyptian forts shed considerable light on activity between Egypt and Ethiopia and the extension of relations with Crete. At the height of the Seventeenth and Eighteenth dynasties—the Ethiopian dynasties—the relations between the royal houses of Ethiopia and Egypt could not be denied. It can be speculated that they extended as far afield as Troy and Minoan Crete. As Hansberry explains,

"Thus the relation existing between Crete, Late Minoan II, Troy VI and Eighteenth Dynasty Egypt were relationships with a more or less Ethiopianized royal house."[79]

Hansberry provides a twist to the thesis as it is presently debated. With his focus on the Eighteenth Dynasty, a dynasty that is decidedly Ethiopian, Hansberry has shifted Bernal's thesis to an Athena that is also decidedly black. Egypt of the Eighteenth Dynasty is Ethiopian. It is an Ethiopian Egypt that is at the height of it powers and international relations with states such as Minoan Crete. It is this Ethiopian Egypt that Hansberry argues is the key to Minoan expansion on the Greek mainland.

Hansberry was not content to rest his case on Ethiopia's ancient prowess. His extended argument was that the power of Ethiopian influence was felt forcefully in the medieval and Renaissance periods, and was critical to the formation of modern thought.

In his essays "Ethiopia in the Middle Ages" and "Ethiopian Ambassadors to Latin Courts and Latin Emissaries to Prester John," Hansberry articulated a position that was reiterated in the primary sources of European explorers and undergirded by contemporary medievalists

77. *Hansberry Notebooks 1*, 44.
78. Ibid., 45.
79. Ibid., 45–51.

such as Robert Lopez. Ethiopia was still a critical feature in the quest for "European" and Christian identity.[80]

It was within the context of this historiography that Hansberry could question conventional epistemology. Here he recognized the impact of Ethiopia on the retrieval and rational restructuring of knowledge in the Enlightenment.

Hansberry questioned the invention of Europe, modern or otherwise. He posed the issue of ownership. The West, he argued, is in good measure a construction of Africa. Yet in implications that are quite instructive to contemporary Afrocentrists, he also asks, to what degree are Africans "Westerners"? Or, more importantly, to what degree African is the West, from its inception? The questions, more so than their answers, lead to new conceptualization. They move us away from the facility of the bipolar categorization that characterizes modern thought to a much richer and more nuanced analysis of ourselves and Africa in the history of the world.

In his assessment of Africa's role in the construction of the history of the world, Hansberry was unwilling to see Africa as marginal to that process. Africa was not simply Egypt, even in the Classical Age; nor were all of its achievements Egyptian. In fact, in Hansberry's analysis, Egypt was descended from the African core: Ethiopia, "Central Africa."

As early as Homer, Ethiopia was known to what would become the European world. By the eighth century B.C., by way of Egypt, Ethiopian dynasties were a dominant world power. The literature of this period was confirmed by the archaeological finds that Hansberry articulated as a central component of his historiography. In spite of

80. Francisco Alvares, *In the Land of Prester John*. William Leo Hansberry, "Ethiopia in the Middle Ages," *Ethiopian Review*, 1 (September and November 1944), William Leo Hansberry, "Ethiopian Ambassadors to Latin Courts and Latin Emissaries to Prester John," *Ethiopian Observer*, 9, 2 (1965), 90–99. Robert Lopez, *Medieval Trade in the Mediterranean World* (New York: Columbia University Press, 1955). Robert Lopez, *The Commercial Revolution of the Middle Ages, 950–1350* (Englewood Cliffs, N.J.: Prentice Hall, 1977). In a 1958 essay, "Mohammed and Charlemagne," in Alfred T. Havinghurst, ed., *The Pirenne Thesis* (Boston: Heath, 1958), Lopez acknowledged the ways in which Ethiopian economic prowess profoundly influenced the development of the commercial relationships in the Eastern Mediterranean basin and with the Byzantine state in particular. So intense were the relations and the level of competition, Lopez relates, the emperor of Ethiopia was the only ruler that the emperor of Byzantium regarded as his equal. Of consequence, the emperor of Ethiopia was the only one addressed in Byzantine correspondence of the period as *"Basileis"* and *"brother"* (61–62).

The impact of the Ethiopian on the construction of medieval social reality is seen in the writers of the age. This can be illustrated pointedly in Arthuriana and surrounding works on chivalry right through the nineteenth century and the historical novels of Sir Walter Scott.

this, until quite recently little or no research or scholarly production could be found on Ethiopia of the Classical Age.

In this light, we might ask, were Hansberry and his work also over-looked because of his emphasis on Ethiopia as opposed to Egypt? The question is two-edged. It relates as much to Afrocentrists as it does to Classicists and Egyptologists. Here we have a black man studying the quintessential black space. What are the implications of his actions (his research) and their consequence on our understanding of the Classical Age? Given how little we know and the scholarly neglect, Hansberry's work, if shown the proper regard, would do exactly as he intended. It would provide, through the development of a new historiographic approach, a new epistemology. Hansberry's work would not only change history as we think we know it; it would change knowledge itself.

SEVEN

Frank M. Snowden, Jr.

Africa is always producing something new.

Greek proverb

Who ever believed in the Ethiopians before actually seeing them?

Pliny the Elder

The past is heavy. To face it, to assume it, facts must be brought candidly to light. The making of a more human world requires rigorous studies.

Dominique de Menil

There stood the Horse, there stood the people all around, doubtful what to do.

Homer, *The Odyssey*

For many of us, the works of Frank M. Snowden, Jr., are like a Trojan Horse. This is particularly true for those who do not take his work seriously, those who wish to discount his efforts, and those who view his work superficially as a gloss for their own arguments. Yet even a careful, diligent, and nuanced reading of Snowden may be at odds with Snowden. Critical reading is done at peril and in light of the various interpretations that Snowden as text might elicit.

The danger of Snowden's work is that it is deftly crafted, detailed like Vergil's Trojan Horse. This is a peril for those who castigate Snowden and those who use his work to their own ends (sometimes with his permission). Yet here, Snowden and his work point up wonderfully the question that is central to this discussion: why has the work of Snowden and his colleagues—African Americans all—not been seriously analyzed by the academy at large?

Frank M. Snowden, Jr., has been one of the most vocal critics of Martin Bernal and the Afrocentrists as a group. The nature of his criticism revolves around the definition of who is "black" or Negro within the context of classical time and space, and the use of modern racial paradigms to describe the relations of this ancient world. His critique also rests on the primacy of Ethiopia in understanding the classical period at large.

It is ironic that much of the data that Snowden presents supports a generalized Afrocentric position. However, what are really at stake here, from all sides, are questions of interpretation and focus. Even within the context of what might be termed variations and contradictions in his analysis, Snowden remains focused.

"Bernal's Blacks": The Question of Race

Nowhere are the dangers inherent in Snowden's work more evident than in the issue of race. Like Woodson, Du Bois, and Hansberry, Snowden accepts the conventional classifications of race. His main task has been the provision of a formula in which the modern characterizations of Negro cum black is equated with the Greek and Latin *Aethiop* and *Aithiop,* our commonly known Ethiopian, Kushite, or Nubian.

Snowden is adamant about the stringency of his Ethiopian/Negro paradigm. It is here that he gives no quarter, especially to Afrocentrists who suggest otherwise and specifically to Martin Bernal. In the *Black Athena* controversy, Snowden has taken exception to Bernal's assertion that the First, Eleventh, Twelfth, and Eighteenth Dynasties "were made up of pharaohs whom one can usefully call black."[1]

Over the years, Snowden has argued forcefully that the terminolo-

---

1. Bernal, *Black Athena,* 242. Frank M. Snowden, Jr., "Bernal's 'Blacks,' Herodotus, and Other Classical Evidence," (author's draft, undated), 1. Also see "Bernal's 'Blacks'" in *Arethusa* (special edition, fall 1988), 83–95; and Mary R. Lefkowitz and Guy MacLean Rodgers, eds., *Black Athena Revisited* (Chapel Hill: The University of North Carolina Press, 1996), 112–128.

gies for "black" and "blackness" used in classical texts have no modern currency as we understand "Negro" or "black" unless the word "Ethiopian" and its qualifiers are present. Asserting that "[i]t is clear that Professor Bernal is using black in the contemporary sense of Negro," Snowden goes on to say that Herodotus's use of *"melachroes"* in describing the Egyptians is not equal to "'Negro' in twentieth century usage."

> Indeed, the clarity of classical authors in their descriptions of the African blacks they called Ethiopians provides the model for many modern commentators who are imprecise and often inaccurate in their use of the terms Negro, black, and African as applied to populations of the ancient world.[2]

The preoccupation with making such an equation, Snowden argues, is illustrative of the ways in which researchers allow modern racial theory and attitudes to cloud their analyses. It is also reflective of one of Snowden's primary concerns: the precise use of terminology.[3]

In a fairly heated, three-way exchange among Bernal and S. O. Y. Keita, Snowden reiterated that "Ethiopians" are not to be equated with Egyptians.[4] Keita's work, which challenges Snowden on both the issues of race and the physical nature of the ancient Egyptians, also serves as a serious counterpoint to the general discussion on the usefulness of race as a scientific descriptor and the specific debates on the blackness or "Negroness" of the Egyptians.[5] It also goes to the heart of a very important position that Snowden took early on: Egyptians were not Ethiopians, or from his point of emphasis, Ethiopians were not Egyptians. This was implied as early as 1970 in *Blacks in Antiquity* in Snowden's discussion of the *Ethiopian* Dynasty that ruled Egypt. He reinforces this dichotomy with references to Ethiopians in the Egyptian military; in discussions of Egyptians and Ethiopians taking Ethiopian and Egyptian wives, respectively; and in consideration of issues related to Egyptian court life.[6] In 1976, he was emphatic in his

2. Snowden, "Bernal's Blacks," (draft) 1–2.

3. Ibid., 1–2.

4. Frank M. Snowden, Jr., "Response," *Arethusa* 26 (1993), 320. S. O. Y. Keita, "Race, *Black Athena*: Bernal and Snowden," *Arethusa*, 26 (1993), 295–314. S. O. Y. Keita, "Response to Bernal and Snowden," *Arethusa*, 26 (1993), 329–334. S. O. Y. Keita, "Studies and Comments on Ancient Egyptian Biological Relationships," *History in Africa*, 20 (1993), 129–154.

5. See C. Loring Brace, David P. Tracer, Lucia Allen Yaroch, John Robb, Kari Brandt, and A. Russell Nelson, "Clines and Clusters Versus 'Race': A Test in Ancient Egypt and a Case of Death on the Nile," in Lefkowitz and MacLean, *Black Athena Revisited*, 129–164.

6. Snowden, *Blacks* 109, 113–119, 128–129, 189. Frank M. Snowden, Jr., "Asclepiades' Didyme," *Greek, Roman, and Byzantine Studies*, 32 (Autumn 1991), 240–241.

separation of Egypt and Ethiopia when he described the Egyptians as "among the first of several *predominantly white* peoples who had extended contacts with blacks living in the lands south of Egypt."[7] This position would be reiterated several times over before the appearance of Bernal's *Black Athena*.[8]

It is Snowden's contention that the Egyptians were "predominantly white"—that they were not "black" in the conventional sense. This statement has sparked the ire of Afrocentrists and the embrace of their critics. On both sides, most have failed to assess the space in which Snowden leaves himself open for interpretation, if not contradiction. Snowden's work allows for this in a number of ways.

First among them is Snowden's assertion of the "true" or "pure" Negro. On a number of occasions Snowden argues that the Ethiopians of classical texts are representative of the "true" or "pure" Negro. Within the "classical 'color scheme',", Ethiopians were the blackest of the black; yet they also varied in color from "reddish-brown to deep brownish-black." They were also identified by their "tightly curled and wiry hair described as wooly, frizzy, or kinky" (though Herodotus also tells us of the "eastern Ethiopians" who differ from their western relatives only by the fact that their hair is straight). Ethiopians, in general, also possessed a "broad, flattened nose," "thick lips," and "prognathism."[9]

By implication, Snowden's most strident argument against the "blackness"/"Negroness" of the Egyptian relies on this characterization of the Ethiopian/Negro. Yet this characterization also allows for considerable variation elsewhere. It is to this variation that friend and foe should give particular attention. Snowden pursues it through literary, artistic, and historical analogy.

The area of Snowden's characterization of the Egyptian is where both Bernal and Keita attack. Bernal alludes to Snowden's "misplaced precision." Even Snowden acknowledged that "specialists . . . have given too much attention to the 'pure' type and not enough to the effects of racial crossings of blacks and whites."[10] In fact, the translated

7. Frank M. Snowden, Jr., "Ethiopians and the Graeco-Roman World," in Martin L. Kilson and Robert I. Rotberg, eds., *The African Diaspora* (Cambridge: Harvard University Press, 1976), 12; italics added.

8. Snowden, *Before Color Prejudice*, vii, 16. On this position, S.O.Y. Keita acknowledges what he regards as the erroneous classification of Egyptians as "Mediterranean whites." "Race," 302–305.

9. Snowden, *Blacks in Antiquity*, 8.

10. Bernal, "APA," 30. S.O.Y. Keita, "Race," 309. Snowden, "Response," 324. Snowden, *Before Color Prejudice*, 65–66. Frank M. Snowden, Jr., "Iconographical Evidence on Black Populations in Greco-Roman Antiquity," in Ladislas Bugner, gen. ed., *The Image of the Black in Western Art* (Houston: Menil Foundation, 1976), 133.

passage of Herodotus for which Snowden takes Bernal to task (a translation that we might assume meets Snowden's approval) provides two of the criteria by which Snowden identifies the "black, " the "Negro," or the "Ethiopian." Herodotus observes that his subjects are "dark" and "woolly haired." Snowden has argued that hair, more so than color, is a defining racial characteristic.[11] In a discussion of variation among blacks in his earlier work, Snowden indicated that it is "safe to assume that a given passage refers to a Negro . . . [w]henever a passage mentions two or more of the physical characteristics accepted by modern anthropologists."[12]

In many ways, Snowden, Bernal, and Keita are closer on the issue of race than, perhaps, Snowden might care to admit. Where Keita asks "at what village along the Nile does 'black' become 'white' categorically speaking?" Snowden supports the arbitrariness of Nile Valley racial classification by citing B. G. Trigger, who "considers the division of peoples of the Nile Valley into Caucasoid and Negroid stocks 'an act that is wholly devoid of historical or biological significance.'"[13]

Keita summons Jean Vercoutter's remarks at a 1974 Cairo Symposium: "'Negro' is a caricature"; "[T]he 'Black race' is highly variable"; and "'Negro' is one variant of the range of real biological Africans." He then relies on sources that Snowden has used, Arthur Thomson and David MacIver, who argue that blacks were an essential element of the ancient Egyptian population in spite of the prejudices of modern theorists.[14]

Writing of those whom he defined as "Ethiopian," Snowden asserts:

Regardless of modern opinions as to the precise racial identity or proper anthropological classification of Kushites, Nubians or Ethiopians, the blacks of ancient artists often bear a close similarity to racial types designated in the modern world as "colored," "black," or "Negro." And many of these, had they lived at a later time, would have been regarded as black or Negro and subjected to prejudice because of their color.[15]

In spite of his intent, Snowden's research indicates that there can be no precise characterization. Opening up both *Blacks in Antiquity* and

---

11. Frank M. Snowden, Jr. "The Negro in Classical Italy," *American Journal of Philology*, 68 (1947), 267, 270. Snowden, *Blacks*, 1, 6–7. Snowden, "Response," 320.

12. Frank M. Snowden, Jr., "The Negro in Ancient Greece," *American Anthropologist*, 50, (1948), 31–32.

13. Snowden, *Before Color Prejudice*, 16.

14. Keita, "Response," 329–331.

15. Snowden, *Before Color Prejudice*, 17.

Before Color Prejudice, Snowden tells us that his Ethiopians are both "dark and black-skinned peoples." He goes on to state that there are three types of blacks in late classical period artistic representation. Their variety, in itself, "make[s] precise racial classification difficult." Snowden then lists the "so-called true or pure Negro"; "a type with less pronounced Negroid features" (e.g., Nilotics, though these are sometimes described as "blue-black");[16] and "pygmies." Later Snowden reduces these types to two.[17]

It is here that a critical examination of Snowden's racial construction should occur. The implications of the terms "Negroid" and "Negrolike" are wide open. The inclusion of "Nilotic," and "Hamitic," as Sanders has shown, beg for interpretation. Snowden characterizes his Nilotics as the blackest of Ethiopian types and yet the less "Negroid." He then instructs us that "mixed-race" types should also be included as part of the Ethiopian variation. So from ancient parlance we are treated to "Libyan Ethiopians," "*Leucaethiopes*," and "*Melanogaetuli*," as well as "several peoples . . . designated as Ethiopians": Mauri and Garamantes among others.[18] So why not "black Egyptians" or "Egyptian Ethiopians"?

Certainly, this broad characterization might pose problems with the precision Snowden hoped for:

> The term Ethiopian embraced a variety of brown, dark and black peoples, including the so-called true or pure Negro, a type with less pronounced Negroid characteristics, sometimes called Nilotic, and various mixed black-white types. . . . [W]hether classified today as Hamites, Nubians, or Negroes [they] were *all* Ethiopians, or persons with burnt faces.[19]

Literary, Artistic, and Historical Analogy

The apparent inconsistencies and complexities of Snowden's Ethiopian characterization should not put us off. On the contrary, they should open up a whole range of analytical prospects for us. Besides this, there is always the possibility that Snowden's construction is purposeful.

We should, from here on, look to purpose. Snowden has observed, in what must be the signature of his work (not the physical attributes of Egyptians), that scholars have shown a constant reluctance to relate

16. Snowden, *Blacks in Antiquity*, 8.

17. Snowden, "Iconographical Evidence," 133.

18. Snowden, "The Negro in Classical Italy," 273; Snowden, *Blacks in Antiquity*, 3, 8, Snowden, *Before Color Prejudice*, 8–9; Snowden, "Bernal's 'Blacks'," 11.

19. Snowden, "Ethiopians," 12.

the Ethiopians of the classical texts to the "Negroes of the graphic and plastic arts."[20] For most scholars Ethiopia and Ethiopians of the classical period have been "figments of a fertile poetic imagination." A. J. B. Wace and F. H. Stubbings seemed to follow on the heels of Glidden, Nott, and Samuel G. Morton in substantiating the reasons that Egypt and the ancient world in general must be freed from "Greeks and unscientific tourists." After all, Ethiopia "was on a borderline between fact and fiction."[21] Even Beardsley's pioneering 1929 work made meager use of the literary sources. Here Snowden points out that

> one of the most serious shortcomings in traditional approaches to blacks in classical antiquity has been the scant consideration given to the experience of these peoples in Africa and its pertinence to the classical evidence. Another weakness has been the failure to appreciate the full import of the combined documentary and archaeological evidence.[22]

According to Hesiod, from Epaphus, child of the "almighty son of Kronos[,] . . . sprang the black Libyans and high souled Ethiopians." Epaphus was the fruit of the union between Zeus and Io. Zeus, Snowden concludes, among the Ethiopians might be equated with Amun, and Dionysus with Osiris.[23]

Snowden begins with a listing that gives us from Hesiod, Epaphus; from Aeschylus, *The Suppliants* and Danaans; from both Hesiod and Aeschylus, a dark Perseus (Libyan and Egyptian); and from Herodotus, through Perseus, the Dorian kings, mothered by an Ethiopian princess: "Perseus married the dark-skinned Andromeda." Further, as Snowden tells us, the "black lover of Aurora was the father of Memnon"—Memnon, until whom, Philostratus remarked, "black men were only found in myth." "Argos begot four Ethiopians by Celaeno, daughter of Atlas," according to the tradition of Philodemus.[24]

Within the mythology and the literature it generated was an African

---

20. Ibid., 11.

21. Snowden, "Iconographical Evidence," 135. A. J. B. Wace and F. H. Stubbings quoted in Frank M. Snowden, Jr., rev. of *Blacks in Ancient Cypriot Art*, by Vassos Karageorghis, *American Journal of Archaeology*, 94 (1990), 162.

22. Snowden, "Ethiopians," 11.

23. Snowden, *Blacks in Antiquity*, 149. Snowden, *Before Color Prejudice*, 46. Snowden refers to Richard Carder, who "has suggested that Zeus, called Ethiopian by the inhabitants of Chios, may have been the black or dark-faced stranger in the *Inachus* of Sophocles (ca. 496–406 B.C.)" (94).

24. Frank M. Snowden, Jr., "*Romans and Blacks*: A Review Essay," *Journal of Philology*, III, 4 (Winter 1990), 555. Frank M. Snowden, Jr., "[*Melachroes*] and *Niger-candidus*: Contrasts in Classical Literature," *Ancient History Bulletin*, 2.3 (1988), 61. Snowden, *Blacks*, 150. Lionel Casson, rev. of *Before Color Prejudice: The Ancient View of Blacks*, *Archaeology*, 36, 72 (Sept.–Oct. 1983).

presence. An Olympian-Ethiopian consortium of sorts oversaw a significant portion of the construction of a mythic and chronological genealogy that included black gods and heroes. In this genealogy "[t]he presence of black gods and heroes and their interracial amours presented no embarrassment." Black Zeus; black Hera, Aphrodite, and Heracles; why not a black Athena?[25]

From this point, for the Greeks, myth and literature are reworked as history. "Beginning with Herodotus," Snowden notes, "Greek knowledge of the Ethiopian type becomes more accurate." Herodotus is responsible for "the Greek image of Ethiopians not only in his day but later":

> From the time of Herodotus onward, classical authors, despite some unreliable reporting and occasional fanciful creations, were often dealing with African realities and were much more knowledgeable than has been realized.[26]

Snowden gives credence to the works of scholars like Herodotus and Diodorus. His forceful usage of these two and other classical historians suggests, and in many instances states outright, an Ethiopian/Egyptian affinity. As Keita points out, "ultimately the question is, with what external populations do the ancient Egyptians of various periods and/or regions have the greatest biological affinities?"[27] I would argue that these affinities go beyond mere biology.

With Diodorus, Snowden provides an almost emphatic usage. The Egyptians are Ethiopian colonists. Snowden does not attempt to counter this. In fact, earlier he presented Diodorus's argument referencing "Egyptian institutions as derivatives of their [Ethiopian] civilization." He saw in the possibilities of the Isiac cult support for the notion of Ethiopian colonization of Egypt.[28]

Snowden allows that Diodorus's work is corroborated by Homer, who, B. H. Warmington argued, in the Greek world was "authoritative."[29] Snowden's willingness to give some merit to Herodotus's "black, woolly haired Colchians . . . as [an interpretation of] evidence of a classical tradition that there were Ethiopians among the

25. Snowden, "The Negro in Ancient Greece," 34. Snowden, *Blacks in Antiquity*, 161. Snowden, *Before Color Prejudice*, 94.

26. Snowden, "The Negro in Classical Italy," 268. Snowden, *Blacks in Antiquity*, 104–105. Snowden, *Before Color Prejudice*, 56.

27. S. O. Y. Keita, "*Black Athena*: 'Race,' Bernal and Snowden," *Arethusa* 26 (1993), 297.

28. Snowden, "The Negro in Ancient Greece," 37. Snowden, *Blacks in Antiquity*, 109, 189.

29. Ibid., 147. B. H. Warmington, rev. of *Before Color Prejudice: The Ancient View of Blacks*, *International Journal of African Historical Studies*, 17 (1984), 520.

troops of the Egyptian Sesotris" must give some pause regarding Bernal's treatment of the same passage in Herodotus.[30]

This interpretation of the Colchians also brings up the fact that there are spaces in which Snowden allows Egyptians to be Ethiopians if only "poetically" or for reasons of literary license. Again we see this with his treatment of Diodorus in *Blacks in Antiquity*, in the image of "swarthy . . . Egyptians and Ethiopians—as well as the wooly-haired" others and in his reference to Horace's use of "Ethiopian . . . loosely for an Egyptian."[31]

Snowden then gives us this interpretation of the historical record by way of art: "[M]ost blacks who appeared in early Greek art were probably of Egyptian origin directly or indirectly." This assertion supposes a tradition of Ethiopian and Egyptian intimacy historically, culturally, and biologically.[32]

Snowden speaks to this intimacy in his reflections on the Twenty-fifth Dynasty. The Ethiopian pharaoh Taharqa was not regarded as an outsider. He was viewed by Egyptians as "one of their own. . . . *"To many Egyptians, Napatans appeared 'Egyptian' not foreign."* Snowden re-inforces these notions by arguing that "once a foreigner came to live in Egypt, learned the language, and adopted Egyptian dress, he or she was accepted as one of the 'people.'" The implications of these statements are indicative of the Ethiopian as integral to the defense of the state and the expansion of its borders. They suggest that Ethiopia was a place of refuge and a protector for an Egypt under siege, and that Ethiopia was also a source of "Egyptian nationalist sentiment."[33]

So the Egyptian petition to Taharqa might be illustrative of this set of affinities: "Let there be peace between us and let us come to mutual understanding; we will divide the country between us, no foreigner shall be ruler among us!" "In other words," as Snowden puts it, "Taharqa was a native son, not a foreign invader like the Assyrians."[34]

The Ethiopian of fifth-century art and literature was, in part, the in-spiration of mythology stimulated by Egyptian contact. Greek mythi-cal construction "turned to the mythological [*and* historical] past of blacks." Ethiopians, I might argue, had "become" Egyptian, in part, because they "had conquered and ruled Egypt."[35]

---

30. Snowden, *Blacks in Antiquity*, 121.

31. Snowden, *Blacks in Antiquity*, 179. Snowden, "The Negro in Ancient Greece," 38.

32. Snowden, *Blacks in Antiquity*, 122. Snowden, "Iconographical Evidence," 146.

33. Snowden, *Before Color Prejudice*, 41–42, 72, 89; italics added. Snowden, "Asclepiades' Didyme," 241.

34. Ibid., 41–42.

35. Snowden, "Iconographical Evidence," 144, 148–150.

Snowden's historiography brings us back to Bernal and his choice of "Black Athena." Here Snowden's observations on the ancestry of Delphos, the oracle, might shed some light. Snowden recalls that Delphos's "mother was named 'Black'" and uses this name as the point of speculation on his background. This speculation, of course, is supplemented with other artifactual evidence, none of it conclusive but all of it thought provoking. And this stimulation of thought, I believe, was Snowden's intention: we should speculate not only on the historical import of the Ethiopians and "blackness," but on their spiritual and allegorical qualities as well. Delphos's origins, including the blackness of his mother's name, were possibly Greek allusions to the notions of wisdom associated with blackness (the Ethiopians as the oldest and, therefore, the wisest of all men—certainly the most pious).

Here we are treated to vintage Snowden, even if it is a Snowden who contradicts what some would regard as the central premise of *their* work—the "blackness of Egypt." This quality is Snowden's ability to amass a formidable array of data, to analyze it, and then to speculate on its implications vis à vis the most important social constructions of our times. It is the willingness to speculate on the "blackness"/"Negroness" of many of the subjects of classical literature from Hesiod's "dark men" to Heliodorus's "genuinely black-skinned" folk.[36]

It is also here that Snowden leaves many of us genuinely perplexed. If, as in Richard Carder's assessment, Sophocles, in his *Inachus*, is willing to make Zeus Ethiopian, why is the proposition of Athena (who springs from Zeus's brow) as "black" so difficult as a speculative premise for cultural and intellectual sharings?[37] Snowden relates that within the Kaberic tradition, artists produced renderings of "Negroid" Aphrodite, Hera, and Cephalus, among others. While the intent of the artists is "not clear," the willingness of Greek artists to make such interpretations must be given some account. In the same light, the interpretive position that must be given to Bernal's choice has implications for the African impact on classical formation.

If Aphrodite and Hera might be interpreted as black; if, as Bernal argues, the return of the *Hera*clids is in fact a reference to Danaan presence in the Peloponnese, then why not a "Black Athena," and what of its implications?

36. Snowden, "The Negro in Ancient Greece," 32–33.
37. Snowden, *Before Color Prejudice*, 14.

Historiography and Epistemology

We need a fresh look at modern interpretations of ancient evidence.[38]

Historiography

If historiography is about choice, then Snowden's choice of a"white" Egypt is secondary to his having us know that Ethiopia is *black*. The blackness of Snowden's Ethiopia is a historiographic choice. Here, Snowden—in an interesting juxtaposition, in both segue and departure, in the diligence of collection and documentation—illustrates an African past and an African presence. He is adamantly opposed to the construction of "Afrocentric mythology," yet he has been equally critical throughout the life of his work of those who would embrace his critique of Afrocentrism because of their ignorance of his agenda. A close reading of that work should make this abundantly clear.

In this, witness is given to his purposeful construction of Ethiopia and Ethiopians within the formation of the classical world. Snowden's work marks a historiographic shift in its attempt to chart the formation of the classical world through Ethiopian (e.g., "black") presence and agency, and the use of that presence and agency to critique contemporary racial and racist attitudes. On this count he quotes H. L. Shapiro: "[M]odern man is race conscious in a way and to a degree certainly not characteristic previously."[39] Snowden goes on to add that

> [t]he relationship between blacks and whites continues to be a critical problem of the twentieth century. *Not without meaning for this vital question is the experience of the Ethiopian in classical antiquity*—the first major encounter in European records of blacks in a predominantly white society. The Greeks and Romans counted black peoples in.[40]

Snowden argues that conventional scholarship has either neglected or deliberately covered up that presence. Again, in *Blacks in Antiquity*, Snowden listed the historiographic and methodological keys of his work and their importance. Snowden's interdisciplinary approach to the subject was what he defined as "comprehensive." He argued that a "less than comprehensive approach" had at least two deleterious effects: it dismissed the fact that the Ethiopian was a known quantity in the classical

38. Ibid., 79.
39. Snowden, *Blacks in Antiquity*, 176.
40. Ibid., 218: emphasis added.

world, and it encouraged the misinterpretation of classical texts because of modern racial prejudice. As a consequence, Snowden argues that a "fresh and comprehensive look at what the Greeks and Romans had to say about Ethiopians from Africa has perhaps yielded something new."[41] Snowden's introduction of Africanists into classical discourse should, perhaps, make wary some classicists who might otherwise embrace him. It should also cause some Afrocentrists to take note. Historiographically, it is indicative of another major shift promoted by Snowden.

To understand the importance of this shift we might use the following example. It is taken as a given that Herodotus's account of Egyptian greatness is a reference, primarily, to the period of Egyptian imperial expansion that preceded the reign of Psamtik I (Psammetichus). The period to which Herodotus refers is the Twenty-fifth Dynasty— the Ethiopian Dynasty. *It is the reign of Ethiopians and their notions of themselves within the construction of Egyptian life that guides Greek thought on the question of Egypt.* We are reminded again of Snowden's assertion that Herodotus is responsible for the Greek image of Egypt, Egyptians, and Egyptian culture. We might conclude that that image is quite dark, indeed. The irony here is that the image of Egyptian culture and prowess is borne in the arms of Ethiopian pharaohs.[42]

With that observation, Snowden wants the inquiry removed from one step further Egypt. He makes this case by reminding us of the immense amount of time and energy that has been spent on the Egyptian debate. He emphasizes that there are other black presences outside of Egypt that are formidable in their own right, *and they must be studied*.[43] Africa has a centrality for Snowden, one reminiscent of his colleague William Leo Hansberry's "central African" thesis.[44]

Almost twenty years before the appearance of *Black Athena*, Snowden wrote that we should "let the ancients speak for themselves."[45] While he does not endorse a "black" Egypt, Snowden is a staunch advocate of a "black" Ethiopia. His "Ethiopians in the Graeco-Roman World" was an extremely important essay in the assertion of black agency in the classical period. In this work, Snowden optimizes the notion of the black diaspora in both temporal and spatial respects. He allows us to contemplate the importance of Africans *in European space* in contrast to our contemporary and conventional notion of the times

41. Ibid., vii–x.

42. Ibid., 104–105, 122. Snowden, "[Melachroes]," 63. W. Robert Conner, rev. of *Blacks in Antiquity*, in *Good Reading: Review of Books Recommended by Princeton Faculty*, 21, III (May 1970) (reprint, no pagination).

43. Snowden, "Whither Afrocentrism?", Georgetown (Winter 1992), 8.

44. Snowden, rev. of *Blacks in Ancient Cypriot Art*, 161.

45. Snowden, "Ethiopians," II.

and space to which Africans must be relegated. Snowden offers the opportunity to explore the impact of that diaspora by casting a much wider net for an African presence in the classical world. Again, with certain irony, Snowden makes many Afrocentrist concerns plausible. The underlying issue, fundamental to Snowden's perspective and key to his historiography, is the recognition of the ways in which Ethiopians shaped the classical age; their presence is literally global.

How could such a presence not have an impact? How could such an impact not be historical? What were the choices that opted for the exclusions of this presence? How does one effectively articulate that presence in light of the previous historiographic choices? Snowden illustrates the "how" and "why" in an intellectual lifetime of choices that began with his 1947 essay "The Negro in Classical Italy." The "how" is framed by meticulous scholarship that makes the case for an African presence in the classical world. This allows the weight of that presence to make explicit the implications of that impact. Those implications are seen in the plausibility of a thirteenth-century B.C. presence of Africans on Cyprus; the extension of that presence to Crete by the second half of the century, and the definitive appearance of Ethiopians in the sixth century B.C. on the Greek mainland.[46]

The thoroughness of Snowden's fact-centered documentation and his familiarity with the primary sources in their original languages are key here. Snowden is focused and singular in his purpose in much the same way that Hansberry was, and possibly to a greater degree, given, by comparison, the discreteness of his subject. The documentary nature of Snowden's work is awe inspiring, if not overwhelming. It is a compilation of data that is difficult to dispute, though some of the assumptions and theory, as well as the conclusions that they generate, may be open to question.

Snowden poses issues of methodology and historiographic choice that are underlined by his use of multidisciplinary resources, particularly art and literature. His critique of Beardsley and those who follow her, in terms of their inability to draw the linkages between artistic and literary production, were noted in his 1947 essay.[47]

This approach to the work allowed him to make the observation that "representations of Negro peoples appear in *every* major period of classical art."[48] Yet those works are virtually excluded from the "handbooks" of art, and therefore their historical import would be lost if not for scholars like Snowden. And it is because of scholars such as Snow-

46. Snowden, rev. of *Blacks in Ancient Cypriot Art*, 161. Snowden, *Before Color Prejudice*, 14.
47. Snowden, "The Negro in Classical Italy," 266.
48. Snowden, "Iconographical Evidence," 133.

den and Hansberry that the historiographic import is not. In this attempt to integrate disparate sources and methodologies, Snowden's approach parallels Hansberry's. Where there was historical data, the two sought artistic, literary, architectural, and archaeological evidence to substantiate it. As Snowden noted, the literary reference takes on new meaning when it is coupled with the "iconographical evidence."[49]

Snowden's historiographic and methodological keys and their importance are argued in *Blacks in Antiquity*. Snowden speaks to the impact of a less-than-comprehensive approach on the writing of history and the construction of knowledge. He then outlines his own choices. They are to focus on Ethiopia as the key to correcting misreadings of classical texts including iconography, architecture, and archaeology. The yield of ancient scholarship would speak to the fallacies of modern racism.

Amadou-Moktar M'Bow, the former secretary general of the United Nations Educational, Scientific, and Cultural Organization (UNESCO), noted Snowden's success and the significance of his literary and iconographic approach: "Some authors have nevertheless attempted to establish a closer correlation between these series of images and the general history of Africa, which they reflect in some respects."[50] However, the contention of Egypt as "black" Egypt did not escape M'Bow's remarks either. Yet it was quite clear, M'Bow continued, that Snowden had been able to extract remarkable insights from this material evidence. The volume of artwork examined, particularly the statuettes, held indications of the size of black populations in various classical locales. Individual pieces, such as portraiture, and their media were reflective of the stature of the persons portrayed. Graphic displays of religious and ritual observances in ancient venues, matched with textual description, reveal issues of origin, and confirm crucial ideas of cultural dissemination and its impact. Snowden's work speaks directly to the intimacy and the degree of familiarity that existed between Africans and the various populations and sectors of the classical world, specifically Greece and Rome.[51]

Snowden summarized the impact of his research in this way:

> To regard, therefore, classical references to Ethiopians in Egypt and below as valueless or the Greco-Roman image of Ethiopians as a glorification of a distant, unknown, mysterious people is to miss the mark. *There is in many instances a remarkable coincidence between certain*

49. Ibid., 135.

50. Amadou-Moktar M'Bow, foreword to Ladislas Bugner, gen. ed., *The Image of the Black in Western Art* (Houston: Menil Foundation, 1976), vii.

51. Snowden, *Blacks in Antiquity*, 184–189.

*classical observations on sub-Egyptian Ethiopia and the facts as recon-
structed by Africanists.*[52]

This is certainly not a position that would make those concerned with
"radical Afrocentrists" rejoice. Consistently, over years of research and
writing, Snowden indicates that he understands the biases that precede
his work. Dispelling the notion of African absence, Snowden lays out
the possibilities and potentials for African presence, African and
Ethiopian histories, and, therefore, black history from the time of earliest recorded history.[53] Snowden places blacks at the beginning and center of the historical process and the production of knowledge. The implications of this placement are the same as those that have been argued
for American history: we are incapable of any comprehensive historical
understanding without acknowledging and exploring the African, the
Ethiopian, the *black* within the context of the classical period.

The broadness of Snowden's historiographic approach is seen in the
use of both Egyptologists and Africanists to construct the Ethiopian
presence in the classical world. He indicates this need for their input by
asserting:

> Classical scholars, in their interpretation of what the Greeks and Ro-
> mans had to say about the Ethiopians below Egypt, have in too many
> instances overlooked the history of these peoples as reconstructed by
> Egyptologists and other Africanists. Such an approach has often re-
> sulted in a failure to appreciate properly the full significance of classi-
> cal references to Ethiopians.[54]

Again, among the many ironies found in Snowden's works is the use
of Egypt to verify the Ethiopian presence. An interesting rejoinder
here is speculation on the implications of the Ethiopian population in
Egypt proper. It is also interesting that Snowden calls upon Africanists
whose agenda seems quite distant from that of both Egyptologists and
Classicists. Africanist research is dominated by a decidedly modernist
bent, and Africanist projects, in part, fuel the Afrocentric debate.

Snowden's data and conclusions allow us to argue two important
points in relation to Bernal's "blacks." First, the experience of the
Twenty-fifth Dynasty was an Ethiopian Egypt. As Snowden has put
it, "Assyria's Egyptian enemy was the Negro."[55] Second, the period
in which Egypt would have its greatest impact on Greek, and there-

52. Ibid., 119; italics added.
53. Ibid., 5.
54. Ibid., 113.
55. Snowden, *Before Color Prejudice,* 43.

fore European, consciousness was the period of the Twenty-fifth Dynasty—the Ethiopian Dynasty, the period when Ethiopia "had conquered and ruled Egypt."[56]

Epistemology

The contradictory notion of Snowden's declaration that the Egyptians were "white" has unexpected consequences for both Afrocentrists and their antagonists. The "mixed" nature of the Egyptians' physical makeup (by Snowden's own accounts and those of others, and the notion, as Snowden proposes, that to be Egyptian is a cultural device as well) is replaced by the physical surety of Ethiopian "pureness." It is the Ethiopian that Snowden wishes to elevate to the stage of world history as an architect and key player in the construction of that history. In the Ethiopian, Snowden assumes, there can be no doubt that those in question are "black," African, and worthy.

Snowden understands that the historiographic and epistemological investment in Egypt is huge. He wishes to circumvent it and defuse it by focusing on Ethiopia. This approach gives a centrality to the black, the African, in the construction of the world. The Ethiopian focus is the fresh and comprehensive look that dominates his historiography. It is also the lynchpin in his construction of knowledge. It is the "fresh look at the interpretation of modern evidence."

It might be argued that Snowden's is a *preceding* refinement of Bernal's thesis. By focusing on Ethiopia as Egypt's source (e.g., the Twenty-fifth Dynasty), Snowden makes the case for Egyptian blackness, albeit, it seems, against his will. Again, with the "blackness" of Zeus, Hera, Aphrodite, and others, Athena's blackness can be anticipated in Snowden's epistemology, if not by him, then certainly by others.

His interpretation of Hesiod's "just city" and the evocation of its Ethiopian character, that is, its justice, its righteousness, its piety, and, we must assume, its wisdom, suggest that it is reflective of Augustine's "City on the Hill." Both are equally African in either their imagery or their authorship. The two are instructive and epistemological in what we think we know of ourselves from an ethos rooted in Greek thought, or Judeo-Christian analysis, or both.

Snowden's treatment of Beardsley is as much epistemological as it is historiographic or methodological. The critique is a consistent one that runs from Beardsley through Thompson.[57] Snowden's fundamen-

---

56. Snowden, "Iconographical Evidence," 150.
57. Snowden, "*Romans and Blacks*: A Review Essay," 543–557.

tal argument is that the body of knowledge must be amended. The Ethiopian, the African, the black, was not, and therefore cannot, be rendered as a servile and negative presence in the classical world. The data does not bear out such a conclusion.

Snowden's assertion flies in the face of the Pounders of the world who argue that blacks could have no significance in the formation of the classical civilization. Snowden moves beyond these notions by insisting on the recognition of African agency in the classical age and recording it. Snowden produces not just the obvious—Ethiopian participation in the construction Ethiopian civilization—but his sources cast Ethiopia as the *civilizer* of the world.

If such a conclusion is too strident, then a more prudent caption underlines the image of "men and women who . . . attained wealth and rank," men and women whose "biographies would read exactly as those of many other persons of foreign extraction who achieved distinction in Greece and Italy.": "[B]lacks could overcome the 'barbarian obstacle' if they were inclined to do so."[58]

Even in his notions of race with all their perplexities, Snowden still leads us to the fundamental questions about the construction of identity in the ancient period and the hindrances of modern assumptions. If the usage of the term "black" by ancient writers is not in accord with modern parlance, then how should we understand it? Even more to the point, however, is if "black" is not in accordance with modern parlance then what should we understand "white" to be? In that light, Snowden's "white" Egypt is subject to more interpretation and nuance than even he seemed to suspect.

However the definition might be drawn, the epistemological wall that Snowden breaches allows us to conclude, in spite of conventional thinking and teaching, that "classical antiquity" was not solely the purview of white folk. The 3,000-year history from Egypt on is one of blacks in the classical record, and that is a record of consistency,[59] one that, as Hansberry commented, should change our notions of what we think we know.

By the end of the ancient period, Snowden concludes, the Ethiopian was symbolic of the cosmopolitan nature of the age and the empire that came to represent it:

[W]orks found from England to Meroe and Spain to Asia indicate that Negroes were a common sight in more than one province. . . . [T]he frequency with which the Negro was portrayed, especially

58. Snowden, "Iconographical Evidence," 238.
59. Snowden, *Before Color Prejudice*, 37.

when taken in relation to classical literature, justifies a reassessment of the number of Negroes in the population of the ancient world."

Also justified is a reassessment, of course, of their impact on that world.[60]

The cosmopolitan nature of the period also allows for a historical and historiographical reevaluation of one of the key concepts used to describe the experiences of peoples of African descent in the modern age. Snowden allows that the diaspora for the black was a convention of life in the ancient period. This is another postulate that should cause a serious rethinking of the African in the history of the world and the issue of agency.

It is clear, however, that many of these points were lost to a large number of Snowden's colleagues, including those who shared the same textual space with him. Ladislas Bugner is an illustration of this. Yet even Bugner is aware of the epistemological importance of Snowden's work: "The time has come to reconsider the opposition of the 'white man' and the 'black' which History has made the vehicle of opprobrium."[61]

Bugner goes on to argue that Snowden is just the man for the task. As he puts it, Snowden "leaves it to be understood that those who deny the relevance of a piece of evidence should produce their own proof." For Bugner, Snowden establishes the black "up and down the Nile" and extends his analysis to the farthest areas that black people penetrated."[62]

Along with Warmington, Bugner recognizes Snowden's most important epistemological contribution. They look at Snowden's evidence and ask of the ancients, "Why the Negro?" Snowden's work is a rejoinder that asks, "Why not?" As Warmington observes in his considerations of the construction of knowledge and the historiographic choices that help to build it, "[T]heir [the Ethiopians] real importance lies in the fact that they were there at all."[63]

Texts and Their Reception: A Critique

In the foreword to *The World and Africa*, Du Bois writes that he would have found it quite useful to have had access to the works of Frank Snowden:

60. Snowden, "Iconographical Evidence," 242–244.
61. Ladislas Bugner, preface to Bugner, gen. ed., *The Image of the Black in Western Art* (Houston: The Menil Foundation, 1976), 1.
62. Ibid., 6.
63. Ibid., 19. Snowden, "Ethiopians," 28–29.

I should like to have used the researches on the Negro in classical Europe of Dr. Frank Snowden of Howard University. But classical journals in America have hitherto declined to publish his paper because it favored the Negro too much, leaving the public to rely on Beardsley's stupid combination of scholarship and race prejudice. . . . I tried to get Dr. Snowden to let me see his manuscript, but he refused.[64]

Snowden was emphatic in his refusal, but for reasons that might be construed as high-handedness on the part of Du Bois. Snowden is equally emphatic on the issue of the positions of the classical journals in relation to his work. Du Bois's assessment is "completely incorrect," Snowden has said. The first of two extremely important articles that would set the tone for Snowden's work over the next five decades appeared in print in the 1946 publication of *Transactions of the American Philological Society*. Snowden indicates that he was not able to share this work with Du Bois at the time Du Bois requested it because it was in press.[65]

Du Bois's assertion, however, points to two things about Snowden's work. As early as 1946, if not before, there was a recognition of the importance of what might now be called the "Snowden Thesis"—that is, the role of Africans in the construction of classical civilization. Second, directly related to this thesis, was the controversy Snowden's work would engender.

From Snowden's dissertation two seminal articles, the basis for two books, emerged. These works were the core for numerous other articles that characterized the Snowden Thesis. That thesis might read as follows:

1. First was the establishment of an African presence in the classical world, a presence that was neither menial or servile, and that continually implied, often stressed, the agency of Africans in this age.
2. Second, this body of work, while accepting of conventional racial categorization, refuted the notion that race was a determinant of any group of people's ability to contribute to the development of any given historical period.
3. Third, Snowden's work signaled the emergence of a new epistemology based on knowledge *of* black peoples, constructed of data and materials that were in many instances, created *by*, if not about them. The historiographic nature of this epistemology was harsh criticism for those who would "fabricate" knowledge and who refused to accept the evidence of an archaeological and literary past.

64. Du Bois, *World*, x.
65. Frank M. Snowden, Jr., Interview, Feb. 28, 1996.

In his explication of an African presence and the consequences of African action, Snowden's last point was one of contention on both sides of the spectrum. It was an affront to conventional classicists and so-called radical Afrocentrists.

Classicists and historians failed to grasp the central premise of Snowden's work and its importance in challenging their own historiography and epistemology. The Afrocentrists in question see Snowden's "white" Egypt and his pointed castigation of their "fabrication" of Egypt as a betrayal of the race.

Snowden indicates that his social economic interest in the ancient world was spurred by an accidental find he made in Pompeii. That find led to his doctoral dissertation, "Slaves and Freedmen in Pompeii." From this came the two defining articles of his career: the 1947 *American Journal of Philology* essay, "The Negro in Classical Italy," and the 1948 *American Anthropologist* essay, "The Negro in Ancient Greece." In part, the way in which these articles established the African presence in the ancient world was through critique and criticism of the methodological approach of his predecessors in the field. While he did not go as far as Du Bois in characterizing Beardsley's work as "stupid" and prejudiced, he was quite strong in his contention that hers and works like it were deeply flawed because they had made no attempt to link iconographic and literary sources.

Snowden's work was not only built around that linkage. It placed more importance on interdisciplinary research as the key to revealing the fact that "Negroes were not uncommon"; both the Greeks and Romans were "well acquainted" with the "Negroid" type.[66]

In the intervening years, up to the publication of *Blacks in Antiquity* and *Before Color Prejudice*, and beyond, Snowden would continue to build the case for a "black population in other Mediterranean areas, especially northwest Africa and Italy [that] was also greater than traditional estimates." He also noted, ironically, that that population was "obviously much larger in Egypt."

While he did not openly speculate on the implications of this Egyptian dynamic, he was more than willing to do this for other areas of the world. Primary among those speculations was the conclusion that these demographics, coupled with literary and iconographic data, showed the absence of racial sentiment. It was the fabrication of that very racial sentiment that "colored" the historiography and epistemology of the modern era, and skewed the understanding of history and blacks' role in the construction of that history.

66. Snowden, "The Negro in Classical Italy," 285. Snowden, "The Negro in Ancient Greece," 31.

The reception of Snowden's 1947 and 1948 works can only be implied by the sources of their publication. I have discovered no contemporary commentary on them. However, the fact that they were published in two of the leading establishment organs of the time gave considerable merit to Snowden's arguments. The same arguments would be witnessed in *Blacks in Antiquity*, *Before Color Prejudice*, and the essay "Iconographical Evidence on Black Populations in Greco-Roman Antiquity," in *The Image of the Black in Western Art*. These three works are signature pieces in that Snowden's thesis is fully articulated and illustrated here, more so than in any of his other works.

Yet even here the reviews indicate that in some spaces forty years of consistent work, of the articulation and rearticulation of the same points, of the enhancement and refinement of these points, has not been quite enough time for old attitudes to die. Forty years of Snowden's work has also pointed to the rather "Foucauldian" ways in which that work has been read and used, by both Snowden and others, on either side of the debate.

Blacks in Antiquity received the Charles J. Goodwin Award of Merit in 1973 from the American Philological Association. Interestingly enough, it was before that association that the germ of that work was presented twenty-seven years earlier.[67] The reviews congratulated Snowden for "an excellent work of scholarship" in the presentation of a "lifetime's labor of love." One reviewer argued that *Blacks in Antiquity* was the "only exhaustive and impartial study on the attitude of Greeks and Romans toward colored people." Another, underlining that importance, said that this was a "work . . . which will find its place in all libraries and will be cited again and again."[68]

This kind of praise could be cited as recognition of the epistemological ground Snowden had broken. As Robert Conner noted, *Blacks in Antiquity* "surprises us . . . by the sheer mass of material. He [Snowden] cites over 150 ancient authors whose testimony helps clarify the role of blacks in classical antiquity." It was this "unlikely topic, the black man in classical antiquity," that Snowden opened up. And in opening it he, just as Hansberry had done in his work, gave broad implications for "Africans among the first Europeans, [and] Moors mak-

67. Snowden, interview. Frank M. Snowden, Jr., Correspondence with Maghan A. A. Keita, 14 February 1996.

68. B. H. Warmington, rev. of *Blacks in Antiquity: Ethiopians in the Greco-Roman Experience*, *African Historical Studies*, 4 (1977), 383–386. Paul MacKendrick, rev. of *Blacks in Antiquity: Ethiopians in the Greco-Roman Experience American Journal of Philology*, 94 (1973), 212–214. Mirielle Cebeillac-Gervasoni, rev. of *Blacks in Antiquity: Ethiopians in the Greco-Roman Experience*, *L'Antiquite Classique*, 44 (1975), 781–782. Henri Metzger, rev. of *Blacks in Antiquity: Ethiopians in the Greco-Roman Experience*, *Revia des etudes anciennes*, 83 (1971), 496–498.

ing their first acquaintance of Italy."[69] Here Snowden had reiterated his colleague's long view of the African in history.

The reviews of *The Image of the Black in Western Art* and *Before Color Prejudice* were equally laudatory. John Russell, writing in the *New York Times Book Review,* commented that "this book [*Image of the Black in Western Art*]—and foreseeably this whole series—is a gift to humanity." Paul Ducrey, writing specifically of Snowden's essay "Iconographical Evidence on Black Populations in Greco-Roman Antiquity," stated that "Frank Snowden . . . is the best contemporary specialist on the depictions of blacks in classical art. . . . [H]e considers untenable the racist image which moderns sometimes project in Greco-Roman art." The American historian David Brion Davis called Snowden "a notable exception" who saw in the iconographic evidence "an unanswerable challenge to the later racist societies that had relied on dehumanizing caricature as an instrument of social and economic oppression."[70]

Before Color Prejudice was itself a critique of "caricature as an instrument of oppression." As the review in *Choice* noted, *Before Color Prejudice* was "an introduction to the absence of color prejudice in antiquity." Ettore Lepare argued that the book was "important reading for new perspectives not only for the student of the ancient world (and the African in particular) but also for anyone interested in racial questions." Hans-Joachim Dienner went to the core of the Snowden thesis when he observed that the "broad gauged work is destined to inspire broader research . . . especially that which will fix more precisely the role of Negroids and other dark-skinned peoples in the intellectual and cultural development of antiquity."[71]

In Snowden's work, Bernal was prophesied. This relationship makes Snowden's strident criticism of Bernal that much more difficult to fathom. Yet in other ways that criticism is quite natural given the history of Snowden's work. Snowden's vehemence is directed at specificity: the Egyptians were not "black." The Ethiopians most assuredly were.

In part, the difficulty in gaining real insight into Snowden on the issue of *Black Athena* arises from the cognitive intimacy many attach, intellectually, to any discussion of Ethiopia and Egypt in antiquity.

69. Robert Conner, rev. of *Blacks in Antiquity,* n.p.

70. John Russell, rev. of *The Image of the Black in Western Art, New York Times Book Review* (5 December 1976) 5–101. Pierre Ducrey, rev. of *The Image of the Black in Western Art, Journal de Geneve* (12 December 1976). David Brion Davis, rev. of *The Image of the Black in Western Art, New York Times Review of Books* (5 November 1981). 38–42.

71. Anonymous rev. of *Before Color Prejudice: The Ancient View of Blacks, Choice* (July/August 1983) 1632. Ettore Lepare, rev. of *Before Color Prejudice: The Ancient View of Blacks, La Parola del Passato: Rivista di Studi Antichi,* 89 (1984). Hans-Joachim Dienner, rev. of *Before Color Prejudice: The Ancient View of Blacks,* Gnonom, 56 (1984).

Snowden, in his "white" Egypt, has not rectified for us an Egypt whose black population—according to Snowden—was the largest in all the lands of the classical world with the exception of Ethiopia itself. Nor has he helped us to reconcile Egyptian "whiteness" with what Lionel Casson notes, on Snowden's behalf and at his behest, was the "powerful Napatan Kingdom" that made Egypt its own and was the inspiration for countless classical authors' image of Egypt in antiquity.[72]

There is difficulty because Snowden himself celebrates this black presence and uses it to imply how one might be both black and Egyptian. He forces us to revisit his own observations. What should we make of his statement that "to many Egyptians, Napatans appeared Egyptian, not foreign"? Or that "once a foreigner came to live in Egypt, learned the language, and adopted Egyptian dress, he or she was accepted as one of 'the people.'"[73] We might add to this his comments on the rulers of the Twenty-fifth Dynasty and the ways in which he believes they were characterized by contemporary Egyptians, their enemies, and their admirers.

Given the size of Egypt's black population and the levels of intimacy, cultural and otherwise, some of us should be taxed by a notion that allows Egypt to be simply "white." In the final analysis, even Snowden's own arguments cannot justify such a conclusion. In part, from these observations, we find the root of our difficulty concerning Snowden's criticism of Bernal.

This criticism is taken up in "Bernal's 'Blacks,' Herodotus, and Other Classical Evidence," published in a special edition of *Arethusa* and in "Bernal's 'Blacks' and the Afrocentrists," in Mary R. Lefkowitz's and Guy MacLean Rogers's *Black Athena Revisited*. Again, the specificity of Snowden's argument centers on Bernal's statements that Herodotus "thought that the Egyptians and some Libyans were black" and that according to Herodotus, again, "many of the most powerful Egyptian dynasties . . . were made up of pharaohs whom one can usefully call black." Bernal ends by stating that "Egyptian civilization was fundamentally African."[74]

Snowden is at pains to emphasize, forcefully, that the *only* blacks of the classical world who satisfy the modern definition are identified by the *rather* specific term "*Aethiopian*."[75] Herein lay the natural order of

72. Lionel Casson, rev. of *Before Color Prejudice*, 74.

73. Snowden, *Before Color Prejudice*, 72, 89.

74. Snowden, "Bernal's 'Blacks,'" (draft, undated), 1; "Bernal's 'Blacks,'" *Arethusa* 83. "Bernal's 'Blacks' and the Afrocentrists," in Lefkowitz and Rogers, *Black Athena Revisited*, 116.

75. I have used the qualifier *rather* here because Snowden has indicated in his own writings that the term Ethiopian is not as specific as implied or even desired.

Snowden's position and hence his criticism of Bernal. Snowden's entire career has been built on the blackness of Ethiopia, not Egypt. He has meticulously constructed that image and argument, and with it he has unequivocally placed the African, the Negro, the black, on the stage of the classical world, *in Ethiopia*. Through that image and argument he has imparted agency. In Bernal and others, Snowden argues, there is the ill-founded attempt to strip Ethiopia of its position in the Classical Age through a misconstrued emphasis on the "blackness" of Egypt.

By the same token, when faced with Bernal and the "Afrocentrists," Snowden, in his passion for detail and nuance, and the meticulous nature of his research, has given us an Ethiopian physical type whose characteristics span an incredibly broad range. And so some of us remain confused by his response to a work that it might have been assumed he would have embraced in large measure.

Snowden's definition of the Ethiopian and his insistence that the Egyptian was not black has been the source of the most pointed criticism of his work. Snowden's definitions prompted a forum in the journal *Arethusa*, which included Snowden, Bernal, and Keita, an anthropologist. Parts of this forum have been mentioned elsewhere in this chapter. However, it is useful to note that Keita begins his critique of Snowden from the basis that Snowden has adopted a definition of race based on the assumptions of someone who is not an anthropologist, and from those assumptions has concluded "that the early northern Nile Valley peoples were biologically and culturally somehow unconnected to the 'real Africa.'"[76]

From this point, Keita introduces several other assumptions related to the concept of race and the ancient Egyptians that have arisen from the *Black Athena* debate. Keita returns us to the issue that began this work: "'[R]ace' explains little in the way of human variation or achievement."[77] Yet "[t]he persistence of race as an explanatory variable . . . still has a socio-political-ideological component and *raison d'etre* divorced from alleged objective inquiry or science."[78]

Citing the contentious passage from Bernal—a passage that ironically Snowden seems to confirm in *Before Color Prejudice*[79]—Keita notes

76. S.O.Y. Keita, "Race," 295.
77. Ibid., 295.
78. Ibid., 296.
79. Keita writes, paraphrasing Bernal, "at least a large portion of the ancient Egyptian *population* was in today's (scientific?) parlance, 'Black.'" Ibid., 298. In *Before Color Prejudice*, on pages 16–17 Snowden speaks to the inadequacies of racial categorization and then goes on to say in two passages that indeed a modern racial categorization might aid the reader in understanding his characterization of the Ethiopian:

> The ancients were acquainted with a wide range of types whose physical characteristics were not unlike those of the highly mixed American Negro described by

the arbitrary nature of racial categorization using Snowden's own criteria. Citing one of Snowden's sources, Keita points out, "Even Seligman (1930, 1966), by no means an 'Afrocentrist,' stated that 'Negroes' were clearly present in the proto-dynastic palettes."[80]

Keita then refers to V. Guiffrida-Ruggeri (1922) and his citation of Jean Capert. Together, the Guiffrida-Rugerri and Capert arguments read that the "Upper Egyptians were real African Ethiopians. . . . First Dynasty leaders defeated the north with negro [sic] troops who comprised the population of Upper Egypt."[81]

Keita calls on Petrie, who argues that "the Third Dynasty, among others came from the Sudan," and on the patriarchs of the "New American School of Ethnography," Nott and Glidden, who argued that the "Old Kingdom Egyptians [were] 'Negroid' re. African, but not 'akin' to any 'Negroes.'"[82]

Keita concludes simply: it is problematic and ahistorical to insist that ancient Egyptians were "white" and Bernal is correct: "[A]ncient Egypt is fundamentally African. . . . [C]ulturally, the core remains Saharo-Sudano-Nilotic (African) to the end."[83] This is just another way of saying that Egypt was and is black. As Keita puts it in a rejoinder to Snowden: "[A]t what village along the Nile does 'black' become 'white' categorically? How 'black' is black?"[84] Keita's is also a useful question for the "Afrocentrists."

Never at a lost when it comes to answering his critics, Snowden's response to Keita and others has been as caustic as ever. Witness his essay in the Lefkowitz and Rogers volume. In many ways, Snowden dismisses Keita's criticism. However, his countercritique is most meaningful when he refers to attempts to describe Egyptians in modern terms with all of their connotations. This he regards as a major shortcoming.[85]

M. J. Herkovits as varying from 'the man of dark-brown skin and African appearance to the man who is almost white, and from the broad-nosed, thick-lipped black man to the Caucasoid-looking, thin-lipped, narrow-nosed "technical" Negro . . . from . . . tightly coiled hair to that of Indian-like straightness.

Snowden concludes by asserting:

[O]bviously much larger in Egypt than elsewhere [was] the black population. . . . [P]eople from three continents often formed their views of blacks on the basis of what they saw and heard in *Egypt, where for centuries the black element in the population was obviously sizable.* (66; italics added)

80. S.O.Y. Keita, "Race," 300.
81. Ibid., 305.
82. Ibid., 305.
83. Ibid., 311.
84. S.O.Y. Keita, "Response to Bernal and Snowden," 332.
85. Snowden, "Response," 319–320.

Yet even in this Snowden never frees us from the impediments of modern classification. As much as he would like to escape this classification, he still clings to its implications, if not the form itself. If there are "intermediate populations," "black-white mixtures," how are we to understand those populations? What do they say to us, if anything, about who is Egyptian or Ethiopian? Snowden's guidance is not clear here.

This is especially the case in his attempt to classify the "Ethiopian" in the most specific and particular fashion as a category that at one moment does not overlap the Egyptian, yet at another moment has variants so broadly dispersed that Snowden is found contradicting himself.[86]

Yet in the midst of the racial debate there is the need to identify Snowden's contribution. What is it? Snowden has established black presence in this time and space—in the classical world. He has attempted to make his blacks indisputably black by casting them as Ethiopians. Given that blackness, that "Ethiopianness," he has provided them with other characteristics that could only be derived from the lexicography of the ancients: Snowden's blacks, his Ethiopians, his Negroes, his Africans, are defined by a virtuousness and wisdom without peer.

In the Bernal/"Afrocentrists" debate, given this almost Du Boisian construction of race that Snowden presents,[87] the ferocity of Snowden's counterpoint leads to another far more poignant speculation. Snowden has been wounded through misunderstanding by those he might serve best and by a voice that implies legitimacy because of its genealogy. Martin Bernal put it best when he said, "[I]f a Black were to say what I am now putting in my books . . . they would be . . . dismissed."[88] What Bernal has put in his books is this: "[M]ost Blacks will not be able to accept the conformity to white scholarship of men and women like Professor Snowden."[89] No matter how inadvertent, Bernal has named names. He has done it as a "white" academician in a context that valorizes whiteness, even by Snowden's standards. He has confirmed in "white" print what many "Afrocentrists" have said of Snowden in other venues: he is a traitor to the race.[90]

Again, irony seems to be a prevalent theme here. Snowden, a supposed "dupe of white scholarship," is victim to the very conventions of

86. Snowden, "The Negro in Classical Italy," 273. Snowden, *Blacks in Antiquity*, 4, 11, 12. Snowden, *Before Color Prejudice*, 8–9.

87. See Du Bois's notion of the construction of race, i.e., the "idea," "ideal," and "spirit" of race and its implications as presented in "The Conservation of Races."

88. Bernal, *Black Athena*, 17–18, 20.

89. Bernal *Black Athena*, vol. 1, 436; italics added.

90. Snowden, "Bernal's 'Blacks' and the Afrocentrists," 116–117.

the epistemology of blackness he opposed. Black criticism of his project was easily overlooked in conventional circles. It was the work of crackpots, "radical Afrocentrists," whose publications were hardly the stuff of mainstream academic review or scholarly exchange. Snowden himself was almost cavalierly dismissive of their claims and their attacks. Yet in the "white" voice of Bernal's historiography and epistemology, Snowden is challenged and wounded in the arena in which he wishes most to contend, the arena in which he has been an undisputed champion, of sorts.

Afrocentrism

In spite of it all, and probably much to his chagrin, there are qualities that endear Snowden to some Afrocentrists. First among them is his attitude. It reflects a bearing and demeanor that emerges from an almost mythic line of black intellectuals beginning in the late nineteenth century. This attitude is epitomized by scholars such as Woodson and Du Bois. They were, and Snowden is, intellectuals who come to do battle. The attitude is one that brooks no nonsense and gives no quarter. All this is done in recognition of the less-than-hospitable reception for one's works as well as one's person. He is caustic and irascible in defense of his position. And it is an attitude, I suspect, that even gains a reluctant smile from many of Snowden's Afrocentric adversaries.

Snowden's is an attitudinal stance that defers to a sense of history. It is a reminiscence of the intellectual past from which many Afrocentrists would claim descent. Snowden is a "scrapper" even if the side he scraps for is of questionable merit to them.[91] In many ways, the core of Snowden's thesis has been both excluded from mainstream academia and ignored by many in the Afrocentric camp. There is a glossing of the validity of his ideas within the context of traditional epistemology, a failure to accept his historical position and what that entails: African agency and a partnership in the creation of the ancient world. Attitudinally, Snowden is in the mode of the best of black intellectual heroes. He is representative of the generation of scholars they sired, scholars who rose to the defense of their work—race men and women.

It seems a bit of supreme irony that Snowden's response to his critics in either camp issues from the same source as Levine's response to "radical Afrocentrists." If there is any doubt, one might look at Snowden's response to Keith Hopkins's review in the *Times Literary Supplement* (October 21, 1983) and at Snowden's own review of Lloyd Thomp-

---

91. Bernal, *Black Athena*, 436.

son's *Romans and Blacks*. These are indicative of Snowden's fire in print and in public fora.

His treatment of Thompson's work and his rejection of its "unwarranted negative attitudes" as a "distorted view of Roman attitudes toward blacks" is tied to his castigation of Hopkins's assertion that Snowden has "cleverly created" a "foundation myth for Black History."[92] Snowden's criticism of Thompson, Hopkins's criticism of Snowden, and Snowden's retort point to another sense of confluence between Snowden and Afrocentric thinkers. Snowden's material, aside from Egypt, is an unabashed praise for African genius in the Classical Age and the ways in which that genius contributed to the construction of classical civilization—that, in fact, is the source of Hopkins's criticism and a position that allows Hopkins to tacitly address Snowden as an Afrocentrist.

As Lawrence Angel notes, Snowden may very well be a source, perhaps even a hero, for some Afrocentrists, because of the meticulous nature of his research *and* his subject matter. Angel notes:

> The fact that it stresses the mixture and cultural interaction of Blacks and Whites may not make it popular among today's Black militants although this is just the group who could use Snowden's data and ideas to best advantage.[93]

The data, the ideas, the methodology are key to Snowden's rebuke of Hopkins. They are also a stern warning to Afrocentrists on the issue of mythologizing the African past. For Snowden, there is no need to fabricate history—no need for "foundation myths," in light of all the evidence of African existence, agency, and interaction in the Classical Age. As Snowden writes

> Afrocentrists maintain that the history of blacks has been distorted or neglected in traditional curricula. As many historians and educators have pointed out, this has often been the case; however, the correction of this defect should not take place at the expense of accurate or balanced history, as it sometimes has. Nor does a proper corrective mean that the study of Western civilization is irrelevant for all students, and it is demeaning to blacks to assume that their intellectual life should not *encompass the whole of human experience.*[94]

92. Frank M. Snowden, Jr., *"Romans and Blacks*: A Review Essay," 557. Keith Hopkins, "Chromatic Harmony," *Times Literary Supplement* (October 21, 1983), 1152. Copy of Snowden letter to the *Times Literary Supplement* (November 7, 1983).

93. J. Lawrence Angel, rev. of *Blacks in Antiquity: Ethiopians in the Greco-Roman Experience. American Anthropologist*, 74 (1972), 160.

94. Snowden, "Whither Afrocentrism?," 7; italics added.

He goes on to say,

> [E]ven when stripped of Afrocentric myths, the black experience in the ancient world—Egyptian, Greek, Roman and early Christian—is itself a fascinating chapter in the history of Mediterranean antiquity. *It is unfortunate that no Afrocentric study has given attention to the significance of* this *experience.*[95]

Here, in finality, is the ultimate source of Snowden's angst and outrage. It is that Afrocentrists have failed to embrace what is "truly" African in this age. They have failed to realize that Ethiopia is their true "center."

---

95. Ibid., 8: italics added.

EIGHT

Through a Glass Darkly

Afrocentrism

. . . Trivializing Afrocentrism

Alison and Ed Corley, Letters

Afrocentrism is another weed fertilized by the idea that there
is no such thing as truth.

George Will,
"Intellectual Segregation"

. . . captives of peculiar arrogance

Molefe Kete Asante,
The Afrocentric Idea

In what George Will certainly knew would not be "the last word," before a national audience far broader than any Afrocentrist might
dream, Afrocentrism was reduced to "meritricious misrepresentations
. . . for ideological purposes." Will wrote this as part of his endorse-
ment of Mary Lefkowitz's *Not Out of Africa: How Afrocentrism Became
an Excuse to Teach Myth as History*. Lefkowitz enjoined the essential aspects of the debate by prompting Will's observation that Afrocentrism
threatens the construction and the "dissemination of knowledge." The
debate is both epistemological and historiographic.[1]

I am hard pressed to find as damning and would-be devastating a critique of Edward Said's work on Orientalism in the popular media,

---

1. George Will, "Intellectual Segregation," *Newsweek* (February 19, 1996), 78.

though his work broaches the same issues. Both *Orientalism* and *Culture and Imperialism*, along with several essays on Palestinian concerns, are epistemological and historiographic in nature. They also pose the very questions that Will finds so repugnant in Afrocentrism: questions of identity, power, and the motives of those who write, particularly those who write what might receive validity as history.

Having said that, I must address Said here on at least two counts: first, there is a relation between Said's critique of Orientalism and the Afrocentric critique and the validation the academy and "official" media give one over the other. This has certainly been a historical paradigm that has played itself out in the over a century and a half of African American scholarship devoted to the construction of African American and African history and identity.

Second, Said's work is also important because it points to and reemphasizes, for the careful reader, the historical relationship, the contiguity, between the emergence and construction of Egyptology and Orientalism as fields of study, a contiguity that by the nineteenth century allowed Egypt to become a metonym for the Orient. The Orient epitomized Egypt and the Egyptian as African became "Oriental," historically and in the contemporary sense of the fields' formation.

The linkage of Said's critique of Orientalism with the Afrocentric critique also leads us back to Du Bois's observation concerning Egyptology's debut as both the child of and justification for the rise of empire and the extensive modern traffic in African bodies.[2] Said and Asante agree that here the hardening and crystallization of racism would occur in the cracks and fissures of intellectual and academic discourse. The mortar and many of the bricks of at least one house of knowledge, constructions "privileged" by "white hegemony," as Will was shocked to learn, is racism.

What Will and other critics overlook in their accusations of Afrocentric mythmaking is the exact point that Snowden makes: given the historical record, mythmaking is unnecessary: "[T]he black experience in the ancient world . . . is itself a fascinating chapter in the history of Mediterranean antiquity." And then to paraphrase him, it is unfortunate that very few, Afrocentric or otherwise, have given attention to the significance of this experience.[3] Will and others, sometimes implicitly referencing Snowden—in particular his attack on Afrocentrism—conveniently ignore the essence of this statement. If Snowden is ig-

---

2. "One must remember that Egyptology, starting in 1821, grew up during the African slave trade, the Sugar Empire and the Cotton Kingdom." See Du Bois, *Black Folk, Then and Now*, 25.

3. Snowden, "Whither Afrocentrism?," 7–8.

nored, Asante and the Afrocentrists are dismissed outright. The Afrocentrists are dismissed, in fact, without so much as a reading.

In most accounts on Afrocentrism, analysis of the positions is based largely on secondhand, anecdotal data rather than a critical reading of the sources themselves. This is exactly the way the Will essay opens; it is good journalistic style, but the article, as Will alleges of Afrocentrism in toto, is not scholarship. So Afrocentrism is analyzed in the popular press in articles such as "Teaching Reverse Racism," in which Leon Jaroff's opening line is " the teachings are sheer fantasy." Jaroff does go on to tell us that he is writing of "extremists within the Afrocentric movement," but he, like most critics, never goes on to identify those who might be more "responsible" and to say what in their thought and scholarship gives them such a credential. Jaroff simply proceeds with the warning that "Afrocentrist myths have taken hold of higher education. . . . Even some well-educated black professionals are not immune to the odd tenets of Afrocentrism." Among those "odd tenets" is the notion that "all Egyptians were black."[4] Jaroff's "extremists" are as undifferentiated as Levine's "radical Afrocentrists." And they are presented with the same reluctance to examine the "why" of their "extreme" or "radical" positions.

What Jaroff, Will, and others write of is at the core of the debate. Stripped of journalistic flourish and academic etiquette, the critique, the criticism, the attacks, focus on the threat that Afrocentrism poses to our way of knowing from the primary grades through graduate education. In its mildest form the threat is articulated as "feel good" or "inspirational" education for black students. The implication is still the same: such education is bogus, a sort of "ethnic cheerleading."[5] At another level, Afrocentrism is "grossly inaccurate and racially inflammatory."[6] The implication here is that Afrocentrism should be dismissed as such. As Frank Yurco, Egyptologist at Chicago's Field Museum has put it, some Afrocentric claims are "baloney" and "sheer distortion."

For others, the real danger of Afrocentrism and all that is attendant to it or follows in its wake is its challenge to Western knowledge, the canon that has become the foundation of that knowledge and our way of knowing *ourselves*— not simply as Westerners, but more particularly as Americans. It is in this context that intellectual, academic, and political heavyweights like Schlesinger, Lefkowitz, and Bennett appear. Their critiques, however, seem less based on a careful critical and his-

---

4. Leon Jaroff, "Teaching Reverse Racism," *Time* (April 4, 1994), 74–75.

5. Suzanne Daley, "Inspirational Black history Draws Academic Fire," *New York Times* (October 10, 1990), A1; B6.

6. Gary Putka, "Curricula of Color," *Wall Street Journal* (July 1, 1991), 1; A2.

torical reading of what has come to be called Afrocentrism than on a pandering to the sensational elements that lend themselves to these critics' particular agendas.

If we return to the popular press accounts, we must recognize that there are elements that have no basis in intellectual discourse, no matter which side articulates them. Some Afrocentrists themselves have turned such comments aside, and some critics of Afrocentrism have acknowledged that not all Afrocentrists are the same.[7]

Some regard Gerald Early's "Understanding Afrocentrism: Why Blacks Dream of a World Without Whites" as just that sort of sensationalism from its provocative subtitle through its core to its end. If Early's work is an "understanding" of Afrocentrism, it is deficient in its analysis. Early's is an attack on Afrocentrism, yet even as such, it is one that retreats as much as it advances on the issues that Early defines as essential to Afrocentrism. It is hardly capable of carrying out what Henry Louis Gates of Harvard University's Department of Afro-American Studies thinks is of necessity in regard to Asante and Afrocentrism in general. That is the need to "kick Asante's ass" in the intellectual sense of the parlance. Yet Early's attempt, possibly and particularly because it is the act of a black intellectual, underlines the facility with which those in disagreement with Afrocentrism might label it *"dat* course" as opposed to discourse, to use Ann duCille's terminology.[8]

Early acknowledges, somewhat to his dismay, that Afrocentrism cannot be easily defined. This seems to me to be a key element of any attempt at serious academic discourse: the theoretical premises are just that—theoretical. They are open for debate and analysis; they are fluid. For Early, this is almost lamentable: "Afrocentrism is many things and has many degrees of advocacy," a great deal of it commercial, shallow, and pretentious. Early illustrates this by declaring that

> Afrocentrists will feel their triumph to be complete when black actors portray Beethoven, Joseph Hayden, Warren G. Harding, Alexander Hamilton, Hannibal, Abraham Lincoln, Dwight Eisenhower, Cleopatra, Moses, Jesus Christ and Saint Augustine.

Early's attempt at *ad absurdum reductio* quickly reduces a great deal of his argument to absurdity. Even when the points are lucid and cogent, Early's disdain for the Afrocentric project compels him to comparison

7. Frank Yurco, Correspondence with Eric King (July 20, 1994). Frank W. Snowden, Interview, Feb. 28, 1996.

8. Ann duCille, *Skin Trade* (Cambridge: Harvard University Press, 1996), 122.

and analysis of positions so arcane and trite that no self-respecting Afrocentrist would deign to argue them.[9]

In fact, the responses recorded in the "Letters" section of *Civilization* for September/October 1995 bear this out for the journal's readership as well. Mel Huang wrote from Ithaca, NY:

> Gerald Early's article on Afrocentrism which presented separatist visions and counterintuitive ideas was out of place in a magazine which I thought promoted good taste and tolerance. I am saddened that even intellectuals in the black community can write such angry pieces.

Jerome Carter of Birmingham wrote:

> I was shocked by your July/August cover story. Lumping together the black middle class, serious scholars and college students with political opportunists, anti-Semites and other fringe personalities, as if they represent a monolithic cabal of misguided dreamers who think Western civilization was invented in Africa is unforgivably insulting and a disservice to your readers.

Probably the most trenchant comment was Frank Wernick's ironic anticipation of *Civilization*'s "upcoming article 'Understanding Eurocentrism: Why Whites Dream of a World Without Blacks.'" As Alison and Ed Corley put it, a "better title for Gerald Early's article would have been 'Trivializing Afrocentrism.'" E. Ethelbert Miller, director of the African American Resource Center at Howard University moved the issue center once again by pointing out that Early's comments were part of a much larger debate on historiography and epistemology that was concentrated in great measure on the construction of African American history and identity as it is played out in the debate over Afrocentrism. The contentions of that history and identity are representative of the contentions in and the potential for American identity, writ large.[10]

A much more thoughtful, judicious, and compelling critique emerges from the pen of Kwame Anthony Appiah. In his "Europe Upside Down: Fallacies of the New Afrocentrism," Appiah treats us to two very important dimensions of Afrocentrism that are hardly reviewed. First, by referring to the "new" Afrocentrism, Appiah implies

9. Early, "Understanding Afrocentrism: Why Blacks Dream of a World Without Whites," *Civilization* (July/August 1995), 32. Molefe Asante, "Reading Race in Antiquity: The Many Fallacies of Mary Lefkowitz," *Blacks in Higher Education* (March 7, 1996), 31–32.

10. Alison and Ed Corley, Letters, *Civilization* (September/October 1996), 10.

that there is an "old" Afrocentrism, and indeed, he goes on to explicitly illustrate that Afrocentrism is historically grounded. Appiah also picks up on Early's dismaying epiphany: Afrocentrism is not monolithic.[11]

Appiah also provides another immense service when he points out that "[a]t least as important as any published work is the body of Afrocentric lore transmitted in public lectures and discussion groups."[12] This popular dispensation of Afrocentricity—another form of "public intellectualism"—allows critiques of Afrocentrism to concentrate on what Appiah describes as the enormous differences "in the variety of thought and writing as well as their factual reliability." Again, Appiah notes that "like most cultural movements at full flood, this Afrocentrism is a composite of truth and error, insight and illusion, moral generosity and meanness."[13]

And while Appiah criticizes Afrocentrism for adhering to "the frameworks of nineteenth-century European thought," in particular its construction of race, racism, and racialism, he finds merit in some Afrocentric work. A case in point is Clinton M. Jean's *Behind Eurocentric Veils*, which Appiah calls "among the best-written and argued Afrocentric books I have read." Yet, according to Appiah, Jean's shortcoming is fundamentally that ascribed to Afrocentrists broadly, again without the benefit of the critical reading Appiah has undertaken, and laboring mightily under Afrocentrism popularized: the inability to learn "to think beyond race."[14]

In many ways, Appiah's critique is representative of what one might expect of intellectual discourse on the issue: thoughtful, balanced, and direct in its criticism, and Marked by a willingness to undertake the issue as a point of intellectual discourse rather than reduce it to the absurdity of its lowest common denominator. If, however, the *Chronicle of Higher Education*'s review of Mary Lefkowitz's *Not Out of Africa* is any example, then neither debate nor discourse have advanced from what is "low" or "common." As Asante's comments in the piece indicate, Lefkowitz and company seem to "miss the larger point," choosing to focus on "'nonsense things'—whether Greeks 'stole' their philosophy, whether Cleopatra was black. . . . Most Afrocentrists . . . do not take such claims literally."[15]

The American tendency to focus on the "nonsense things," the in-

11. Kwame Anthony Appiah, "Europe Turned Upside Down: Fallacies of the New Afrocentrism," *London Times Literary Supplement* (February 2, 1993), 24.

12. Ibid., 24.

13. Ibid., 24.

14. Ibid., 25.

15. "Not Out of Africa," Editorial, *Chronicle of Higher Education,* 42 (February 16, 1996), A6–A7.

ability "to think beyond race," the great difficulty in entertaining the possibility that Afrocentric discourse might lead to a deeper understanding of the classical world, are traits that Shelley Haley describes as "deeply racist." These traits are a reflection of the ways in which many scholars "read the historical evidence."[16] They exist in marked contrast with Ann Macy Roth's observations on the legitimacy of Afrocentric discourse in the rest of the world, particularly France, and Afrocentrism's potential for rejuvenating Egyptology.

Roth deserves particular attention for several reasons. In her "Building Bridges to Afrocentrism: A Letter to My Colleagues," Roth notes that few Egyptologists have seriously considered the "contentions of the Afrocentric movement." There is a certain "curiosity and discomfort that American Egyptologists feel about Afrocentrism, yet, "'Afrocentric Egyptology' . . . has an international scholarly literature behind it."[17]

While Roth believes that "Afrocentric Egyptology is less a scholarly field than a political movement," she argues that "the Afrocentric movement has a great potential to advance or to damage our field." The effect will be dependent in large measure on the attempts of "traditionally-trained American Egyptologists . . . to understand and adapt to its existence."[18]

To illustrate her contention regarding the importance of Afrocentrism and its potential impact on Egyptology, Roth emphasizes the point by stating that she was "amazed at the quantity of Egyptology that was already being taught" at Howard University, one of the United States' preeminent historically black universities. Study in the field, she remarks, "continues to grow in importance and influence." She tempers these remarks by noting that much of this is popularized Egyptology that "has little to do with the Egyptology that . . . professional Egyptologists practice." However, she continues, by simply regarding its "exponent[s'] . . . aggressive and seemingly irrelevant questions" as "nuisance," traditionally trained Egyptologists may be "missing an opportunity." What Roth suggests is an alliance, which in the scheme of developing constituencies for certain bodies of knowledge seems quite logical. Initiates to all fields of study come to them by way of popular ideas concerning those fields. Egyptology is no different. Rather than dismissing Afrocentrism as "nonsense" and "disparaging the knowledge of its proponents," Roth sees Afrocentrism as

16. Ibid, 23.

17. Ann Macy Roth, "Building Bridges to Afrocentrism: A Letter to My Colleagues," pt.I (ftp://oi.chicago.edu/pub/papers/AMROTH_Afrocentrism.ascii.txt,26 January 1995), 1–2.

18. Ibid., 1–2.

a possible seedbed of beginning interest and support for Egyptology. From there the ideas, techniques, and methodologies of Afrocentric students might be refined and enhanced. The implication is that traditionally trained American Egyptologists might have something to learn as well.[19]

Roth's observations concerning most of her colleagues' reactions to Afrocentrism is fundamentally the same one that Bernal acknowledges. Those reactions rise from the same source. However, what Roth says concerning the utility of Afrocentrism, its variety, the possibilities of its scholarship, and its legitimacy has many implications. Among them is the notion that Afrocentrism has been summarily dismissed in most quarters of the academy. It has been dismissed not so much without a "hearing" as without a "reading"—a critical reading.

We need to return to the comparison that began this discussion. That comparison asks about the privileging of certain discourses and knowledges, and in doing so introduced Said and his critique of Orientalism and Asante's articulation of Afrocentrism as illustration. Said's position has certainly been subjected to hostilities, but none as derisive nor as petty as those aimed at Asante and Afrocentrism in general. A rejoinder to the latter observation might be that the "pettiness" of Afrocentrism elicited this response. In that light, I argue, again, that Afrocentrism has not been *critically read*.

In that regard, a foundation is laid by the implicit and explicit remarks of Afrocentrism's critics. Implicit in the criticism Levine and others direct against those labeled "radical Afrocentrists" is the idea that there must be "nonradical" Afrocentrists." Roth indicates that Afrocentrism is international and that that in itself provides for a certain variety politically and scholastically. Appiah, speaking of the "new" Afrocentrism, implies and then briefly addresses the older, historical discourse. The point is that Afrocentrism is variegated, and in light of this, its most recent and prominent critiques have failed to seriously consider that variety and what it means in terms of the complexity and the theoretical and historical depths of the concepts it represents. This means that very few of its critics thus far have attempted a wide and critical reading of the sources that address the subject in both the historical and the contemporary senses.

It is also evident that in regard to the readings that have been attempted, most—the overwhelming number—have hardly been critical in the intellectual sense in terms of their assessment of the source or sources they have chosen to critique. Afrocentrism is simply not taken

19. Ibid., 1–2.

seriously. If we focus on the work of the one person most widely critiqued in regard to Afrocentrism, Asante, we see that even within the context of a *single* author, the critics have failed to thoroughly read the source. In essence, as both Roth and Asante observed, the work has been reduced to "nonsense."

Epistemology and Historiography

Asante's work is fundamentally epistemological. At its core is a recognition of and concern for ways of knowing. Here again, if we look to Said, we find a corresponding argument. Said argues that "Orientalism" is, indeed, a way of knowing the "Orient." The terminology that both Asante and Said employ implies that there are other ways of knowing this space, defining it, naming it. Afrocentrism is simply one articulation of a way of knowing.

In some ways, what Asante has articulated in Afrocentrism moves beyond Said's critique in Orientalism in terms of attempting to define what another way of knowing might be—what its spatial parameters might be and how it might be named. If we address Asante and Said in concert, we are back to Du Bois. There is the consonance, the simultaneous genesis and development of Egyptology and Orientalism. They are, in many ways, twins. Said implies as much when he states that "what are striking in these discourses are the rhetorical figures one keeps encountering in their descriptions of 'the mysterious East' as well as stereotypes about the 'African mind.'" All this, Said continues, is "part of the general European effort to rule distant lands and peoples." And though the discourses these acts generate are seen as essentially European, we are reminded that "no American has been immune from this structure of feeling . . . the extraordinary global reach" of the imperial project.[20]

The epistemological nature of these works and their concern for the construction of knowledge is contentious. People do contend for knowledge: the control of it, the control over it, and the control that it consigns. A. Daudi has argued that "discourse is 'object of the struggle for power'"—that there is "power in the discourse." So to contend over epistemology is to contend over power. As Octavia Paz has put it, "power . . . is reserved only for those who have knowledge." Therefore, as Asante observes, contending for knowledge is the struggle to reorder power.[21]

20. Edward Said, *Culture and Imperialism* (New York: Vintage Books, 1994), xi, xvii.
21. Quoted in Molefe K. Asante, *The Afrocentric Idea,* (Philadelphia: Temple University Press, 1987), 14, 29.

He is quite clear about this point when he writes that "Afrocentricity . . . proposed as a critique of domination and hegemony . . . has challenged the imposition of Eurocentrism as universal."[22]

Again Said makes the same argument. He challenges "Orientalism" as a European construct. Said's work is a critique of the ways in which Europeans have constructed the "Orient."[23] Asante's work is a construction of "Africa" by a segment of the African world in opposition to what EuroAmerica has constructed. There is little doubt that Africa is a construction. Works such as Dorothy Hammond and Alta Jablow's *The Africa That Never Was*, or Valentine Y. Mudimbe's *The Invention of Africa* and *The Idea of Africa* confirm this.[24] It was Du Bois who argued that Africa, along with Asia and, by extension, Europe, was truly an invention of not simply the modern age but the twentieth century.[25] This Africa is obviously not without variation. Asante acknowledges this variation when he discloses that his "African" is a composite. In all this, however, it is quite clear that in many ways, the works of both Asante and Said "recognize" and play on one another.

Yet the real dilemma lies in the attempt to have the academy consider Asante and the work on Afrocentrism in the same ways that we do other scholarly discourse: by serious comparison. Consider the following as a basis for the construction of such a comparison. Said, Bernal, and Roth, as examples, have led us to the following conclusions: the Orientalist and Egyptological discourses are as old as the Enlightenment. Bernal notes, in much the same way as Said, that "Egyptology" is, in large measure, the construction of Egypt by Europe. Certainly, it is a construction under contention because, as Roth indicates, it is a "Eurocentric" discipline.[26] Du Bois spoke to this very notion when he sharply characterized the political economic genesis of Egyptology as Imperialism and King Cotton.

Said's pronouncements in *Orientalism* simply mirrored Du Bois's remarks: "Orientalism coincides exactly with the period of unparalleled

22. Molefe K. Asante, "Multiculturalism and the Academy," *Academe*, 82,3 (1996), 22–23. Molefe K. Asante, *Kemet, Afrocentricity, and Knowledge* (Trenton: Africa World Press, 1990), vi. Asante is in good historical company here. His notion that "opposition . . . re-orders the structure of power" is not far distant from Frederick Douglass's "power concedes nothing without demand."

23. Said, *Orientalism*, 97,117,147.

24. Dorothy Hammond and Alta Jablow, *The Africa that Never Was: Four Centuries of British Writing about Africa* (New York: Twayne Publishers, 1970). Valentine Y. Mudimbe, *The Invention of Africa: Gnosis, Philosophy, and the Order of Knowledge* (Bloomington: Indiana University Press, 1988); *The Idea of Africa* (Bloomington: Indiana University Press,1994).

25. William Edward Burghardt Du Bois, "The Pan African Movement," in Elie Kedourie, *Nationalism in Asia and Africa* (New York: Meridian Books, 1970), 372.

26. Roth, pt. 2, 14.

European expansion. . . . Every continent was affected, none more so than Africa and Asia." Orientalism and Egyptology are manifestations of the knowledge that Lord George Nathaniel Curzon recognized as a "part of the necessary furniture of Empire."[27] The sharpness of the critique crystallizes in light of its historical development.

Asante defines the historical root of the problem in the same way. He identifies the Enlightenment, and he focuses on Hegel in particular. This focus is important in light of the superficial critiques made of Asante. They overlook, dismiss, ignore; they are ignorant of the fact that Asante grounds his critique in Western philosophical tradition (this might be the key to one of the substantive critiques: Afrocentrism, in light of its own analysis, is a Western thesis, yet this Westernness does not detract from its viability as theory or discourse). Because of this superficiality there is no assessment of the implications of this array of sources. There is no assessment of how Asante's work or Afrocentrism speaks to the world rather than the presumed narrow audience that most critiques imply. Yet the implications are seen in his discussions of the "problems of methodology" and Hegel's impact on Western tradition.

Hegel's definition of history privileges a certain form of discourse and denigrates others. Those others are dismissed as myths and orality, as "obscure modes . . . peculiar to obscure peoples." As Asante points out, "In Hegelian terms Africans are an obscure people, obscure because Europeans do not know them but certainly not obscure to their own recorders, musicians, historians, epics, myths, and chronicles." What Asante has outlined here in terms of "obscurity" is the fact that history as Hegel defines it is rooted in modernism and the emergence of the modern age. Africa becomes unknown; it becomes terra incognita not because it *is* so but because it *needs* to be so in order to satisfy the conditions necessary for the construction of European hegemony.[28] Europeans do not *know* Africa or Africans in the modern period because they cannot afford to. References to premodern history, historiography, and epistemology must be forgotten, "obscured," because not to do so would question the morality and, therefore, the rationality of the modern age.[29] Here, Asante seems quite philosophical, and the philosophical nature, contemporarily, might be referenced by reading Sartre, Foucault, and Mudimbe.

Asante's critique of Hegel allows him to link historiography (Hegel's "philosophy of history") and epistemology. From Hegel, Asante fash-

27. Said, *Orientalism*, 41, 123, 214.
28. Georg Friedrich Hegel, *Reason*, 3. Quoted in Asante, *Kemet*, 31, 23, 32.
29. Ibid., 31, 23, 32.

ions a dialectic concerning Eurocentric historiography and epistemology in the forms of Orientalism and Egyptology versus the question of Africa in these discourses. While Africa is "irrelevant to knowledge acquisition" in conventional Eurocentric discourse, there is a compulsion for the "total acquisition of Egypt intellectually."[30] Asante continues,

> "Indeed, the idea embedded in European thought, partially in the seventeenth, eighteenth, nineteenth and twentieth centuries[,] that Africans were inferior . . . has tainted most of what passes for social sciences in the west.[31]

Yet even this quest would not allow Hegel to "admit that Egypt was high culture." It was simply not part of his historical world.[32] Regardless, as Burton put it, "Egypt is a treasure to be won," all within the creation of a "domain of . . . scholarly rule." Fourier understood this when he wrote that his purpose was to "exclaim on the significance of Egypt to knowledge in Europe."[33] If Denon, Volney, and Gregoire were to be believed, the "blackness" of Egypt could have altered European ways of knowing fundamentally.

So what does a critical reading of Asante reveal? A critical reading moves the reader away from shallow pronouncements, pro or con. It might be argued that Afrocentrism's supporters are just as much in need of such a critical reading as are its detractors.

Asante's questioning of Eurocentric "universality" and the primacy of science is a challenge to the "Eurocentric way of seeing reality," to the "last five hundred years" of "conventional epistemology."[34] Along with the association that many chose to make in terms of Afrocentrism's relation to the questions of Egypt and Egyptology, it is crucial to recognize that Afrocentrism is also a central component of postmodernist discourse. Without Asante having to say it (though he does), a historical analysis of postcolonial/postmodernist theory reveals that much of the discussion that is taken for granted today is rooted in the Enlightenment discourse on race. The earliest challenges to that Enlightenment discourse are fundamentally African and African American discourses. These are the texts that are acknowledged here beginning in the early nineteenth century and before. They are the very texts that mark the emergence of an alternative epistemology.

30. Ibid., 32, 37, 128. Said, *Orientalism*, 76–85.
31. Asante, *Kemet*, 21.
32. Ibid., 32.
33. Said, *Orientalism*, 196–197. Asante, *Kemet*, 128–129.
34. Asante, *Idea*, 4, 21–22.

That we might claim for Africans and African Americans an inaugural and central role in the postmodern/postcolonial debate can be argued in this way. The colonization of the Americas intimately and extensively involved Africans, soon to be African Americans, writ large. Africans as chattel, early on, became both subject and object of the colonial enterprise that was to characterize the colonization of North, Central, and South America, and the Caribbean. The resistance of these Africans, from the first day, was also the beginning of a postmodern/postcolonial discourse that would question the very tenets of Enlightenment philosophy as it pertained to race and as it manifested itself in print in the words of the Accompongs, the Phyllis Wheatleys, the Olaudah Equianos, Benjamin Bannekers, the Tousaint L'Ouvretures, and the David Walkers of this experience. Theirs were well-reasoned, lucid, philosophical attacks on one of the most dominant and reprehensible aspects of the Enlightenment: the construction of race to deny various groups of people access to resources and the denigration and degradation of these people as the rationale for their expropriation—*racism*. Asante and other Afrocentrists are heir to this intellectual construction right through the works of Snowden.

If one studies Asante's references to Sartre and others, what might occur from a critical reading is a realization that the evolution of Afrocentrism is witness to the movement of power in the postcolonial/postmodern critique. One begins with an Afrocentric critique; the other is the result of it.[35]

The discourse begun by Africans in the Americas is a discourse on place, race and identity, and the political economy of slavery as the upshots of imperialism and colonialism. Afrocentrism can be defined, in this long historical, historiographic, and epistemological view, as a "movement toward decolonizing information and approaches to information." It is the decolonization of "the structure of knowledge itself."[36]

So one of several critical readings of Afrocentrism might reveal that postcolonial/postmodern studies such as Said's critique of Orientalism need not and, in most senses, should not be viewed as competitive. They are globalized manifestations of the same phenomenon with regional specifics, and yet, as Said has pointed out, with many of the same actors. It should go without saying in the critique that such a postcolonial/postmodernist critique offers the view that not all of these actors are colonizers.

That postcolonial/postmodern discourses do compete. That they

35. Asante, *Kemet*, v; *Idea*, 159, 162–163.
36. Asante, *Kemet*, 40.

are *forced* to compete—that their legitimacy within the academy lies in their competitions—lends itself to the main thesis of this work: there are favored discourses and they are witnessed in the legitimacy granted to some ideas and not to others within the academy and its adjuncts.

While Asante engages in and sometimes encourages that very competition, in other ways, ways that belie the combative rhetoric of much of Afrocentrism, his vision is much broader; much more encompassing; much more inclusive: "If African American theory follows the same path [the narrowness of Eurocentric theory] what would happen to progressive theory? . . . How can the oppressed use the same theories as their oppressors?[37] These notions come directly from Paulo Freire (at least, he wrote them before Asante)[38] yet they are hardly received as such when they are encountered in an Asante volume. We might wonder if they are even read there at all.

Asante argues that there is a "legitimacy of criticism based upon a plurality of cultural views." In many ways, this idea is exactly what his critics object to: the principle of relativity that will result in the "disuniting of America." The concept of such plurality is unimaginable for Will and company. Yet the concept seems terribly reasonable when Asante speaks of a coexistence of cultures.

So what is the task of Afrocentrism? In the same ways that Afrocentrism might be contentious, Asante searches for "a paradigm of complementarity." In doing so, he attempts to recognize Thomas Kuhn's "harmony of opposites," a recognition that not all thinking is dialectical, dichotomous, or oppositional.[39] It is an essentially postmodern argument that states that "one must often use different sensibilities to gain access to knowledge." Quoting Marvin Harris, Asante underlines his argument for the acknowledgment of different ways of knowing that might be identified as postmodern when Harris argues that there are "domains of experience of knowledge that cannot be achieved by adherence to the rules of scientific method."[40]

Asante's opening to complementarity and harmony is an interrogation of Eurocentric "universality." The issue of objectivity is broached and described as "collective European subjectivity." Asante's attack here is on the "traditional ideology of empiricism." It is an attack on postmodern critical theory that Asante calls the "post-Eurocentric

37. Asante, *Idea*, 165.
38. Paolo Freire, *Pedagogy of the Oppressed* (New York: Seabury Press, 1970).
39. Asante, *Idea*, 12, 16.
40. Asante, *Kemet*, 37; *Idea*, 15.

idea," an idea that allows for "transcultural analysis" and even sees the possibilities of "post-male ideology."[41]

The need for such an idea is recognized within the context of what Roy Preiswerk and Dominique Perrot regard as the ethnocentrism of most Western histories. As Brodkey has put it, "all scholarship recognizes that researchers are implicated in their own research." Asante underlines this idea by stating that "no field of human knowledge can be divorced from the authors' involvement as a human being in a given context. . . . [E]pistemologically what has been presented as 'objective' fact reveals itself as a value judgement." There is a "valorization inherent in the choice of facts and concepts."[42]

This valorization and the choices that it reflects are indicative of the "inability to 'see' from several angles"; this "is perhaps the one common fallacy in provincial scholarship" and the issue central to "Western standards imposed as interpretive measures on other cultures."[43] We must assume that at its best, this constriction is what Afrocentrism seeks to avoid. As Asante explains, "I am not questioning the validity of the Eurocentric tradition within its context." That tradition simply cannot claim a "universal hegemony as it has frequently done in the social sciences."[44]

There are, Asante argues in boldface, "Other Ways of Knowing."[45] This argument is an acknowledgment that "almost all knowledge has cultural relevance and must be examined for its particular focus." Other ways of knowing imply other contexts. The examination and comparison of those contexts imply the "emergence of parallel frames of reference" and the "legitimacy of criticism based upon a plurality of cultural views."[46] The context may be identified by the "fact that certain political constructs impose definite limitations in concepts and content on all discourse about reality." That reality, as Berger and Luckman indicate, is socially constructed. The role of Afrocentrism is to expand "the repertoire of human perspectives on knowledge." Afrocentrism insists on new perspectives that "create new ways of seeing data" in such a way that they promote the "decolonization of information and approaches to information." If this insistence is linked to the issues of Egyptology and Orientalism, to epistemology and historiography, it is done in recognition of the fact that "few early Egyptologists

---

41. Asante, *Idea,* 8.

42. Brodkey, quoted in Asante, *Idea,* 139, 25, 157. Asante goes on to argue that "all analysis is culturally centered and flows from ideological assumptions" (159).

43. Ibid., 3, 11.

44. Ibid., 4.

45. Ibid., 163; *Kemet,* 36.

46. Asante, *Kemet,* 167–168.

could divorce their hegemonic attitudes towards knowledge about other people from their political position in the world."[47] This is a position that Roth supports when she acknowledges that Egyptology is a Eurocentric discipline.

This observation prompts Asante's conclusion that "the last five hundred years of world history have been devastating for the acquisition of knowledge about other than European cultures." As Woodson asserted, it has been devastating to the very construction of knowledge itself given the fetters imposed by Western hegemony.[48]

Asante's epistemological notions are clearly related to Woodson's and Du Bois's critiques of Western education, American education in particular, and the ways in which it marginalizes Africa, Africans, and peoples of African descent. Asante points out that "Woodson . . . provided the Afrocentric paradigm with critical interpretations of what Western education does to African people" and "provides us with a general discussion of the entire educational enterprise." Woodson awakened a recognition of the "need for transforming Western education."[49]

Again, the issues of choice and "valorization" indicative of Hegel's discussions and construction of history are key here. Asante argues that Hegel had the benefit of reading the accounts of the French expedition to Egypt, yet he chose not to use them in his construction of the history of the world in general, and that of Africa in particular. This information could not prevent him from concluding that the "Egyptian Spirit" was "imbruted." However, even its brutish nature would not allow Hegel to link it to Africa, which had neither history nor culture. But it did imply that Egyptian culture could not be considered "high culture" and therefore could in many ways be dismissed.[50]

The "valorization inherent in the choice of facts and concepts" is historiographic, both in terms of the construction of history and in terms of critiquing that construction. Afrocentrism, in part given the way that Asante has presented it, is a critique that receives a certain epistemological and philosophical mooring because of the ways in which he employs his sources. That employment reveals the basis for the writing of new histories while recognizing older histories, historiographies, and epistemologies. Afrocentrism as it is presented here also recognizes that the writing of history is key to ways of knowing.

47. Ibid., 21, 16, 40, 57, 139.
48. Ibid., 21.
49. Ibid.,161, 150.
50. Georg Wilhelm Friedrich Hegel, *The Philosophy of History*, translated by J. Sibree (London: Colonial Press, 1900), 219. Asante, *Kemet*, 32.

Within the context of African America, those new ways of writing history, of constructing knowledge, have been historically validated by almost two hundred years of historical discourse carried on by peoples of African descent in the Western hemisphere.

The historiography (historiographies) represented in approximately two hundred years of African American historical writing is a critique of historians and the histories they have written, both within and without this specific community. As important, it also proposes new ways of writing histories, recognizing that history is the "fundamental integrater" of our experiences—of our ways of knowing.[51]

In many ways, like a good student of history, Asante anticipated Will:

[T]he neglect of African origins and contributions to the world's intellectual history in effect misrepresents much knowledge and perpetuates a narrow scholarship. . . . A parochial, ethnocentric, xenophobic view of the world constitutes a serious problem for multicultural realities.[52]

It might be asked when the Afrocentric project is evaluated in toto, whose histories are "meritricious misrepresentations . . . for ideological purposes"? We may find that *neither* side is lacking in partisan debate; but further investigation also reveals that the Afrocentric position is neither as static nor as monolithic as some of its most strident critics imply.

The historiographic concerns are evident. Asante indicates that the call for Afrocentricity is a call for a "new historiography" whose central concern is the "place of Africa as a real and imagined fact in the rediscovery of our past." I construe that "past" to be global when Asante goes on to add his concern for the expansion of *human history* by "creating a new path for interpretation."[53] This position is akin to the that of Eric Wolf in his work *Europe and the People Without History.*[54]

In this light, Asante and the entire Afrocentric project assert that "a people who have been relegated to the fringes of society must now be looked upon as players in the field." Such a perspective, from all sides of this discourse, becomes part of the "historical process of humanizing the world . . . the active . . . self-conscious advancement of the humanizing motif in every sector of society." This is a process that

51. Asante, *Kemet*, 30.

52. Asante, *Idea*, 166.

53. Ibid., 9.

54. Eric R. Wolf, *Europe and the People without History* (Berkeley: University of California Press, 1997).

Afrocentrism helps make possible, a process that through the reinterpretation of history will give whites "a new way out of their collective dilemma." Here, the reclamation of Egypt begins "the necessary reconstruction."[55]

This "reconstruction" is essentially what Du Bois sought, according to Asante. And though Du Bois was not "Afrocentric," he "prepared the world for Afrocentrism. . . . Afrocentricity was the most logical end of his brilliant growth pattern." Du Bois's intellectual and political life was the evolution of an "unyielding mission" whose goal "was the humanizing of the world through the humanizing of America" while wrestling with the "contradictions of [the] Eurocentric view."[56]

55. Asante, *Idea*, 32. Asante, *Afrocentricity* (Trenton: Africa World Press, 1988), 48, 96, 104.
56. Ibid., 16–17.

NINE

The Thesis and Its Refinement

I consider myself a "Diopian."

Molefe Asante, Idea

Cheikh Anta Diop

What does such a statement as the epigraph to this chapter mean? What is its import and implications? It is in the consequence of writing this work a provocative declaration. It is also a fundamental starting point for understanding much of what has emerged as Afrocentric or Africa-centered thought and discourse in the United States. It implies, as Roth has pointed out, that this discourse is international in scope; it is dynamic and diverse in its formation, perspectives, and interpretations. To declare oneself a "Diopian" is also a statement of declaration as to where one believes the critical theory begins. It declares the theory as political—a theory that has a specific agenda that centers on an Egypt that is "black" in the conventional, modern, racialized definition of the term. Yet this blackness in descriptive and discursive terms also attempts to transcend the conventional. To make such a declaration is to be combative.

In 1956, at the First International Congress of Black Writers and Artists, Cheikh Anta Diop laid down the first proposition of his thesis: "We have come to discover that the ancient Pharaonic Egyptian civilization was undoubtedly a Negro civilization."[1] Diop's statement was that

---

1. Mercer Cook, translator's preface to Cheikh Anta Diop, *The African Origins of Civilization: Myth or Reality* (New York: Lawrence Hill, 1974), ix.

much more important in the circle in which he delivered it because he became respected, as Theophile Obenga would argue, as "the only Black African of his generation to receive training as an Egyptologist."[2] Diop's writings, particularly in translation, became critical to the construction of Afrocentrism as an American paradigm. The America "Nile Valley School" emerged from it as one of several modes of thought that would be associated with Afrocentrism as a broader phenomenon.

Diop's statement needs to be given some contextual and historical bases. Diop's remarks were delivered in the charged atmosphere of post–World War II political activity marked by challenges to colonialism and imperialism. Diop, a Senegalese student, was a product of the French colonial enterprise and had been one of the leaders of the student opposition to French rule. Understanding this context, some scholars attempt to dismiss Diop's work or discredit him because of his activism. They need to, however, give "serious attention to his Egypt-centered scholarship." It is a body of scholarly material that deserves the same scrutiny and intellectual analysis as the work of Bernal. After all, Bernal is an heir to Diop's legacy and an illustration of Diop's effort and the validity of his thesis. As Valentine Mudimbe has argued, though Bernal has been "reproached . . . for having played down Cheikh Anta Diop," Bernal's work "strongly accented Cheikh Anta Diop's hypothesis by diffusing the Senegalese scholar's 'black factor' into 'Afroasiatic roots' of classical Greco-Roman civilization."[3]

Serious examination of Diop's work also points to a fundamental point of divergence with Bernal, a point of divergence that can also be read as complementary and globalizing in terms of granting Afrocentrism a wider purview. Kenneth Curtis defines this difference as "directional": a difference regarding the directions of cultural diffusion.

Bernal's thesis, though hardly discussed as such, is a diffusionist thesis. The diffusionist aspect of Diop's work is one of the areas in which he has received the greatest criticism. This difference of direction is related to the fact that Bernal's thesis focuses on Egyptian impact on Europe. Diop, recognizing that impact, also raises the same issue concerning Egyptian cultural dynamic in relation to Africa. It is within the difference of these contexts that Curtis argues that Bernal's thesis is Eurocentric while Diop's seeks a new interpretation for his analytical synthesis.[4]

2. Ibid., ix.

3. Valentine Y. Mudimbe, *The Idea of Africa* (Bloomington: Indiana University Press,1994), 24, 101.

4. Kenneth Curtis, "The Historiography of Centrism and Diffusionism in African History: Diop's Legacy," paper presented at the Second International Conference of the World History Association, Florence (June 1993), 4, 11, 33, 47.

For some, such a notion is specious and speculative at best. Yet for others it holds real possibilities, which Diop attempts to illustrate graphically. Curtis points out that Diop's post–World War II critique was devoted to "a critical examination of African history" at a time when Africans were "not considered important enough to have history." We need only refer to the Trevor Roper citation that opens this work to see what Curtis has in mind. Only four years separate Trevor Roper's contention from Diop's declaration. Diop's work indicates that not only is there such a thing a African history, or histories, but there is also such a thing as "African conceptions of ancient history."[5]

Though Bernal attempts to distance himself from Diop, Diop's work, as Curtis puts it, is an "anticipation" of Bernal. Through Bernal, because of the racial dynamics of American intellectual discourse in particular, a major theoretical premise is placed in the main arena of American intellectual life. This was witnessed in the widespread willingness to take up serious scholarly debate on Black Athena. It was also seen in the little-noted inclusion of Diop and fellow African Egyptologist, Theophile Obenga, among the scholars who wrote the UNESCO History of Africa. Within the context of volume 2 of the UNESCO work, Ancient Civilizations of Africa, of equal critical import was the inclusion of the "Annex to Chapter 1: Report on 'The Peopling of Ancient Egypt and the Deciphering of the Meroitic Script.'" Within this volume, particularly in this annex, some serious debate ensued that illustrates the parameters of the current discourse.[6]

The annex consisted of documentation on a symposium held in Cairo January 28 through February 3, 1974, predating Bernal's work and the UNESCO volume by a decade or more. The symposium discussions outline the complexity and convolutions of the arguments presented on all sides of the debate. They are also an indication of racialized thinking in every quarter, including among "Egyptian" Arabs. So here, even Asante's criticism of Said receives some historical relief. One instance that is particularly illuminating is the reversion on the part of some participants to speculate on the "whiteness" of Nubia in the last quarter of the twentieth century.

It is not clear what impact, if any, these discussions had on Bernal and the production of Black Athena. They were, however, certainly an extension of and amendments to a thesis that Diop had begun to ar-

5. Ibid., 4, 5.

6. "Annex to Chapter 1: Report of the Symposium on 'The Peopling of Ancient Egypt and the Deciphering of the Meroitic Script,'" in G. Mokhtar, ed., General History of Africa, Volume 2: Ancient Civilizations of Africa (Berkeley: University of California Press, 1990) (abridged edition).

ticulate as early as 1948 and that had its earliest culmination in the publication of *Nations negres et culture* (1954) and the subsequent volumes *L'Unite culturelle de l'Afrique noire* (1959) and *L'Afrique precoloniale* (1960). Interestingly enough, these three volumes were published in Paris by the *Presence Africaine* group. *L'Anteriorite des civilizations negres: mythe ou verite historique* followed in 1967.

Nations negres et culture and *L'Anteriorite des civilizations negres* became the centerpieces for Diop's most influential English translation, *The African Origins of Civilization: Myth or Reality*. Interestingly, the translated title and its tone provide an attitude in English that may or may not have been intended in French. Where Bernal, in hindsight, saw "Black" as opposed to "African" Athena unfortunate, the "African Origins of Civilization" may have been incendiary. It is here that the American discussion of Afrocentrism begins in earnest. The only drawback to its commencement is that so many regard it as having no precedent.

As Mercer Cook wrote in the translator's preface to *The African Origins of Civilization*, the volume was a "refutation of many ideas of Egyptologists, anthropologists," and the like. As Cook points out, Immanuel Wallerstein had noted that Diop's thesis of Egyptians as Negroes

> "has the interesting effect of inverting Western cultural assumptions.
> . . . [I]f the ancient Egyptians were Negroes, then European civilization is but a derivative of African achievement."

Wallerstein also noted that Diop was not the first to make such an argument. Du Bois had made it several decades before, as had Woodson.[7]

With all this talk of "Negroes," however, Diop informs the reader that his work is about "culture" more so than race. It is the rehabilitation of the "cultural concept," that is key to "restoring the collective African personality."[8] Asante's construction of the "composite" African is an echo of Diop's collective personality. The terms also suggest that there is little here that might be regarded as essential. The cultural core of the thesis is learned and therefore consciously transmitted if it is to have optimal impact.

Just as Diop anticipated Bernal, he also anticipated many of his critics. To charges of myth-making and historical extravagance, he answered that those who promoted his thesis could not attempt to "delude the masses . . . by unveiling a mythical, embellished past." By

7. Ibid., ix, x.
8. Diop, *Origins*, xiii.

the same token, he held that he would not be barred from using the same tactics to address his critics as they used to criticize his position.[9] In this regard, Mudimbe has commented that Bernal and others underexploit "potential powerful 'allies'" such as Sir James Frazer, E. A. Wallis Budge, Seligman, and Henri Frankfort.[10]

Diop called for the "formation of teams . . . of honest, bold research workers, allergic to complacency and busy substantiating and exploring ideas expressed in our work." This appeal carried particular weight for those Diop called "young American scholars." It was his belief that "the American contribution to this final phase could be decisive."[11]

These scholars would substantiate the thesis that the "history of Black Africa must be connected to the history of Egypt." The implications of such substantiation were feared and foreshadowed in Diop's notion that the world would no longer be able to view Africa as an "insolvent debtor" but as the "very initiator" of Western civilization. The world would be compelled to recognize Egypt as "the Mother of all civilization." It was this exact bias that prompted James Carter's objection in his letter to *Civilization* in the wake of the Gerald Early article "Understanding Afrocentrism." Carter feared that just this sort of assertion would lend credence to the idea that Afrocentrism was espoused solely by a "cabal of misguided dreamers who think Western Civilization was invented in Africa."[12]

This is, however, exactly what Diop wished; that the academy come to grips with the fact that Africa was indeed the seat of Western civilization. To accomplish this task he began the reconstruction of Herodotus and other Greeks. Diop maintained that Herodotus was "not a passive reporter of incredible tales and rubbish, 'a liar'" but that he helped to inaugurate commentary on Egypt's sustained role in initiating Mediterranean peoples in civilization.[13]

Diop follows Du Bois; he is echoed by Bernal; Roth speaks to him by implication. In fact, Bernal reads in much the same way when we pick up Diop: "The birth of Egyptology [was] marked by the need to destroy the memory of a Negro Egypt at all costs and in all minds."[14] To substantiate this claim, we need only refer to the impeti of imperialism and slavery, and Nott, Glidden, Morton, and the New School of

9. Ibid., xiii.
10. Mudimbe, *Idea*, 102.
11. Diop, *Origins*, xiii, xvii.
12. Cf. 13; italics added.
13. Diop, *Origins*, 4, 10.
14. Ibid., 45.

American Ethnography's attempt to take the question of Egyptian identity "out of the hands of the Greeks."

Diop's thesis operated at cross purposes with the idea that

"we are not accustomed, in fact, to endow the Black or related races with too much intelligence, or even enough intelligence to make the first discoveries necessary for civilization."[15]

To do this in the case of Egypt would be a recognition of the "essential identity of genius, culture, and race"; it would mean that "all Negroes can legitimately trace their culture to ancient Egypt and build a modern culture on that foundation."[16]

This is exactly Levine's criticism of "Egypt as metonym," the ability and probability for all peoples of African descent, no matter where they are, no matter where they hail from, to claim Egypt. Yet her argument against such an act has little veracity unless she and all the other critics of this notion are willing to forgo American, Anglo-Saxon, Teutonic, Nordic, and so on, claims to a Greco-Roman paradigm fashioned from nineteenth-century Romanticism.

The cultural diffusionist aspects of Diop's thesis also can be summarized in this way from the ancient to the present: in spite of imperialism and colonization, and even in some ways because of modern racial slavery, there is no interruption in African history. Mudimbe, relying on Foucault, explains it in this way: "[T]here is no such thing as a history of silence, which does not imply that there is no way of writing a history of silenced experiences." Foucault goes on to say:

The description of a statement does not . . . consist in rediscovering the unsaid whose place it occupies; or how one can reduce it to a silent, common text; but, on the contrary, in discovering what special place it occupies, what ramifications for the system of formations make it possible to map its localizations, how it is isolated in the general dispersion of statements.[17]

Diop maps the "localizations" and declares that "Egyptology will stand on solid ground only when it unequivocally recognizes its Negro-African foundation."[18]

15. Ibid., 78.
16. Ibid., 140.
17. Mudimbe, *Idea,* 71.
18. Diop, Origins, 148.

UNESCO: General History of Africa

Some critical evaluation of the importance and impact of Diop and his thesis should emanate from the position that it retained in the UNESCO debates that provided impetus to the opening chapters of volume 2 of the *General History of Africa*. In an incremental fashion, the entire UNESCO project is a witness to the attempt to construct an Africa-centered history of the continent. Diop's drive is central here. It becomes manifest in the most simple way through his inclusion and that of his protégé, Theophile Obenga, among the team of authors that began explorations into the "Ancient Civilizations of Africa." Diop and Obenga's efforts are underlined by the inclusion of a "dissenting" report of a sort, in terms of the annex of the "Report of the Symposium on 'The Peopling of Ancient Egypt and the Deciphering of the Meroitic Script.'" As I mentioned before, the inclusion of this report emphasized the contentions and their levels that are still prevalent in the current discourse. This might also be considered a new debate, given the forum in which it occurs. If nothing else, however, it is a re-constituted debate, given the focus on race and its utility (at least as articulated by most of the participants) in the attempt to construct a comprehensive history of Africa from the prehistoric to the present.

In this regard, the most remarkable, though probably not unexpected, aspect of the discussions of the 1974 symposium that find their way into the volume in question is the way in which all parties seemed wedded to a scientific construction of race, while denying both its plausibility and possibility. Curtis attempts to pull Diop from this morass by maintaining that Diop recognized that the concept of race has no scientific validity but used it to attack Eurocentric interests who themselves use the concept to meet their needs. Curtis notes that "race is an important factor in history" and, for Diop, "a fundamental one."[19]

This rationale has a fair amount of credibility in some circles; however, in others, it points to one weakness in the Afrocentric thesis that these critics argue is still bound by Eurocentric prescriptions—Afrocentrism and Afrocentrists themselves have not yet escaped the very Enlightenment that they criticize.[20] Diop's usage is both interesting and oxymoronic. It brings to mind his declaration that his critics will not themselves be allowed to use outmoded concepts like race

19. Curtis, "Historiography," 50.
20. See Appiah, "Europe Turned Upside Down: Fallacies of the New Afrocentrism," *London Times Literary Supplement* (February 2, 1993), 24. Mudimbe, *Invention of Africa* and *The Idea of Africa*.

while criticizing Diop and company for using the concept of race in regard to the sources they might employ.

Diop's chapter in the UNESCO volume offers little that is new or controversial. He moves from Louis Leakey's premise regarding the peopling of the Earth—a premise recently supported by DNA and mitochondria studies—to argue for a monogenetic origin for humankind "at the sources of the Nile."[21] From there, using sources—some of which might be regarded as "outmoded," and yet be applauded, on the other hand, by scholars such as Mudimbe—Diop establishes the phenotypic, if not racial, characteristics of the ancient Egyptians. Relying on Emile Massoulard, Falkenberg, Petrie, G. Elliot Smith, Giuseppi Sergi, and others, Diop equates the "brown race" Egyptians and Sergi's "'Mediterranean or Eurafrican race'" as "simply a euphemism for negro."[22]

The historiographic and epistemologic nub of the entire debate, not simply Diop's perspective on it, is racial. As Diop points out, "[I]n current textbooks the question is suppressed: in most cases it is simply and flatly asserted that the Egyptians were white and the honest layman is left with the impression that any such assertion must have a prior basis of solid research."[23]

If we couple this statement of racial assumptions and "impressions of solid research" with notions of black incapacity and Curtis's observation, repeated in Trevor Roper's dictum, that there is no history of Africa worthy of representation, then a critical, yet possibly unintended aspect of Diop's work emerges. Diop, in spite of the ambivalences seen in his denial and use of race, undermines racial assumptions in the very way that Shelley Fisher Fishkin suggests it might done through the "interrogation of whiteness." Diop compels "whiteness to speak its name" by questioning the assumption of Egyptian whiteness. At another level, the interrogation might conclude in this manner: "accepted: given modern racial classifications, the Egyptians could not have been "black," or conceived of themselves as "black", how could they, then, given modern racial classifications, have been "white" or conceived of themselves as 'white?'" Again, when we refer to one of the specific purposes of the Afrocentric project, a challenge to European, and therefore "white," universality, Diop and others move to a challenge of the "assumptions" of Europe and "whiteness" as the sole arbiter of civilization. The project emerges as much grander, much

21. Cheikh Anta Diop, "Origin of the Ancient Egyptians," in Mokhtar, *General History of Africa, Volume 2* (abridged edition), 15.

22. Ibid., 16.

23. Ibid., 17.

more complex, and much more diverse than many of its detractors or champions have envisioned. This is illustrated in the refinement of the approach that Diop has set out.

More than a decade before *Black Athena,* scholars, most of whom would not be characterized as Afrocentrists, characterized Egypt as African. Their definitions of this characterization left room for considerable discourse and debate over what this meant. It is clear, however, that there were those other than Diop and Obenga who would have allowed this characterization to shade itself with the implications of modern, racial "blackness."[24] The nature of those 1974 discussions also spoke to the implications of Diop's appeal for "teams . . . of honest, bold, research workers" that must be linked to the call for new methodologies[25] within which the theoretical premises of Afrocentrism must be addressed. Diop explicitly found encouragement in the emergence of scholarship in the United States, especially, though not exclusively, among African Americans.[26]

Refinement

A reading of Asante alone reveals that there is much more to Afrocentrism than simply a pejorative and narrow nationalism, an exclusionary and xenophobic blackness–racism in the reverse. A reading of other Afrocentric authors might reveal what Appiah has stated about the diversity of the body of work and its quality. An extended reading of Afrocentrism also points to the way that it has evolved as a body of work and the ways in which that evolution has been the product of the conscious refinement of the thesis.

Early's depiction of the commercial, pretentious, and shallow Afrocentrism and its implications of a static, if not degenerate, intellectual endeavor is in keeping with Long's observations in his 1774 *History of Jamaica.*[27] Indeed, Long's was the historical notion applied to most black intellectual activity, and Early's tone and approach to a critique of Afrocentrism mirrors this.[28]

24. "Annex," 34–35, 38–45.

25. Ibid., 35, 36, 55.

26. Diop, *Origins,* 16.

27. See Long, *History of Jamaica,* vol. 2, 349, 351–365.

28. Having said this, I need to emphasize that my objections to the Early piece are lodged in just that: his tone and his approach to Afrocentrism, not the fact that he has chosen to critique it, pro or con. Early seems not to find any intellectual merit in the thesis of an Africa-centered discourse; to that degree, his work comes across as flippant. I contrast his work with that of Appiah.

An examination of the evolution and refinement of Afrocentrism might yield some rather interesting results if we were to begin with Maulana Karenga, given the fact that Karenga has been directly involved with so much of what for Early illustrates the intellectual vapidity of Afrocentrism. Among the things Early references are Kwanzaa and the Kawaida movement.

Tied to these popular conceptions, the fact that Asante finds "Karenga's concept of historical fundamentalism" as "the key discipline in providing a knowledge base" could hardly make Early respect Afrocentrism. It does, however, give insight into what Asante finds essential to the construction of theory and the utility of history and its construction in the development of Afrocentrism. Karenga's insight into history and historical construction—black history, black historical construction, black historiography—is crucial to Afrocentrism's intellectual currency.[29] Karenga articulates what Afrocentric history is supposed to do.

In linking Karenga to Woodson, Asante establishes a historical continuity. He sets the parameters for the evolution and refinement of theory. Afrocentrism is contextualized by historiographic and epistemological construction. It is Karenga who calls for the "reconstruction" of history within the context of "reconstructing African-American life and history."[30] It is essentially the same call that Woodson made some seventy-three years earlier with the establishment of the Association for the Study of Negro Life and History.

Karenga's chapter "Black History" in his work *Introduction to Black Studies,* begins with the declaration that black studies' "Core task . . . is the rescue and reconstruction of Black history and humanity." It might be construed that Karenga's "humanity" is solely black, but I believe that further reading of Karenga, even in a way that is not particularly nuanced or analytical, reveals that the terminology is inclusive— inclusive in the same ways that Asante argues that Afrocentrism will liberate Europeans and Eurocentric thinkers.

Karenga has chosen the "rescue" of humanity, not solely of black people, through the reconstruction of black history, a history that is illustrative of the potential of humankind. This history and, therefore, the act of conceptualizing and writing this history are part of the process of "humanizing the world," shaping the world in a human image. The reconstruction of black history, within this context, also recognizes that in a very natural manner "Africans shape the world in a particular way . . . in their own image and interests."

29. Asante, *Kemet,* 31.
30. Asante, *Afrocentricity,* 20.

Such shaping is merely an addition to "the richness and beauty of human diversity."[31]

It is interesting to point out here that just as critics of Asante have noted, a considerable portion of Karenga's paradigm is also rooted in Enlightenment doctrine with its discussion of shaping the world in a human image and its assumption of struggle with and control over nature. Yet it might be assumed that such similarities might make Afrocentrism more accessible to its critics or at least exhibit a shared set of sensibilities that might make dialogue that much more possible.

For Karenga, "history reveals itself as human practice." Its "motive force is struggle," yet that struggle has its own diversity that need not be dominated by race, class, gender, and so on. This is an interesting proposition given the way in which Afrocentrism is conventionally read and historical formation is generalized. Karenga summarizes "four major oppositions" in his construction of history: nature, society, other humans, and the immediate self.[32]

Karenga argues that history is the "key social science, the social science on which all other social sciences depend." And, he continues,

> as the mirror and avenue of human struggle and progress, history has a special relevance for blacks which is rooted in its contribution to their intellectual and political emancipation. This contribution takes on its special meaning due to the challenge posed by gross denial, deformation and destruction of Black history as both a record and process.[33]

One need not necessarily agree with the argument, but even in disagreement it would take a considerable stretch to characterize it as far-fetched, "radical," or "extreme." A critical reading of Hegel, Marx, Spengler, or Toynbee would support Karenga's position. Within the context of critical readings, Karenga argues that black history is a "corrective for the self-indulgent myths of racism." Again, I would argue that this goal is not beyond the pale; it is in keeping with the "enlightened" discourse of the day. Where it might part company with some who engage that discourse is its reference to Diop's conceptualization of the black world as the "initiator of 'western civilization.'" Aside from this, there are not many who would even contest Karenga's questioning of the validity and utility of Eurocentric histories of Africa and

31. Maulana Karenga, *Introduction to Black Studies* (Los Angeles: University of Sankore Press, 1989), 42–43.
32. Ibid., 42, 47.
33. Ibid., 47–48.

peoples of African descent, and the ways in which the historians who construct these histories have evaluated data.[34]

Refocusing our attention, Karenga moves us back to the central point of contention in our own culture wars. In looking at the scholarship in black history for the last half of the 1970s, Karenga notes that Egypt is central to his argument. Again, he centralizes it in a way that is all too familiar to students of the evolution of African American historiography. Karenga indicates that what he is most taken by in terms of the black historical scholarship of the late 1970s is the assertion that Ethiopia is the root of Egyptian origins.[35] Unfortunately, Karenga makes no indication that he is celebrating a historical and historiographic tradition that preceded him by decades when both Hansberry and Snowden offered the same conclusions. He does, however, let us know that he is quite aware of Du Bois's "African Egypt."[36] Here he summarizes and strikes a familiar theme that by extrapolation places him in the company of David Walker and others. Karenga concludes that the goal of black history is the representation and presentation of "Blacks in the roles of both producers and products of history, those who make and are made by these historical experiences."[37]

Even within the framework of contention, Karenga's aspirations for black history certainly make these elements of Afrocentrism reasonable. Ali Mazrui has referred to Afrocentrism as "an antithesis . . . a dialectic seeking to negate the negation." The negation is Eurocentricity. Mazrui asks if Afrocentrism might in fact be in search of a " synthesis" as "an aspect of multiculturalism." And though Mazrui is willing to speculate that Afrocentrism and multiculturalism may be "parallel themes, separate but equal," he also sees in the work of Karenga a "bridge building between the two."[38]

While Mazrui poses real questions about the ability of Afrocentrism to be multicultural, he recognizes that the facility to enjoin the issue of Africa from an "African perspective" is a valuable asset shared by the challenges of both Afrocentrism and multiculturalism to Eurocentrism. He muses whether or not multiculturalism is, in fact, the synthesis of the Afrocentric/Eurocentric dialectic.[39]

Part of what Mazrui suggests in his critique and refinement of Afrocentrism focuses on the vehicle. Mazrui argues that the Afrocentric

34. Ibid., 51, 54.
35. Ibid., 55.
36. Ibid., 57.
37. Ibid., 73.
38. Ali Mazrui, "Afrocentrism Versus Multiculturalism? A Dialectic in Search of a Synthesis," address delivered at the James S. Coleman African Studies Center, May 5, 1993. 2.
39. Ibid., 2.

project is much larger than the American arena (the African American arena); this is, in large part, the argument taken up by Paul Gilroy. In this light, African American studies is limited in that it confines its area of deliberation to the United States. "Black studies" could also be argued as problematic, given the various definition that might apply to "black," especially outside of the United States. Mazrui prefers "Africana Studies" as representative of a "globalized Africa"; Africa and its diaspora.[40]

Mazrui argues that Afrocentrism's "Gloriana Afrocentricity" and "Proletariana Afrocentricity," the notions of "the captured African as a co-builder of modern civilization," might be better posited in and given proper direction within the framework of Africana studies. This contextualization would provide for the possibility of seeing "Afrocentricity as a perspective on world studies . . . a method for looking at the history of the world."[41]

Mazrui has taken an interesting position, given that some Afrocentrists, such as Asante, have dismissed him and his work as it pertains to Afrocentrism. C. Tsheloane Keto seems to have anticipated Mazrui's argument and answered quite positively in terms of delineating the ways in which Afrocentrism (Keto's "Africa-centered perspective") lends itself to multiculturalism and the possible variations on telling the history of the world, inquiry into historiography, and explications that expand our ways of knowing.

Keto's work is extremely important as an illustration of the paths of refinement that Afrocentrism might take, showing Afrocentrism as a working thesis that is being critically evaluated by its advocates. It is a thesis open to self-criticism.

Keto moves the refinement of Afrocentrism further. He picks up on Karenga's statement of the obvious: different peoples will see and construct the world in their own images. This construction, for Karenga, is historical, historiographic, and epistemological. Any attempt to understand Africa and peoples of African descent must take this fact into account. Any attempt to understand world history must acknowledge it.

Keto's quest, through "Africa-centered" histories, is for histories of Africa and peoples of African descent that focus on Africa as context and actor, specifically and globally. Keto is engaged in the construction of "nonhegemonic" history. In the same way that Asante acknowledges the utility of Eurocentric scholarship in its context, Keto speaks to the possibilities for scholarship that have emerged from the develop-

40. Ibid., 1. Paul Gilroy, *The Black Atlantic: Modernity and Double Consciousness* (Cambridge: Harvard University Press, 1993).

41. Mazrui, "Afrocentrism," 4.

ment of non-European, non-Eurocentric scholarship. These are presented by a "perspective within Eurocentric scholarship [that] has left open the possibility of a meeting ground for a nonhegemonic Europe-centered perspective, a nonhegemonic Africa-centered perspective as well as other nonhegemonic perspectives." The possibilities are real in that Keto believes that "we have achieved this theoretical common ground."[42]

Here Keto is referencing the work of scholars like William Appleman Williams, Said, and Wolf. He is certainly aware of the discourses on alternative epistemologies, and postmodern and postcolonial studies. These all represent nonhegemonic discourses of which Africa-centered histories and attendant studies are an integral part.

In defining his Africa-centered approach, Keto emphasizes the importance of defining terminology. He is quite aware of the historical, geopolitical, and temporal dynamics of the construction of "Africa." Having pointed this out, he goes on to argue that

> the Africa-centered approach of history rests on an unpretentious common sense premise that it is legitimate and intellectually useful to treat the continent of Africa as a geographical and cultural starting point, a "center" so to speak that serves as reference point in the process of gathering and interpreting historical knowledge about peoples of African descent throughout the world and people in Africa itself.

From this vantage, point the Africa-centered perspective serves as an "agent for change within a re-emerging school of knowledge . . . a tool for analytical investigation in the human sciences."[43]

Keto reemphasizes the notion that Afrocentrism as theory is as much about historiography and epistemology as it is about anything else. At its most critical levels it is about compelling us to consider what it is we think we know and how we come to know it. Keto feels the need to address the "categorization of knowledge" by referring us to the very initiation of the modern, Western university systems and the partitioning and compartmentalization (departmentalization) of "social sciences" and "humanities." Keto looks at these, in the historiographic sense, as "specialized forms of history" that are replete with their own linkages to the study of the past, to studying the past, and, therefore, their own ways of knowing. And they are being challenged. The Africa-centered perspective is one of the challengers.

---

42. C. Tsehloane Keto, *The Africa Centered Perspective of History: An Introduction* (Blackwood, New Jersey: K. A. Publications, 1991), i.
43. Ibid., 1–2.

In true historiographic fashion, Keto reminds us that history is always to be challenged as a "reconstituted past" that automatically implies a "selective and interpreted" past. In this way, Keto extends the historiographic critique by arguing that the "selective and interpretive" nature of doing history provides a "place for Europe-centered, Asia-centered, and America-centered analysis of Africa and Africans . . . to counteract an overly parochialized view of Africa by Africans that might emerge in an Africa-centered analysis." Of course, "in turn . . . a reciprocal need for an Africa-centered, Asia-centered, America-centered analysis of Europe" corresponds to this notion of doing history. In fact, the implication is that all histories carry validity if they recognize that they cannot claim universality.[44]

And this is just the case. The current intellectual framework relies "too heavily on conceptual products of Europe-centered constructs." These constructs, in the modern age, are derivations of European imperialism; this is indicated by an epistemology that is dominated by a "European centered intellectual hegemony," though George Will and others might object to such a characterization.

Again the refinement of the intellectual discourse is reflected in Keto's take on Du Bois's notion of "twoness." Keto's reading suggests not simply "warring souls," but the device for reconciling the ways in which any one of us might look at the world. Keto argues that Du Bois's project was, in part, an "[a]ttempt to reconcile 'two centers.'" He goes on to argue that "those who know more than one center understand the conflict of frameworks and are sensitive to the diversity of humanity"; they know this because there is a sense of compassion and empathy engendered that allows for the recognition of global constructions rather than simply parochial ones.

"Those who are unaware of the multiplicity of centers or choose to ignore other centers often believe that their center is the only center that makes sense and interprets the world."[45]

Because the consequences of such thinking have been devastating, Keto concludes that "[w]orld history cannot be constructed outside of a polycentric framework." The result of this conclusion is the past thirty years of "in depth, comparative studies" that have challenged and altered the hegemonic, Europe-centered perspectives that dominated intellectual discourses. These comparative studies have challenged the notion of European universality, the "hidden center" as Keto puts it.

44. Ibid., 5.
45. Ibid., 6–7, 9, 12.

However, Keto acknowledges that there are "important contributions of the Europe-centered framework in the construction of the world's knowledge. . . . [w]e should also . . . acknowledge previous contributions." In fact, he goes on, such an acknowledgment celebrates and perpetuates the "intellectual diversity [that] . . . is at the heart of 'America's becoming.'"[46]

This position, one endorsed by as diverse a group of scholars as Williams, John Lukacs, Asante, Karenga, and Bernal, is supported by what Sande Cohen articulates as the realization that "intellectual acceptance of academia as a just player in the overall organization of knowledge" is open to serious debate.[47] Again, among the questions fundamental to such a realization is who is "read" or "heard"? Who is privileged? What discourses are privileged? Within the context of the Africa-centered argument as posed by Keto, the questions are universalized. They are not simply the questions of Afrocentrists.

The Africa-centered position advocates "tolerance and inclusion." Yet, it is also intolerant of assigning a "peripheral role for the Africa-centered perspective in the world's growing knowledge industry." The inclusion of the Africa-centered perspective is a contribution that provides "corrective historical insights."[48]

Keto illustrates many times over that the Afrocentric or Africa-centered perspective that he represents is quite capable of self-criticism. Telling of this is his observation that

> the line of hegemony is not only a temptation to Europe-centered scholarship. The Afrocentric perspective can also carry hegemonic undertones when all claims to progress in all regions of the world are explained in terms of the African presence and the African presence alone.[49]

Keto defines the Africa-centered perspective as "part of a global intellectual movement" involved in the creation of a "pluriversal." It is a movement that is "diversity affirming" in the construction of the "human sciences of the twenty-first century." He argues that such an approach must be "gender sensitive" and nonhegemonic.[50]

Yet Keto is compelled by the Africa-centered agenda to return the reader to the centralizing force of refined theory. Africa-centered his-

46. Ibid., 18–19, 25.
47. Ibid.
48. Ibid., 27.
49. Ibid., 28–29.
50. Ibid., 29, 38.

tory recognizes and stresses the connection between the ancient Nile Valley and the rest of Africa in an "interconnected temporal context rather than on the basis of an extreme diffusionist model." It speaks to this interconnectedness in the desire to explore the history of Africa prior to the dessication of the Sahara and the advent of Islam.[51]

In spite of the ways in which Keto articulates the Africa-centered project most analysis of Afrocentrism reverts to the conflictual. For example, Keto points out that "[n]owhere is the conflict of centers, frameworks and perspectives so vividly portrayed than in Arthur Schlesinger's discussion in *The Disuniting of America.*" Schlesinger's choices of illustration contrast "the American Dream" with what other observers might term "the American Nightmare." For Keto, Schlesinger's is one of the latest in a series of Europe-centered hegemonic works that assign a peripheral role to peoples of African descent as well as many others. These others, along with Africans, are cast as an "enduring problem."[52]

Though the past ten years or so may provide some variation in the reading, the Schlesinger thesis along with that of Daniel Patrick Moynihan and the writings of pundits like Patrick Buchanan and George Will underscore a fundamental tenet of Enlightenment thought that remains prevalent to this day. African American culture has few, if any, positive attributes from the perspective of Eurocentric hegemony. Peoples of African descent are "denied [a] sense of contribution to the formation of America's historical community." The Africa-centered perspective "opposes the silencing of the historical African voices in that debate about the formulation of American culture." That refusal to keep silent is witness to America's ongoing culture wars; it is also witness to the creation of a "new focus for evaluating historical choices." It is a historiographic witness.[53]

The sophistication and refinement of the Africa-centered project, the growth and development of Afrocentrism as an intellectual enterprise, is seen in the inclusive nature of the work as it is outlined by scholars such as Keto. It is also seen in the increasing vigor in which a growing number of Afrocentric scholars exhibit the ability and the desire to critique the excesses and weaknesses of the thesis. As Keto puts it, this project is not about "glorifying pigmentology in academic guise"; it is "not . . . blanket approval" for all utterances that present themselves as Afrocentrism. The exercise centers on the development of what Keto terms a "self-disciplining perspective." This attempt at

51. Ibid., 38.
52. Ibid., 42–43.
53. Ibid., 43–46.

self-discipline and critique is seen at several turns in the later works of Karenga and Asante, and, of course, Keto himself.

The desire is a resurrection of "intellectual discourse that will provide a critique of domination." And though Keto is not overly concerned with Egypt, he maintains that the issue of Egypt cannot be separated from this discourse.[54]

In many ways, a discussion of the refinement of the Afrocentric discourse could have begun with mention of Theophile Obenga. Yet as briefly as he might be mentioned here, Obenga marks a beginning and a bridge in terms of informed critique of Diop's views and the shaping of a refined product, in several spaces, including the United States.

Again, Curtis regards Obenga's work as one critical line in the refinement of Diop's thesis. In fact, the work of the Congolese scholar and Egyptologist might be regarded, in some ways, as the most critical statement regarding the possibilities and potential in the refinement of Diop's work and Afrocentrism as critical theory.

Linkages are also important here. Obenga, as protégé of Diop, also served as a visiting faculty member in Temple University's Department of African American Studies, headed by Asante. Here, we might speculate that what Curtis has termed as reflective of Obenga's "appreciative yet critical attitude" toward Diop's work and the Afrocentric project in general has become manifest. Obenga's work, as Chris Gray has pointed out, moves from "[e]stablishing an African historical identity to linking up this particular identity with the history of the world as a whole." As Curtis observes, "Obenga has moved towards world history."[55]

From here, the critique of Diop and an emerging Afrocentrism are certainly refined with commentary on both sides of the Atlantic. Mamadou Diouf and Mohamad Mbodj point to this when they warn against an uncritical acceptance of Diop's work, which would have the consequence of reducing "his thesis to ideology." They point out that understanding of Diop's work requires "classical academic discussion in which points of agreement could coexist with points of disagreement" in order to deepen and expand Diop's contribution.[56] The refinement, the promotion of open discourse might be witnessed in Asante's move to an exploration of the philosophical and cultural aspects of Diop's work and how they might play out in Afrocentrism.

54. Ibid., 38, 58.

55. Chris Gray, *Conceptions of History in the Works of Cheikh Anta Diop and Theophile Obenga* (London: Karnak, 1989), quoted in Curtis, "Historiography," 35.

56. Mamadou Diouf and Mohamad Mbodj, "The Shadow of Cheikh Anta Diop," in Valentine Y. Mudimbe, ed., *Surreptitious Speech: Presence Africaine and the Politics of Otherness, 1947–1987* (Chicago: University of Chicago Press, 1991). Quoted in Curtis, "Historiography," 37.

This refinement and openness are certainly explored in Keto's historiographic refinement.[57]

This refinement moves along and challenges the three main tenets of Diop's thesis. Sometimes the challenge comes from Diop himself. From wherever the challenge might emanate, it is an indication that the thesis is neither static nor ahistorical. It is an intellectual body of work characterized by a community of scholarship that is dynamic and not monolithic. It defies the possibility of characterizing all contributors to the discourse as "extreme" or "radical" (whatever such terms might mean in the pejorative). And it makes critical reading and analysis of the works of Afrocentric/Africa-centered scholarship imperative.

57. Ibid., 39, 43–44.

TEN

Reprise

Conclusion by Way of Continuity

Discourse and Dat Course

Ann duCille, *Skin Trade*

Knowledge essentially functions as a form of power.

Valentine Mudimbe, *The Idea of Africa*

Epistemology

This chapter opens with a particular indebtedness to the work of Valentine Y. Mudimbe. Valentine Y. Mudimbe is a very learned man. He is a philosopher. His arguments, in part, mirror Daudi's notions on discourse and power. He knows Philostratus and Hecataeus as well as he knows Sartre and Foucault. Mudimbe received the 1989 Herskowits Award for his scholarship. Yet remarkably, or maybe not so, he is seemingly unknown among the critics of Afrocentrism. Is Mudimbe an Afrocentric? Is Mudimbe Afrocentric? The far more important question, however, may be, does Afrocentrism become more "knowable"—more intelligible—through Mudimbe?

If the refinement of Afrocentrism has moved toward inclusion, if it is an examination of the "pluriversal," as Keto puts it, then how does Mudimbe instruct us in its understanding? In some ways he does this by taking us back to our beginnings in this particular discourse. We are forced to entertain questions of epistemology and historiography, questions of culture and ideology. What Mudimbe does for us most forcefully is bring us back to the consideration of the construction of our identity—or any identity—in the modern period. And in the critical reading that must be mandated for any intellectual enterprise he allows us to reflect on how the construction of modern identity has been key to our construction of the past—and our invention of the past and the present.

In his work *The Invention of Africa*, Mudimbe introduces the construction of Africa along the same lines that Said has articulated concerning the construction of "Orientalism." Within this realization, Mudimbe speaks to the need of the African to reconstruct her- or himself. This need is in fact implicit in both of Mudimbe's titles, *The Invention of Africa* and *The Idea of Africa*.

Mudimbe's discussion is epistemological. This characteristic, is seen in the ways in which he relates the European construction of Africa to the creation of a certain type of knowledge. He loosely equates the *gnosis* of his title with *episteme* as ways of knowing.[1] He is quite clear, however, that they reflect two different ways of knowing. What Mudimbe presents here is a critique of "Western epistemological order," to which, he wants the reader to be clear, the "most explicit 'Afrocentric' descriptions . . . knowingly and unknowingly refer." As a critique of the *entire* Western paradigm (if that is possible), Mudimbe wants his audience to note that Afrocentrism has not yet escaped that paradigm, though he also wants the audience to understand that it is witness to the "transformation of types of knowledge" through the discourse engendered by Afrocentrism as well.[2]

This transformation is seen in the very questioning of the "credibility" of Western definitions of Africa:

[T]oday Africans themselves read, challenge, rewrite, these discourses as a way of explicating and defining their culture, history, and being. It is obvious since its inception, Africanism has been providing its own motives as well as its objects and fundamentally commenting upon its own being while systematically promoting a *gnosis*.[3]

The process is somewhat Newtonian. As duCille puts it, "for every doubly conscious racial or ethnic other constructed by institutions, there is a self attempting to assert its subjectivity." The problem is that such Newtonian dynamics have resulted in a "world out of joint," one that presents a "familiar that is foreign and a self that is alien."[4]

1. Mudimbe, *Invention*, ix.
2. Ibid., x.
3. Ibid., xi.
4. Ann duCille, *Skin Trade*, (Cambridge: Harvard University Press, 1996), 120, 121.

DuCille worries that this disjunction might be the fate of Afrocentrism if some forms of the discourse are allowed to dominate others.

While Mudimbe's "Africanism" may be associated with the product of late nineteenth- and early twentieth-century colonialism, I would maintain that its genesis is much earlier. Its beginning goes back to the first moment and the first act of resistance by those peoples who would be *first* defined as "Africans" in the modern sense of the term by their arrival on the Western shore of the Atlantic. In this context, Mudimbe is right, the colonial period did offer the possibility of "radically new types of discourse on African traditions and cultures."[5]

Just as Said argues of the Orient, Africa was invented by colonialism. This representation was, according to Mudimbe, an "organization," an "arrangement" that transformed "non-European areas into fundamentally European constructs." The task of this construction was to "regenerate" African space and consciousness to meet the exigencies of imperialism—that is, the "integration of . . . histories into the Western perspective." This was the ongoing project of the last quarter of the nineteenth century through the 1950s. The result was what Sachs termed "europeocentrism," a "forced deculturalization . . . on the world scale."[6]

Mudimbe follows a general concurrence that in the span of the late Renaissance through the early Enlightenment the West was experiencing the creation of a new epistemological foundation that by the late eighteenth and early nineteenth centuries would have as its hallmark a significant anti-African bias. This bias had no more profound manifestation than in the sciences and philosophy, which granted to this "new epistemological ordering . . . a theory of understanding and looking at signs in terms of 'the arrangement of identities and differences into ordered tables.'"[7]

As Mudimbe explains this construction, "Africa was discovered in the fifteenth century . . . [and] the slave trade narrated itself accordingly." Africa and the African became exceedingly "ugly" as the slave trade intensified; they became the epitome of "alterity [as] a negative." The African became the essential "other." Mudimbe continues, "We do know what is inscribed in this discovery, the new cultural orders it allowed, and in terms of knowledge, the texts that its discourses built."[8]

Much of the discourse was built on travel literature that was re-

5. Ibid., 1.
6. Ibid., 1–4. Sachs quoted in Mudimbe, *Invention*, 4.
7. Ibid., 12.
8. Mudimbe, *Idea,* 16–17; *Invention*, 12.

garded as proof of African inferiority. We have already been treated to the works of Schaw and Long. Works like these formed the core of what Mudimbe refers to as the "colonial library," a library that was reflective of only one viewpoint, the European.[9]

The construction of such a corpus and the institutions to house it— what Lord Curzon referred to as the "furniture of empire"—was the building and reinforcement of what Mudimbe has termed "epistemological ethnocentrism." It is an ethnicized determination of knowledge and its construction that exists right through the present and can even be seen in the works of liberal thinkers such as Carl Sagan.[10] This epistemological ethnocentrism has a direct bearing on the inability to even entertain the notion of a "black" Egypt. And again we are reminded that colonialism is the "epistemological locus of Africa's invention" and one of the forces key to the myth of the "inherent superiority of the white race." This way of thinking is all in line with what Paul Ricoeur calls the notion of "universal civilization" that assumes a "European center." That center assumes a "cultural monopoly," a hegemony that allows for domination in multiple arenas, not the least of which is the construction of knowledge—the very determination of what constitutes knowledge and who is capable of its production.[11]

Foucault enters the discussion once more by reiterating the role of Enlightenment thought in the ways in which it "define[s] what knowledge can offer about human beings." This new epistemology determined *who* was human through the discourses it produced—discourses that were then, and are now, in competition, contention. The construction of epistemology, the building of knowledge, is a way to chart history. It also embodies the recognition that "knowledge functions as a form of power." This means that epistemology—the construction of knowledge—is interdependent on "systems of power and social control." In effect, the "culture wars"—the struggle over what might be considered knowledge–is a struggle over power and social control.[12]

Historiography

Claude Lévi-Strauss argued that anthropology and history are, in fact, a "two-faced Janus." If the "historical process [accounts] for the growth of knowledge," then some of the new historiographies meet

9. *Invention*
10. Mudimbe, *Invention*, 15.
11. Ibid., 16, 17, 19, 20–21.
12. Ibid., 24–26, 27–28.

Lévi-Strauss's criteria for *"episteme* radically opposed to Western norms . . . that could simultaneously undermine a totalitarian order of knowledge and *push knowledge into territories traditionally rejected as supposedly nonsensical."*[13] Here, Mudimbe, through Lévi-Strauss, has encapsulated the issue central to these culture wars. The Afrocentrists' ire is directly related to *what* is nonsensical. From the standpoint of traditional academe, it has always been black folk, blackness, and the questions they raise that are nonsense and not worthy of discussion. This attitude is based on the physical biases that race as a construction of the modern age has provided as a way of knowing. Given this analysis, to entertain the history of, history among, or history by black peoples—peoples who have no history—is *nonsensical.*

Mudimbe asserts that the Africanist discourse is both "challenge" and "commentary" that is as old as the "invention of Africa." If this is the case, then the historiographic treatments associated with Africa's emergence, specifically in the era of modern slavery, push back Mudimbe's Africanist chronology. These treatments also posit the "invention of Africa" and the beginning of new discourse, new historiography, and new epistemology with the landing of "Africans," particularly those who were enslaved, in the western hemisphere.

This perspective satisfies Lévi-Strauss's dictates at the same moment that it anticipates the emergence of Afrocentrism and Afrocentrism's ability to undermine the current discourse and expand the boundaries of knowledge by asking what is, seemingly, nonsensical. Mudimbe might as well single out Will, Buchanan, Lefkowitz, and others by name in illustrating this contention. This new historiography and epistemology have been created to offer resistance to the "tyranny of history" and the "totalitarian order of knowledge."

Mudimbe allows his interpretation of Foucault and Lévi-Strauss to "bring to African consciousness new reasons for developing original strategies within the social sciences." Some Afrocentrists might take exception. Asante would argue the case of African centrality to Foucault and Lévi-Strauss's consciousness; the notion that the postmodern, postcolonial moment was realized with the first act of African resistance in the "new world"—the "modern world." For duCille, Mudimbe's comment is indicative of the strains between postcolonial, postmodern theorists and Afrocentrists.

Yet Mudimbe's way of moving to the "African *prise de parole* about philosophy and knowledge" is a reflection on the post–1970s "notion of epistemological vigilance" on the part of peoples of African descent. That vigilance has been the analysis of the "political dimensions of

13. Ibid., 32–33; italics added.

knowledge and the procedures for establishing new rules in African studies" as imperatives to "strategies for mastering intellectual paradigms." Key among these have been the ways in which African and African American Studies have addressed themselves to critiques of history and literature.

Mudimbe admits that "power is still the objective" in what he terms a "struggle for maturity." This maturity can be read in several ways. One way, probably the most conventional, is the maturity that has come to Africa and peoples of African descent in the wake of colonization and imperialism. Another way of reading the terminology is to think of that maturity in terms of the entire modern project, a project of global dimensions whose refinement has allowed for the emergence of new discourses that have enhanced our senses of identity, singularly and collectively. The question of power, in this light, speaks to a more equitable distribution of the world's resources. That this is one consequence is evident in the most recent discussions across the globe. What Mudimbe alerts us to is a way of recognizing these discourses. By way of recognition we must also come to grips with the genesis of these discourses and realize that they have a history.[14]

In part, that history has been illustrated on these pages. An object of these historical discourses from the very first resistances of the modern age through Woodson, Du Bois, Asante, Said, Mudimbe, and others, has been the decolonization of the "social and human sciences." This project is what Paul Hountondji has called the "critical reinterpretation of . . . African history . . . destroying the classical frame of anthropology." It is the overthrow of Lévi-Strauss's Janus.[15]

The historical ramifications are important. As much as history, or the lack of it, confers identity, then the histories that began the modern age established particular historiographies and epistemologies. What these histories identified was what should be allocated to whom and on what basis. The contention over Egypt began there and remains there.

Mudimbe underlines this point when he tells us that scholars such as Obenga do not spring forth whole cloth. The *prise de parole* of Obenga's generation was the issue of *Negritude*. This was a challenge to Galileo, Locke, and all others in terms of the epistemological changes wrought by the Enlightenment. The question that Mudimbe poses for us, a question quite similar to those posed by Asante and Said—questions that the works of Du Bois, Woodson, and others imply—is what does this movement represent in the sense of adding

14. Ibid., 36.
15. Ibid., 37.

to, changing, or refining the construction of knowledge? What is the import of this movement, this struggle of the latest moment of the modern age? Might this newest construction of knowledge prove as important as the Enlightenment postulates themselves? Could this be the value of the contributions of peoples of African descent to the discourses on postcolonialism and postmodernism?

Examining Obenga again, Mudimbe cites his credentials. This process has often been the way that scholars of African descent begin an interchange, by asserting their right to speak by virtue of their credentials. There is no doubt in Mudimbe's mind that Obenga is more than qualified to address the issues at hand. It is Mudimbe's assertion that Obenga brings to the issues the level of refinement that they demand. Obenga

> brings to African history associations a critical view on Cheikh Anta Diop's theses and at the same time, as director of a major research center in Libreville, fights for "an African perspective" and initiative in history.[16]

Engaging his "critical view on . . . Diop's theses," as Mudimbe puts it, Obenga wished to draw his American colleagues into a discussion of these issues during his stay at Temple. This is reflected in two ways. First is the way in which Obenga is referenced in the publications that follow his stay in the United States, the most prominent of which are the writings of Asante and Keto. There is a reverential tone given to the way in which Obenga is regarded. Second, the works themselves reflect a more critical tone; they are, in significant parts, critiques themselves. At first glance they may appear to yield little or nothing to their adversaries, but more nuanced readings suggest the ways in which Afrocentric/Africa-centered texts and discourse can be regarded as the opening wedge of a globalized discourse that engages historiography and epistemology within the space of debates centering on postcolonial and postmodernist theory and interpretation.

Mudimbe broadens this discourse by making sure that the African voice is included. He cites J. O. Sodipo, Kwasi Wiredu, Paulin Hountondji, Engelbert Mveng, and Ngudu among the producers "of a body of works, which are both difficult, because of the amplifications that explain them, and extremely sophisticated with respect to the relationships between knowledge and power."[17] Mudimbe's sources speak to the internationalization of the discourse. Roth has alluded to this by

16. Ibid., 40.
17. Ibid., 40–41.

giving notice to the serious discussions of Afrocentrism found in French circles. The contemporary American sources also bear this out from Asante through Bernal. And though some of these same sources might see a certain reluctance among postcolonial and postmodernist theorists to embrace Afrocentrism, the links become increasingly clear with each new addition to these discourses.[18] In addition to Mudimbe's African counterparts are the European theorists whom he, Asante, and Keto invoke.

The question here, in light of all this, is do Diop and Obenga bridge the gap between Africans and African Americans in the exploration of similar issues related to power and the construction of knowledge? Do Mudimbe's observations allow for the internationalization of the dynamics—do they illustrate the dynamics—that compel both Africans and African Americans and that at the same time animate discussion and critique from other sectors of the African diaspora as witnessed in Paul Gilroy's *Black Atlantic* or Sidney Lemelle's critique of Asante's work?[19] What we see here are the numerous possibilities for refining and enriching the discourse externally and internally.

If I am accused of overreaching in terms of the importance that might be attached to this discourse both historiographically and epistemologically, I am bearing witness to what Mudimbe defines as a "severe political and ideological confrontation." In terms similar to those of Fishkin, Mudimbe argues that the combined elements of this discourse, from every corner, result in an interrogation of the "European tradition" and its relation to power. Afrocentrism jumps the barriers of "colonial discourses," colonial propositions, and the colonial sciences." The barriers become key to the necessity of knowing Africa.

The colonial necessity is readily understood. It arises from the need to invent (i.e., "the invention of Africa") in order to arrange space, concepts, and resources. The ancient necessity for knowing Africa was imperative for different reasons, if Alain Bourgeois is to be believed. Bourgeois's notions of the ancient need to know Africa are in line with all those scholars who have argued for an examination of Africa as a historical player on the world stage.

In *La Grece antique devant la negritude*, Bourgeois wrote in 1971:

Finally, what to conclude except that the relationships between Greece and Negritude, which one might *a priori* have thought to be

18. duCille, *Skin Trade*, 120–135.

19. Sidney Lemelle, "The Politics of Cultural Existence: Pan-Africanism, Historical Materialism, and Afrocentricity," *Race and Class*, 35 (1993), 94–105. Molefe Kete Asante, "Are You Scared of Your Shadow? A Critique of Sidney Lemelle's 'The Politics of Cultural Existence,'" *Journal of Black Studies*, 26, 4 (March 1996) 524–533.

negligible or almost nil, appear to be of unsuspected richness? It was necessary for [Greek] writers to show off their knowledge of Africa, which was, and necessarily so, limited and fragmented. In fact, they knew much more than one would have expected, and from what they knew, they made the best of it.[20]

The necessity of knowing Africa was rooted in the idea that Africa was integral to the Greeks knowing themselves. This is certainly implied, if not stated, in many ancient texts. And it is underlined and reinforced in the modern conceptualization and invention of Africa; that is where Africa has been presented as the "paradigm of difference," translated to fulfill a "political project."

This political project has proceeded apace, in spite of the fact that

since the 1920s, African scholars, and most notably anthropologists and historians, have been interrogating these landscapes and civilizations and reconstructing, in a new fashion, piece by piece, fragile genealogies that bear witness to historical vitalities that, until then, seemed invisible to students of African affairs.[21]

Clearly, the historiographic range of this project can be extended chronologically simply by giving attention to the late eighteenth-through twentieth-century works produced by African Americans and other peoples of the African diaspora. These works are ancestors to A. Barthelot's 1927 *L'Afrique saheriene et soudanaise ce qu'en ont connu les anciens,* just as Barthelot's work is a precursor for Bourgeois's, and Bourgeois's is for Bernal. Barthelot's work coincides with, and we must assume was influenced by, *Negritude* and its quest for a celebration of the "values of blacks' historical and cultural experiences." In fact, it is from this "intellectual and ideological background" that "Bourgeois discloses and reactivates traces and designations of Africans in Greek texts." As the scholars Bernal designated as his predecessors had indicated, the message that these works "unveil, which has been ignored, blurred, or muted by centuries of Western scholarship, is represented silently to a twentieth-century project: black is beautiful."[22]

Mudimbe has done two things for us here. First, he reminds us of Asante's assertion that the African, in particular the African American, is critical to the postcolonial, postmodernist discourse. Second, addressing the issue of the refinement of the thesis, Mudimbe resurrects

20. Quoted in Mudimbe, *Idea,* 20.
21. Ibid., xii.
22. Ibid., 20.

some elements of the internal debate that has always existed among the generations that constructed this Africa-centered discourse. Focusing on the *Negritude* generation, a broad grouping that if expanded across linguistic and cultural lines could most certainly have included Du Bois, Woodson, Hansberry, and Snowden, Mudimbe examines and argues their intellectual and cultural pedigree.

Given their context, he concludes that their historical and cultural projects, their attempts to reconstruct knowledge, were "progressive," if not "radical." Their works revolved around Africa-centered intellectual movements that we recognize today as *Negritude*, and the Negro Renaissance, the New Negro Movement. Mudimbe legitimates the contributions and the gravity of those contributions to the current debate. It is clear that these intellectuals' efforts helped to shape the present debate, and that in itself obligates their inclusion in the historical and intellectual genealogy as full partners. Embracing Woodson, Du Bois, Hansberry, and Snowden, Mudimbe in his observations on the refinement of the thesis, includes Léopold Senghor, Bourgeois, Eugene Guernier, and, of course, Diop in a project that speaks to the "originality of Egyptian civilization" as an African invention.[23]

Diop is the generational bridge. His origins and rhetoric are clearly determined by *Negritude*. The task, as he articulated it, set on this foundation, as well as other serious historical bedrock, illustrates the importance of his ideas and those of his diasporan contemporaries in the shaping of the current debate. The acknowledgment of Diop's origins and the context out of which Obenga emerges dictates that the creators of *Negritude*, as well as similar intellectual movements, must be critically analyzed in terms of their contributions to the current discourse.

Mudimbe's restoration of these historical and intellectual personalities, coupled with his reading of Bourgeois, reflects a new historiographic and, therefore, new epistemological approach "to today's discourse and perception of history." He leads us back to a basic Afrocentric concern: "[I]n sum the African right to dignity enunciates itself in reactivating ancient texts and by interrogating the objectivity of history."[24]

The consequence of these interrogations by peoples of African descent over the course of the modern age has resulted in real historiographic and epistemological change:

The general movement in which the reactivation of Greek texts takes place is more than a simple revision of traditional scholarship. It signi-

23. Ibid., 24.
24. Ibid., 24.

fies, in fact, the reversal of perspectives, which is the sign of a major epistemological rupture.

To be sure, among the major ramifications of this movement, from the time of David Walker to the present, have been controversy and struggle. These were staples long before Foucault and others. They are fundamental products of African and European interaction in the modern age. In many ways they are epitomized by the American experience, to the degree that, historiographically, the "real issue is not one of theory versus empirical collection. It is rather about the silent and *a priori* choice of the truth to which a given discourse aims."[25] As Bernal put it, what is necessary is not simply the rethinking of the basis of "Western Civilization" but a recognition of the "penetration of racism" and "continental chauvinism" into all our historiography, or philosophy of writing history." And while Bernal may be clear on this point, Mudimbe feels that his clarity might be even greater if his reading of classical sources such as Herodotus was more critical, and if Bernal were able to recognize the "shifting philosophies" that "manipulate the information that we get from ancient texts." Mudimbe is speaking to historiography and epistemology in both directions, recognizing the biases of both ancient and modern writers and arguing that the ancient texts, as historical documents, are governed by their own epistemological contexts.[26]

Critique

DuCille's critique of Afrocentric, postcolonial and postmodern discourses is hard-edged. It is incisive, not blunt. On one hand, DuCille cautions against an African American hegemony of the discourse and the problems that such a singular perspective might create. On the other, she is fully cognizant of the ways in which postmodern and postcolonial discourses have ignored or been ignorant of the African American contributions to the establishment of these fora. While she speaks specifically to the reinscription of "cultural dislocation" for African American theorists, the same danger awaits postmodernists and postcolonialists who fail to realize the "unknowing contradiction of the very cultural traditions they wish to celebrate." DuCille pushes for a recognition of the relation between Afrocentrism, postmod-

25. Ibid., 39.
26. Bernal, *Black Athena*, vol. 1, 2. Mudimbe, *Idea*, 98.

ernism, and postcolonialism. This is, of course, a position that many Afrocentrists, including Asante and Keto, have begun to advocate.[27]

DuCille's argument leads to the need to recognize that the terms of engagement for these discourses and their products are multiple and overlapping. Such a revelation identifies the relation between "post-coloniality and Afrocentrism as intellectual perspectives, as acclaimed and disclaimed discourses respectively." At issue is the disjuncture between the two, a disjuncture that might be illustrated by Asante's criticism of Said.[28] DuCille reflects on that disjuncture, opening her discussion of the perils and possibilities that face this intellectual activity:

> [W]hat does it mean, for example, when Afrocentrism is dismissed as methodologically sloppy, anti-intellectual identity politics while postcoloniality is affirmed as theoretically sophisticated oppositional discourse?

She concludes that the "most critical factor may have more to do with the market than with methodology."[29] DuCille's primary thesis is the commoditization of discourse and the ways in which color makes some discourses less "valuable" than others. She returns us to what has been visible since we posed the question of "why Bernal and not his predecessors?" DuCille points out the danger in the internecine feudings of what should be allied discourses: "Although the designation 'postcolonial' may be new, the study of power relations between colonizer and colonized is not." DuCille implies that the earliest of postcolonial discourses begin among peoples of African descent. She then proceeds to list the great names of the nineteenth century to make her case and to make the postcolonialists and postmodernists take notice. She also makes it quite clear that among her theorists and activists, women do not take a back seat. For DuCille, postcolonial and postmodern discourse can be recognized as an "elegant incarnation" of "resistance narratives," a genre whose earliest forms included the slave narratives of the western hemisphere.[30]

It is here that DuCille issues a similar warning to Afrocentrists. What must be avoided at all costs is any brand of "Afrocentrism" that "perpetuate[s] the same divide-and-conquer ignorance on which imperialism has depended." The necessity for recognition on both sides of this particular discourse is based on the realization that without such

27. DuCille, *Skin Trade*, 121–122.
28. Asante, *Kemet*, 123–125.
29. DuCille, *Skin Trade*, 123.
30. Ibid., 124, 126.

recognition we will see the continued use of postcolonial and post-modern studies to "reaffirm the European or Anglo-American center . . . [as] a form of intellectual imperialism that erases the line between the colonizer and the colonized." In effect, this realization is an expression of the need for an "interculturally oriented African American Studies."[31]

Of course, Mazrui presents the same argument when he suggests that Afrocentrism might require a much more refined "vehicle." The vehicle Mazrui had in mind is Africana Studies. For Mazrui, the Africana model encompasses people of African descent no matter where they might reside in geographical and temporal space. As Mazrui puts it, this model also allows for the formation of alliances with other cultures and Western dissidents. It allows for the creation of space in which postcolonial and postmodernist and Afrocentric "visions" might see how "remarkably similar" they are.[32]

On this point, Asante and Gates are talking *to* each other. Both recognize the centrality of Black studies as a historical and contemporary theoretical exercise that expands accepted epistemologies. It is a demonstration that there are other ways of knowing that, in the end, must and will be acknowledged. Gates concludes that the time has come when

> academe must give Black Studies programs their due . . . [T]he role of Black Studies in the academy has never been more crucial . . . in educating a nation that remains woefully ignorant . . . [W]e have only begun to glimpse its potential for integrating the American mind.

Asante concurs. He argues that the inevitable evolution of the Afrocentric perspective within Black studies "inaugurate[d] an entire system of thinking about social science and criticism, and pointed to the inherent problems of Eurocentric theory." Afrocentrism within the context of Black studies, within the context of DuCille's "interculturally oriented" African American Studies, or Mazrui's expansive Africana Studies, celebrates another way of knowing.[33]

In this context, in the context of this mutual recognition and the knowledge it generates, the epistemological question is renewed: "[W]hat do we do with this knowledge? . . . To what use do we put

31. Ibid., 125, 133–134.

32. Mazrui, "Afrocentrism," 3, 4. DuCille, *Skin Trade*, 135.

33. Henry Louis Gates, Jr., "Academe Must Give Black Studies Programs Their Due," *Chronicle of Higher Education*, September 20, 1989, A56. Asante, *Idea*, 163.

this sense of our multiplicity, our interrelatedness, and our interdependence?" One possibility, DuCille suggests, is "[t]o teach one another about the white academy that both claims and disclaims us."[34]

Disclaimers

In using descriptors like "radical" or "extreme" the critics of Afrocentrism allude to a certain emotional quality, an imbalance, a dysfunction, that hampers the mental applications for even the most mundane task. By allusion, they argue, how can one expect serious scholarship to occur in an atmosphere so charged—an atmosphere that, if not characterized by derangement, is certainly suffused with anger? It is, in fact, anger that is supposedly characterized by the words "radical" and "extreme" in this case—an anger that is suppose to debilitate, that supposedly precludes rational, unbiased intellectual inquiry, that must be anti-intellectual.

Interestingly enough, Lawrence W. Levine has pointed out that the critics themselves are very angry people; in fact, they are people with a historical pedigree of anger relating to projects that seek a more expansive and inclusive history, historiography, and epistemology. Their critiques of the dangers of Afrocentrism, postmodernism, postcolonialism, and so on, are almost interchangeable. As Said has pointed out regarding the "rhetorical figures that one keeps encountering" in colonial narratives, no matter the colony, they tend to read the same. They disregard the concessions they have made over the *longue duree* of this discourse to the fundamental ideas that the discourse promotes: the issues of Africa, Africans, and peoples of African descent; race; and the ways in which all of these have lent themselves to the construction of history and knowledge.

So in the end, works like Lefkowitz's *Not Out of Africa* are ineffectual because they engage in the very *"nonsense"* that they deplore; and they do so in a manner that Levine has described as bereft of the intellectual and scholastic rigor of which they accuse Afrocentrists. They suggest the possibilities of discussing "responsible teaching and academic freedom" while characterizing their opposition as "flat-worlders."[35]

---

34. DuCille, *Skin Trade*, 135.

35. Mary Lefkowitz, *Not Out of Africa: How Afrocentrism Became an Excuse to Teach Myth as History* (New York: Basic Books, 1996), 9; 11. The "nonsense" of Lefkowitz's position is that she clings tenaciously to the idea that she can craft a serious argument against Afrocentrism by illustrating it with examples that even Asante dismisses as not worthy of serious scholarship. Afrocentrism, *as serious scholarship*, is far removed from the questions of whether Socrates, Hannibal, or Cleopatra were "black." A serious and critical reading of Afrocentric texts would reveal a concern for far more substantial and, therefore, consequential issues

Not Out of Africa is indicative of a school of scholastic opinion that either denies or is ignorant of the historical processes that define what is currently called Afrocentrism. These scholars argue that there can be no interpretations other than their own. There is no recognition of the roles that race and imperialism play in the modern construction of histories about the past, ancient or otherwise. Lefkowitz and company believe that they can rely on the same ploy that they disdain. Lefkowitz evokes the same racism that she accuses Afrocentrists of by first dismissing the notion that their ideas might have intellectual merit and then assuming that Afrocentrists and Afrocentric thought constitute one, undifferentiated, monolithic mass. In the end, in spite of the endorsements of Gates and Snowden for Lefkowitz's project, one is forced to agree with Asante: there is no "interest in understanding Afrocentricity" and the question of dialogue or discourse in these circles seems out of the question. For Lefkowitz, "an alternative way of looking at the past" is worse than the production of "pseudohistory."[36]

Yet it may be an apparition that dialogue and discourse are out of the question. There have been concessions; these, in fact, have been the source of dismay for many such as Lefkowitz and Windschuttle. These concessions signal the ways in which the institutions and the very act of doing history have been "undermined." They are reflective of the defections, however slight, that have occurred in the attempt *to understand* the various positions that wish to speak to history, to speak history, and to create history. So when we speak of these particular concessions, it is not in the sense of the capitulation of one side or the other, but in terms of the realization on both sides of the need to secure a new discourse.

First among these concessions has been the moderation of voice on both sides. In some spaces, the speech is not quite so strident. One of the best illustrations is a close reading of Asante's later works in which he recognizes and accepts the validity of all perspectives including the Eurocentric. Both Keto's and Mudimbe's writings signal this as well, as does Roth's argument concerning the possibilities of an Egyptologist/Afrocentrist dialogue. Her acknowledgment of French Afrocentrists invites an examination of Afrocentrism as something other than monolithic "nonsense" spouted primarily by American blacks; it also suggests that serious examination of American Afrocentrism needs to

---

such as historiography and epistemology, and the contributions of peoples of African descent to these over the course of time. Given the evolution of the discourse and its variety, Lefkowitz's attack is disingenuous at best in its focus on "myths of origin and cultural dependency, mystery systems, and stolen legacies."

36. Ibid., xii–xiv.

be placed on the intellectual agenda. This might be considered in light of the fact that nationally and internationally recognized scholars such as David Levering Lewis are using the same terminology to describe such subjects as W. E. B. Du Bois.

Even among the "hard-core" there are signs. Frank Yurco's comments indicate that there is recognition that Afrocentrists vary, and there are indeed those for whom he and his colleagues can muster some levels of respect.[37] It is Yurco who inadvertently challenges Robert Pounder's assertion that there was no "significant role for blacks in Egyptian society" by observing that "many people today who consider themselves Afro-American or 'black' . . . would have no trouble finding physical types resembling their own in contemporary Egypt." I asked, when I first encountered this statement, if, given the iconography, African Americans would have any difficulty finding those same physical types among ancient Egyptians? That was certainly what Du Bois had in mind when he presented his findings. How much should we suppose the ancient Egyptian population has changed? What Pounder, Yurco, and others demonstrate is what Molly Levine has referred to as a "particularly perverse pedantry." I can only ask for whom?[38]

A cursory review of Lefkowitz and Guy MacLean Roger's *Black Athena Revisited* also speaks to the concessions made here, though many are hardly ever overtly recognized by their authors. The attack on *Black Athena* seems content with the issues of chronology and linguistics. The "Africanness" and, to some degree, the "blackness" of the Egyptians has become almost, though not quite, a moot point. On this count, there is the preference to argue the insufficiencies of race as a scientific concept–something the predecessors of Afrocentrism did long ago and that leading Afrocentrists support. Or there is a resort to the specifics and the arcanery of anthropology: "clines" and "clusters." The general agreement, among all engaged, is that ancient Egypt is not what we had conventionally assumed it to be.

Black Athena Revisited, a much more solid piece of work than *Not Out of Africa*, cannot accomplish what *Not Out of Africa* wished to—it cannot bring closure to this debate; it cannot definitively put down the Afrocentrists. The contributions to this work are thorough and technical, but in the end they are unconvincing. They march over much of the same ground the critics covered with the first edition of *Black Athena*, and they hold it in the same fashion. Some are still quite indignant that any suggestion might be made of linkages between Africa

37. Frank Yurco, Correspondence with Eric King (July 20, 1994), 3.
38. See Molly Myerowitz Levine, "The Use and Abuse of *Black Athena*," *AHR*, 97, 2 (April 1992), 454, 39, 51, 66.

and the formation of the classical world; others are querulous about who and what these "Africans" might be and how they might be even remotely related to those making the claims (African Americans). Others are simply dismissive—Lefkowitz perpetuates this attitude in *Not Out of Africa*, though the theories had substantive and historical support well before Lefkowitz put pen to paper or fingers to keypad. In large, we might be left to believe that little has been learned and that little has changed in the years following Bernal's raucous introduction to the Classics, Egyptology, and Afrocentrism.

Who and what Afrocentrists are other than interlopers has hardly been entertained. There has not been much apparent activity in the attempt to find a common ground. *Black Athena Revisited* upholds tradition. It is another attempt to stave off the "untutored," the "uncultured," the intellectually unwashed—the "black." This is done in much the same way as the interpretation of the texts celebrated as the canon has always done.

Yet *Black Athena Revisited* cannot put down the Afrocentrists because among its own legions there is innuendo and contradiction. This innuendo and contradiction are key to the ways in which Afrocentrism is helping to reshape the debate and transform it into a new discourse. This instability may be an inadvertent beginning of the hope that Roth raised concerning the cooperation between Egyptologists and Afrocentrists. While this project has not been engaged in any major sense, the impact of serious Afrocentric scholarship is being registered—if one is willing to take a critical look.

Substantive or not, the scholars presented in *Black Athena Revisited* have fundamentally missed the point when it comes to Afrocentrism. Quite possibly because like Bernal, in many ways, they wish not to see it. They prefer debate over chronology, linguistic form, or clines. Or perhaps it because they are incapable of conceptualizing it. They have not engaged the notion that history has many interpretations or, more important, that there are *epistemologies,* plural. There are many ways of knowing. If they had cared to engage Afrocentrism as a historical and intellectual phenomenon, they might have come across Du Bois's 1903 essay "Laboratory in Sociology at Atlanta University," in which he attempted to acquaint the reader with the notion that there might indeed be a "point of view of the colored races"—a space, a center, from which they might view the world, individually and collectively.[39] Had

39. William Edward Burghardt Du Bois, "Laboratory in Sociology at Atlanta University," from *The Annals of the American Academy of Political and Social Science*, reprinted in Julius Lester, ed., *The Seventh Son: The Thought and Writings of W. E. B. Du Bois* (New York: Vintage Books, 1971), 247–251.v

they cared—if they care—to explore the intellectual history of Afro-centrism, they would find scholars such as William Leo Hansberry cautioning black scholars on the dangers of ethnocentrism. They would recognize in Hansberry and his work a parent to that of DuCille and many, many others.

Yet it has never occurred to the critics of Afrocentrism to ask why these Afrocentrists (at least those that they choose to identify) are so radical; that is, why are they so angry? Perhaps, they might even inquire as to what it is that they are so angry about. Again, such a notion may be inconceivable, given the "center" from which such a question might be posed. From that center—the center of the Wills, Buchanans, Bennetts, Schlesingers, and Lefkowitzes of the world—these people have nothing about which to be angry. In effect, they have no right to be angry (*"after all that has been done for them"*). And such anger is ineffectual anyway, given that they have no intellectual, scholastic, or academic fora in which to express it. How could they possibly be angry; and indeed, angry about intellectual discourse? From such a "center" there is little hope for inquiry, let alone discourse.

The anger is not over the "blackness" of Egypt, or "stolen legacies" per se. It is an anger that concerns attempts to open dialogue, to broaden debate, to engage discourse, that have been dismissed historically and continue to be dismissed as I write. It is a dismissal that "radicalizes" "even some well-educated black professionals . . . to the odd tenets of Afrocentrism."[40] They are radicalized because the historical response to their effort has repeatedly indicated that they are intellectually insignificant, marginal, and menial. Even like Snowden, they can be dismissed as necessity dictates.

Whose "necessity"? For many of the radicalized, it is not about fact. History is not about fact. It is about interpretation—hence, historiography: the *why* and how of writing history. Interpretation is the emperor's clothes. Will may pontificate about the Afrocentrist's rags, but it becomes clear, upon critical inspection, that Will and company are also historiographically and epistemologically naked. Their history, like that which they critique, has a certain transparency.

Who are these Afrocentrists, and why are they so angry? Du Bois describes their charge and its challenges:

In history and the social sciences the Negro school and college have an unusual opportunity and role. It does not consist simply of trying to parallel the history of white folk with similar boasting about black and

40. See Len Jaroff, Teaching Reverse Racism," *Time* (April 4, 1994) 74–75.

brown folk, but rather an honest evaluation of human effort without transforming history into a record of dynasties and prodigies.[41]

As a student of American history and society, Du Bois understood the inevitability of an Africa-centered discourse:

> The civilization by which America insists on measuring us and to which we must conform our national tastes and inclinations is the daughter of European civilization which is now rushing firmly to its doom. . . . [W]hat good can come out of it all? . . . Old standards of beauty beckon us again, not the blue-eyed, white-skinned types which are set before us in school and literature but the rich, brown and black men and women with glowing dark eyes and crinkling hair.[42]

The "old standard of beauty"? How far back does Du Bois wish to go? Is this the standard referenced by the same Herodotus who has been discredited by some who debate here?: "[T]he Ethiopians . . . are said to be the tallest and best-looking people in the world."[43] And, as Molly Levine might put it, *what difference does it make?* It seems that it makes a great deal of difference, especially in a world where the production of knowledge is predicated on the denial of some peoples, and then that knowledge is used to erect social structures and barriers that institutionalize and perpetuate that denial. In the very real and material sense, this epistemology and the accompanying sociology of knowledge guide and justify the resources to which any individual or group might have access. They dictate the quality of life and, in many cases, historically and contemporarily, the existence of life itself.

What difference does it make? The debate is political—political-economic, to be exact. It is contention over the allocation of resources and who is deserving of those resources. To believe that it is not—to argue that knowledge, scholarship, and the academy are without agendas, especially in the ways in which they constitute power—is to be disingenuous or deceitful, or both. The epistemology that is being contested revolves around the ways in which the production and construction of knowledge lend themselves to the making of such decisions.

Martin Bernal has spawned a cottage industry of which I am a part. The most recent pronouncements on Afrocentrism and *Black Athena*

---

41. Du Bois, "Does the Negro Need Separate Schools?" in Lester, *Seventh Son,* 415–416.

42. Du Bois, "The Battle for Europe," from *The Crisis* (September 1916), quoted in Lewis, 525–526.

43. Herodotus, *The Histories,* 211.

are clearly evidence of this. They also return me to my central thesis: the ways in which race has impacted the writing of the history of the classical period, the ways in which some scholars, because of their race, have had their intellectual production ignored, their ideas neglected; their intellectual lives shunted to a junction labeled "Blacks Only."

Mainstream historians, if I may use that term, have missed much of the historical nature of the Afrocentrists' claims because they have failed to study the history—in particular the intellectual history—of black peoples, especially that of black peoples in America. Here, many Afrocentrists might be guilty as well in assuming that theirs is a project of twentieth-century ingenuity and dynamism, and not one of solid historical progression.

My position is not necessarily to prove the cases of scholars such as Carter G. Woodson, William Edward Burghardt Du Bois, William Leo Hansberry, or Frank M. Snowden. Any critical reading of their works allows them to stand on their own merits. I am much more content to point to the plausibility of their arguments in historicizing, enriching, and expanding the discourse. Here, my agenda addresses a more profound and universal issue of modern academic life. That agenda centers on modern historiographic and epistemological construction. In particular, it asks, given the inquiries of Bernal, why have we not addressed in a similar fashion, with similar vigor, the entreaties of Woodson, Du Bois, Hansberry, Snowden, and the rest? It asks, what has been the impact of race on the writing of history in general and the writing of the history of the ancient period in particular? It asks that we riddle the sphinx.

Index